MW01622659

IT'S ALL ABOUT Christmas

Cover and Interior designed by Christina Marcano

Published by Covenant Communications, Inc.
American Fork, Utah

Printed in China
First Printing: October 2015

21 20 19 18 17 16 15   10 9 8 7 6 5 4 3 2 1

ISBN 978-1-68047-624-8

TABLE OF CONTENTS

The Birth of Christ

1 NEPHI 10:4

Yea, even six hundred years from the time that my father left Jerusalem, a prophet would the Lord God raise up among the Jews—even a Messiah, or, in other words, a Savior of the world.

ISAIAH 7:14

Therefore the Lord himself will give you a sign. Behold, a virgin shall conceive and bear a son, and shall call his name Immanuel.

LUKE 1:26–38

And in the sixth month the angel Gabriel was sent from God unto a city of Galilee, named Nazareth,

To a virgin espoused to a man whose name was Joseph, of the house of David; and the virgin's name was Mary.

And the angel came in unto her, and said, Hail, thou that art highly favoured, the Lord is with thee: blessed art thou among women.

And when she saw him, she was troubled at his saying, and cast in her mind what manner of salutation this should be.

And the angel said unto her, Fear not, Mary: for thou hast found favour with God.

And, behold, thou shalt conceive in thy womb, and bring forth a son, and shalt call his name JESUS.

He shall be great, and shall be called the Son of the Highest: and the Lord God shall give unto him the throne of his father David:

And he shall reign over the house of Jacob for ever; and of his kingdom there shall be no end.

Then said Mary unto the angel, How shall this be, seeing I know not a man?

And the angel answered and said unto her, The Holy Ghost shall come upon thee, and the power of the Highest shall overshadow thee: therefore also that holy thing which shall be born of thee shall be called the Son of God.

And, behold, thy cousin Elisabeth, she hath also conceived a son in her old age: and this is the sixth month with her, who was called barren.

For with God nothing shall be impossible.

And Mary said, Behold the handmaid of the Lord; be it unto me according to thy word. And the angel departed from her.

MATTHEW 1:18–25

Now the birth of Jesus Christ was on this wise: When as his mother Mary was espoused to Joseph, before they came together, she was found with child of the Holy Ghost.

Then Joseph her husband, being a just man, and not willing to make her a publick example, was minded to put her away privily.

But while he thought on these things, behold, the angel of the Lord appeared unto him in a dream, saying, Joseph, thou son of David, fear not to take unto thee Mary thy wife: for that which is conceived in her is of the Holy Ghost.

And she shall bring forth a son, and thou shalt call his name JESUS: for he shall save his people from their sins.

Now all this was done, that it might be fulfilled which was spoken of the Lord by the prophet, saying,

Behold, a virgin shall be with child, and shall bring forth a son, and they shall call his name Emmanuel, which being interpreted is, God with us.

Then Joseph being raised from sleep did as the angel of the Lord had bidden him, and took unto him his wife:

And knew her not till she had brought forth her firstborn son: and he called his name JESUS.

ALMA 7:7, 9–10

Behold, there is one thing which is of more importance than they all—for behold, the time is not far distant that the Redeemer liveth and cometh among his people.

But behold, the Spirit hath said this much unto me, saying: Cry unto this people, saying—Repent ye, and prepare the way of the Lord, and walk in his paths, which are straight; for behold, the kingdom of heaven is at hand, and the Son of God cometh upon the face of the earth.

And behold, he shall be born of Mary, at Jerusalem which is the land of our forefathers, she being a virgin, a precious and chosen vessel, who shall be overshadowed and conceive by the power of the Holy Ghost, and bring forth a son, yea, even the Son of God.

LUKE 2:1–20

And it came to pass in those days, that there went out a decree from Cæsar Augustus, that all the world should be taxed.

(And this taxing was first made when Cyrenius was governor of Syria.)

And all went to be taxed, every one into his own city.

And Joseph also went up from Galilee, out of the city of Nazareth, into Judæa, unto the city of David, which is called Bethlehem; (because he was of the house and lineage of David:)

To be taxed with Mary his espoused wife, being great with child.

And so it was, that, while they were there, the days were accomplished that she should be delivered.

And she brought forth her firstborn son, and wrapped him in swaddling clothes, and laid him in a manger; because there was no room for them in the inn.

And there were in the same country shepherds abiding in the field, keeping watch over their flock by night.

And, lo, the angel of the Lord came upon them, and the glory of the Lord shone round about them: and they were sore afraid.

And the angel said unto them, Fear not: for, behold, I bring you good tidings of great joy, which shall be to all people.

For unto you is born this day in the city of David a Saviour, which is Christ the Lord.

And this shall be a sign unto you; Ye shall find the babe wrapped in swaddling clothes, lying in a manger.

And suddenly there was with the angel a multitude of the heavenly host praising God, and saying,

Glory to God in the highest, and on earth peace, good will toward men.

And it came to pass, as the angels were gone away from them into heaven, the shepherds said one to another, Let us now go even unto Bethlehem, and see this thing which is come to pass, which the Lord hath made known unto us.

And they came with haste, and found Mary, and Joseph, and the babe lying in a manger.

And when they had seen it, they made known abroad the saying which was told them concerning this child.

And all they that heard it wondered at those things which were told them by the shepherds.

But Mary kept all these things, and pondered them in her heart.

And the shepherds returned, glorifying and praising God for all the things that they had heard and seen, as it was told unto them.

3 NEPHI 1:19–21

And it came to pass that there was no darkness in all that night, but it was as light as though it was mid-day. And it came to pass that the sun did rise in the morning again, according to its proper order; and they knew that it was the day that the Lord should be born, because of the sign which had been given.

And it had come to pass, yea, all things, every whit, according to the words of the prophets.

And it came to pass also that a new star did appear, according to the word.

MATTHEW 2:1–12

Now when Jesus was born in Bethlehem of Judæa in the days of Herod the king, behold, there came wise men from the east to Jerusalem,

Saying, Where is he that is born King of the Jews? for we have seen his star in the east, and are come to worship him.

When Herod the king had heard these things, he was troubled, and all Jerusalem with him.

And when he had gathered all the chief priests and scribes of the people together, he demanded of them where Christ should be born.

And they said unto him, In Bethlehem of Judæa: for thus it is written by the prophet,

And thou Bethlehem, in the land of Juda, art not the least among the princes of Juda: for out of thee shall come a Governor, that shall rule my people Israel.

Then Herod, when he had privily called the wise men, inquired of them diligently what time the star appeared.

And he sent them to Bethlehem, and said, Go and search diligently for the young child; and when ye have found him, bring me word again, that I may come and worship him also.

When they had heard the king, they departed; and, lo, the star, which they saw in the east, went before them, till it came and stood over where the young child was.

When they saw the star, they rejoiced with exceeding great joy.

And when they were come into the house, they saw the young child with Mary his mother, and fell down, and worshipped him: and when they had opened their treasures, they presented unto him gifts; gold, and frankincense, and myrrh.

And being warned of God in a dream that they should not return to Herod, they departed into their own country another way.

ISAIAH 9:6

For to us a child is born, to us a son is given; and the government shall be upon his shoulder, and his name shall be called Wonderful Counselor, Mighty God, Everlasting Father, Prince of Peace.

Night
Before
Christmas

The Night Before Christmas

'Twas the night before Christmas, when all through the house,
Not a creature was stirring, not even a mouse;
The stockings were hung by the chimney with care,
In hopes that St. Nicholas soon would be there;

The children were nestled all snug in their beds,
While visions of sugar plums danced in their heads,
And Mama in her 'kerchief, and I in my cap,
Had just settled our brains for a long winter's nap—
When out on the lawn there arose such a clatter,
I sprang from the bed to see what was the matter.
Away to the window I flew like a flash,
Tore open the shutters, and threw up the sash.
The moon on the breast of the new fallen snow,
Gave the lustre of midday to objects below;
When, what to my wondering eyes should appear,
But a miniature sleigh, and eight tiny reindeer,
With a little old driver, so lively and quick,
I knew in a moment it must be St. Nick.

More rapid than eagles his coursers they came,
And he whistled, and shouted, and called them by name:
"Now! Dasher, now! Dancer, now! Prancer, and Vixen,
"On! Comet, on! Cupid, on! Donner and Blitzen;
"To the top of the porch! To the top of the wall!
"Now dash away! Dash away! Dash away all!"
As dry leaves before the wild hurricane fly,
When they meet with an obstacle, mount to the sky;
So up to the housetop the coursers they flew,
With the sleigh full of toys—and St. Nicholas too:
And then in a twinkling, I heard on the roof
The prancing and pawing of each little hoof.
As I drew in my head, and was turning around,
Down the chimney St. Nicholas came with a bound:
He was dressed all in fur, from his head to his foot,
And his clothes were all tarnished with ashes and soot;
A bundle of toys was flung on his back,
And he looked like a peddler just opening his pack:
His eyes—how they twinkled! His dimples, how merry.
His cheeks were like roses, his nose like a cherry;
His droll little mouth was drawn up like a bow,
And the beard of his chin was as white as the snow;
The stump of a pipe he held tight in his teeth,
And the smoke, it encircled his head like a wreath.
He had a broad face, and a little round belly
That shook when he laughed, like a bowl full of jelly:

He was chubby and plump, a right jolly old elf,
And I laughed when I saw him in spite of myself;
A wink of his eye and a twist of his head
Soon gave me to know I had nothing to dread.
He spoke not a word, but went straight to his work,
And filled all the stockings; then turned with a jerk,
And laying his finger aside of his nose
And giving a nod, up the chimney he rose.
He sprung to his sleigh, to his team gave a whistle,
And away they all flew, like the down of a thistle:
But I heard him exclaim, ere he drove out of sight—
Happy Christmas to all, and to all a good night.

CLASSIC FAMILY Christmas Books

- *How the Grinch Stole Christmas* by Dr. Seuss
- *The Polar Express* by Chris Van Allsburg
- *Olive, the Other Reindeer* by Vivian Walsh
- *The Night Before Christmas* by Charles Santore
- *The Best Christmas Pageant Ever* by Barbara Robinson
- *The Biggest, Most Beautiful Christmas Tree* by Amye Rosenberg
- *Froggy's Best Christmas* by Jonathan London
- *Christmas Train* by Thomas S. Monson
- *The Christmas Miracle of Jonathan Toomey* by Susan Wojciechowski
- *Christmas Jars* by Jason Wright
- *Forgotten Carols* by Michael McLean
- *The Christmas Box* by Richard Paul Evans
- *The Nutcracker by* Susan Jeffers
- *Yes, Virginia, There Is a Santa Claus* by Chris Plehal and James Bernardin
- *Christmas Oranges* by Linda Bethers and Ben Sowards
- *A Christmas Dress for Ellen* by Thomas S. Monson

Up on the Housetop

Up on the housetop reindeer pause,
Out jumps good old Santa Claus.
Down thru the chimney with lots of toys,
All for the little ones, Christmas joys.

Chorus
Ho, ho, ho! Who wouldn't go.
Ho, ho, ho! Who wouldn't go!
Up on the housetop, click, click, click.
Down thru the chimney with good Saint Nick.

2. First comes the stocking of little Nell;
Oh, dear Santa, fill it well;
Give her a dolly that laughs and cries,
One that will open and shut her eyes.

Chorus

3. Next comes the stocking of little Will
Oh, just see what a glorious fill
Here is a hammer, And lots of tacks
Also a ball, And a whip that cracks.

Chorus

William Studwell, The Christmas Carol Reader

"Up on the Housetop" may have been the first American song of importance detailing the theme of Santa Claus. It is one of the first entirely secular Christmas songs composed in the United States. Written by little-known Benjamin R. Hanby, sometime in the 1850s or 1860s, this vivacious song could possibly predate, "Jingle Bells" (1857).

Hanby may possibly have composed another popular carol, "Jolly Old Saint Nicholas." There is no real evidence that Hanby was responsible for the other song, yet the styles and anonymity of thc songwriter for "Jolly Old Saint Nicholas," elicit the conjecture that Hanby might have authored both.

Now dash away!
Dash away! Dash away all!

One of the most
glorious messes in the world is the
mess created in the living room on
CHRISTMAS DAY.
Don't clean it up too quickly.

~Andy Rooney

Merry Christmas Poem

M. D. Sterling

First boy:
M stands for merry—oh, let us be merry;
M stands for merry—right merry am I.
(Bowing.) With a bow to the right, sir,
and a bow to the left, sir,
Come, now, and be merry, all sadness
defy.

Chorus (by school, to the refrain of "Buy
a Broom")
Christmas dear now draws near,
With song and with evergreen welcome
it here.

First girl:
E stands for evergreen, beautiful ever-
green,
E stands for evergreen, never to fade.
(Courtesying.) With a courtesy to right,
sir, and a courtesy to left, sir,
Bring evergreen garlands for Christmas-
time made.

Chorus

Second boy:
R stands for rollicking—come, then, be
rollicking;
R stands for rollicking—fun's in the air!
With a bow to the right, sir, and a bow to
the left, sir,
In Christmas-day rollicking take now a
share.

Chorus

Second girl:
R stands for rally, a grand Christmas rally,
R stands for rally, where Christmas trees
grow!
With a courtesy to right, sir, and a cour-
tesy to left, sir,
We rally where Santa is likely to go.

Chorus

Third boy:
Y stands for youthful—rejoice, now, all
youthful;
Y stands for youthful—quite youthful
am I.
With a bow to the right, sir, and a bow to
the left, sir,
The youthful make merry when Christmas is nigh.

Chorus

Third girl:
C stands for Christmas—bright Christ-
mas, merry Christmas;
C stands for Christmas—the best of the
year.
With a courtesy to right, sir, and a cour-
tesy to left, sir,
Make merry at Christmas with good
Christmas cheer.

Chorus

Fourth boy:
H stands for happy—at Christmas be
happy!
H stands for happy—right happy am I.
With a bow to the right, sir, and a bow to
the left, sir,
If you would be happy some Christmas
gifts buy.

Chorus

Fourth girl:
R stands for ready—for Christmas be ready;
R stands for ready—are you ready yet?
With a courtesy to right, sir, and a courtesy to left, sir.
To make ready for Christmas, oh! never forget.

Chorus

Fifth boy:
I stands for icy—for winter so icy;
I stands for icy, when Kris drives along.
With a bow to the right, sir, and a bow to the left, sir,
Though icy the weather we'll give him a song.

Chorus

Fifth girl:
S stands for Santa—the children's own Santa;
S stands for Santa, the jolly old dear.
With a courtesy to right, sir, and a courtesy to left, sir,
For Santy to fill we hang stockings each year.

Chorus

Sixth boy:
T stands for thoughtful—of all friends be thoughtful;
T stands for thoughtful—your presents prepare.
With a bow to the right, sir, and a bow to the left, sir,
And be thoughtful those poorer than you have a share.

Chorus

Sixth girl:
M stands for magic—for Christmas-night magic;
M stands for magic filling stockings and tree.
With a courtesy to right, sir, and a courtesy to left, sir,
Who does this fine magic, can any agree?

Chorus

Seventh boy:
A stands for all of us, old and young, all of us;
A stands for all of us looking for Kris.
With a bow to the right, sir, and a bow to the left, sir.
And all of us hope that not one will he miss.

Chorus

Seventh girl:
S stands for smiling—on Christmas morn smiling;
S stands for smiling—all smiling I'll be.
With a courtesy to right, sir, and a courtesy to left, sir,
All smiling, yes, smiling, when presents I see.

Chorus

REINDEER FOOD

Sprinkle this reindeer food outside on Christmas Eve to make sure Santa and his reindeer don't miss your house!

In a small zipper food storage bag or empty shaker container, mix:

- ½ cup uncooked oatmeal
- ½ cup sugar
- ¼ cup red or green sugar crystals (as used for cake decorating)

How "Merry Christmas" is said in . . .

Afrikaans: Geseënde Kersfees
Bosnian: Sretan Božić
Chichewa: Khrisimasi Yabwino
Czech: Veselé Vánoce
Danish: Glædelig Jul
Dutch: Vrolijk Kerstfeest
Esperanto: Felica Kristnasko
Filipino: Maligayang Pasko
Finnish: Hyvää Joulua
French: Joyeux Noël
German: Frohe Weihnachten
Greek: Kala Christouyenna
Hawaiian: Mele Kalikimaka
Icelandic: Gleðileg Jól
Igbo: Ezi Ekeresimesi
Indonesian: Selamat Natal
Italian: Buon Natale
Japanese: Meri Kurisumasu
Latvian: Priecīgus Ziemassvētkus
Lithuanian: Linksmų Kalėdų
Macedonian: Streken Bozhik
Navajo: Yá'át'ééh Késhmish
Norwegian: God Jul
Polish: Wesołych Świąt
Portuguese: Feliz Natal
Romanian: Crăciun Fericit
Slovak: Veselé Vianoce
Slovene: Vesel Božič
Spanish: Feliz Navidad
Swahili: Krismasi Njema
Swedish: God Jul
Thai: Sukhsant wan Khristmas
Turkish: Mutlu Noeller
Uzbek: Rojdestvo Muborak
Welsh: Nadolig Llawen

SANTA FACTS

- Before 1931, Santa had always been shown wearing other colors. A Coca-Cola advertising campaign, showing an image of him in red and white, became the familiar Santa Claus we now know.
- With a global population of more than seven billion people, the elves in Santa's workshop need to make more than five million presents every day of the year to meet demands.
- The American state of Indiana has a town called Santa Claus, and in Alaska there is a town called North Pole.
- Every Christmas Eve, the North American Aerospace Defense Command (NORAD) tracks Santa's trip around the world. The tradition began in 1955. You can track Santa at their website, www.noradsanta.org.
- The largest gathering of people dressed like Santa Claus was achieved by 18,112 people. The event took place in India on 27 December 2014 to raise charitable funds in aid of the poor.

COOKIES FOR SANTA

Have you ever stopped to wonder why we leave cookies and milk for Santa on Christmas Eve? The truth is no one really knows why, but there are a few different theories.

1. During the traditional feast of Saint Nicholas on December 6, children left food and drink for the saint and his attendants. During the night, the offering was traded for gifts. In some cultures, Saint Nicholas Day is still celebrated at the beginning of December, but in other cultures, that holiday has been combined with Christmas.

2. Medieval traditions in Germany included decorating a "paradise tree" with fruits, cookies, and other edible items. Eventually this tradition would merge with Christmas, and Santa would snack on the tasty ornaments. As the decorations changed over time, the idea of leaving the jolly old man with a snack meant leaving something near the tree instead of on it.

3. Many people believe that the tradition of leaving cookies for Santa originated during the Great Depression. Parents, wanting their children to learn generosity, taught them to share what little they had, including leaving snacks for Santa and his reindeer.

What kind of cookies do you leave for Santa? Here are some ideas:

SHORTBREAD COOKIES

1½ cups sugar
½ cup butter or margarine, softened
½ cup shortening
2 eggs
2¾ cups all-purpose flour
2 teaspoons cream of tartar
1 teaspoon baking soda
¼ teaspoon salt
¼ cup sugar
2 teaspoons ground cinnamon

1. Heat oven to 400 degrees F.
2. Mix 1 ½ cups sugar with the butter, shortening, and eggs in large bowl. Stir in flour, cream of tartar, baking soda, and salt.
3. Shape dough into 1¼-inch balls. Mix ¼ cup sugar and the cinnamon. Roll balls in cinnamon-sugar mixture, and place about 2 inches apart on ungreased cookie sheet.
4. Bake 8 to 10 minutes. Remove from cookie sheet to wire rack.

LEMON COOKIES

1 cup butter, softened
1½ cups sugar
1 egg
1 teaspoon lemon juice
1 Tablespoon lemon zest
1 teaspoon vanilla
½ teaspoon salt
½ teaspoon baking powder
2¼ cups flour

LEMON GLAZE

1½ cup powdered sugar
1 Tablespoon lemon juice
1 Tablespoon lemon zest
1 Tablespoon milk
¼ teaspoon vanilla

1. Preheat oven to 350 degrees F.
2. In a large bowl, cream butter and sugar. Add egg and beat well.
3. Add lemon juice, lemon zest, and vanilla; mix. Next add salt, baking powder, and flour. Mix until well incorporated.
4. Roll cookies into 1-inch balls and place on greased cookie sheet about 2 inches apart.
5. Bake for 8 to 10 minutes or until lightly golden on the edges.
6. Combine glaze ingredients in a medium bowl and whisk until smooth. Drizzle as much glaze as desired over slightly warm cookies. Let cool completely before serving.

CHOCOLATE CHIP COOKIES

¾ cup granulated sugar
¾ cup packed brown sugar
1 cup butter or margarine, softened
1 teaspoon vanilla
1 egg
2¼ cups all-purpose flour
1 teaspoon baking soda
½ teaspoon salt
1 package (12 ounces) semisweet chocolate chips
1 cup coarsely chopped nuts (optional)

1. Heat oven to 375 degrees F.
2. Mix sugars, butter, vanilla, and egg in large bowl. Stir in flour, baking soda, and salt. Stir in chocolate chips and nuts.
3. Drop dough by rounded tablespoonfuls about 2 inches apart onto ungreased cookie sheet.
4. Bake 8 to 10 minutes or until light brown. Allow cookies to cool slightly before removing from cookie sheet. Cool on wire rack.

PEANUT BUTTER REINDEER COOKIES

¾ cup peanut butter
1¼ cups firmly packed brown sugar
½ cup shortening
3 Tablespoons milk
1 Tablespoon vanilla
1 egg
1¾ cups all-purpose flour
¾ teaspoon baking soda
¾ teaspoon salt
Chocolate-covered mini pretzels
Mini brown M&Ms
Regular-sized red M&Ms

1. Preheat oven to 375 degrees F.
2. Combine brown sugar, peanut butter, shortening, milk, and vanilla in a large bowl. Beat at medium speed until well blended. Add egg, and beat until just blended. Set aside.
3. In a separate bowl, combine flour, baking soda, and salt. Add to creamed mixture at low speed until blended.
4. Form dough into 1-inch balls. To make reindeer-shaped cookies, pinch the bottom of the ball to form a point, then flatten with your hand. Space cookies about 2 inches apart on a greased cookie sheet. Bake for 7–8 minutes, until just beginning to brown.
5. Remove from oven and immediately (and gently) press two mini pretzels into the tops of the cookies for the reindeer antlers. Press two mini M&Ms in for the eyes and one red M&M for the nose.
6. Allow to cool slightly on the baking sheet before transferring to a wire rack to cool completely.

Yield: 40

CANDY CANE COOKIES

½ cup butter
½ cup shortening
1 cup sifted confectioners' sugar
1 egg
1½ teaspoons almond extract
1 teaspoon vanilla extract
2½ cups sifted all-purpose flour
1 teaspoon salt
Red food coloring

1. Preheat oven to 350 degrees F.
2. Blend shortening, butter, sugar, egg, and extracts. Set aside.
3. In a separate bowl, mix flour and salt and then add to shortening mixture. Divide dough in half.
4. Blend a few drops of red food coloring into one half.
5. Roll 1 teaspoon of the red dough and 1 teaspoon of the white dough on a lightly floured surface into 4-inch strips. Place strips side by side, press lightly together, and twist like a rope. Curve one end down to look like the handle of a candy cane.
6. Bake 9 minutes or until lightly browned. Remove while still warm.

Yield: 2 dozen

The Gift of the Magi

By O. Henry

ONE dollar and eighty-seven cents. That was all. And sixty cents of it was in pennies. Pennies saved one and two at a time by bulldozing the grocer and the vegetable man and the butcher until one's cheeks burned with the silent imputation of parsimony that such close dealing implied. Three times Della counted it. One dollar and eighty-seven cents. And the next day would be Christmas.

There was clearly nothing to do but flop down on the shabby little couch and howl. So Della did it. Which instigates the moral reflection that life is made up of sobs, sniffles, and smiles, with sniffles predominating.

While the mistress of the home is gradually subsiding from the first stage to the second, take a look at the home. A furnished flat at $8 per week. It did not exactly beggar description, but it certainly had that word on the lookout for the mendicancy squad.

In the vestibule below was a letter-box into which no letter would go, and an electric button from which no mortal finger could coax a ring. Also appertaining thereunto was a card bearing the name "Mr. James Dillingham Young."

The "Dillingham" had been flung to the breeze during a former period of prosperity when its possessor was being paid $30 per week. Now, when the income was shrunk to $20, though, they were thinking seriously of contracting to a modest and unassuming D. But whenever Mr. James Dillingham Young came home and reached his flat above, he was called "Jim" and greatly hugged by Mrs. James Dillingham Young, already introduced to you as Della. Which is all very good.

Della finished her cry and attended to her cheeks with the powder rag. She stood by the window and looked out dully at a gray cat walking a gray fence in a gray backyard. Tomorrow would be Christmas Day, and she had only $1.87 with which to buy Jim a present. She had been saving every penny she could for months, with this result. Twenty dollars a week doesn't go far. Expenses had been greater than she had calculated. They always are. Only $1.87 to buy a present for Jim. Her Jim. Many a happy hour she had spent planning for something nice for him. Something fine and rare and sterling—something just a little bit near to being worthy of the honor of being owned by Jim.

There was a pier glass between the windows of the room. Perhaps you have seen a pier glass in an $8 flat. A very thin and very agile person may, by observing his reflection in a rapid sequence of longitudinal strips, obtain a fairly accurate conception of his looks. Della, being slender, had mastered the art.

Suddenly she whirled from the window and stood before the glass. Her eyes were shining brilliantly, but her face had lost its color within twenty seconds. Rapidly she pulled down her hair and let it fall to its full length.

Now, there were two possessions of the James Dillingham Youngs in which they both took a mighty pride. One was Jim's gold watch that had been his father's and his grandfather's. The other was Della's hair. Had the queen of Sheba lived in the flat across the airshaft, Della would have let her hair hang out the window some day to dry just to depreciate Her Majesty's jewels and gifts. Had King Solomon been the janitor, with all his treasures piled up in the basement, Jim would have pulled out his watch every time he passed, just to see him pluck at his beard from envy.

So now Della's beautiful hair fell about her, rippling and shining like a cascade of brown waters. It reached below her knee and made itself almost a garment for her. And then she did it up again, nervously and quickly. Once she faltered for a minute and stood still while a tear or two splashed on the worn red carpet.

On went her old brown jacket; on went her old brown hat. With a whirl of skirts and with the brilliant sparkle still in her eyes, she fluttered out the door and down the stairs to the street.

Where she stopped, the sign read: "Mme. Sofronie. Hair Goods of All Kinds." One flight up Della ran, and collected herself, panting. Madame, large, too white, chilly, hardly looked the "Sofronie."

"Will you buy my hair?" asked Della.

"I buy hair," said Madame. "Take yer hat off and let's have a sight at the looks of it."

Down rippled the brown cascade.

"Twenty dollars," said Madame, lifting the mass with a practiced hand.

"Give it to me quick," said Della.

Oh, and the next two hours tripped by on rosy wings. Forget the hashed metaphor. She was ransacking the stores for Jim's present.

She found it at last. It surely had been made for Jim and no one else. There was no other like it in any of the stores, and she had turned all of them inside out. It was a platinum fob chain, simple and chaste in design, properly proclaiming its value by substance alone and not by meretricious ornamentation—as all good things should do. It was even worthy of The Watch. As soon as she saw it she knew that it must be Jim's. It was like him. Quietness and value—the description applied to both. Twenty-one dollars they took from her for it, and she hurried home with the eighty-seven cents. With that chain on his watch, Jim might be properly anxious about the time in any company. Grand as the watch was, he sometimes looked at it on the sly on account of the old leather strap that he used in place of a chain.

When Della reached home, her intoxication gave way a little to prudence and reason. She got out her curling irons and lighted the gas and went to work repairing the ravages made by generosity added to love. Which is always a tremendous task, dear friends—a mammoth task.

Within forty minutes her head was covered with tiny, close-lying curls that made her look wonderfully like a truant schoolboy. She looked at her reflection in the mirror long, carefully, and critically.

"If Jim doesn't kill me," she said to herself, "before he takes a second look at me, he'll say I look like a Coney Island chorus girl. But what could I do—oh, what could I do with a dollar and eighty-seven cents?"

At seven o'clock the coffee was made, and the frying-pan was on the back of the stove, hot and ready to cook the chops.

Jim was never late. Della doubled the fob chain in her hand and sat on the corner of the table near the door that he always entered. Then she heard his step on the stair away down on the first flight, and she turned white for just a moment. She had a habit of saying a little silent prayer about the simplest everyday things, and now she whispered: "Please God, make him think I am still pretty."

The door opened, and Jim stepped in and closed it. He looked thin and very serious. Poor fellow, he was only twenty-two—and to be burdened with a family! He needed a new overcoat, and he was without gloves.

Jim stopped inside the door, as immovable as a setter at the scent of quail. His eyes were fixed upon Della, and there was an expression in them that she could not read, and it terrified her. It was not anger, nor surprise, nor disapproval, nor horror, nor any of the sentiments that she had been prepared for. He simply stared at her fixedly with that peculiar expression on his face.

Della wriggled off the table and went for him.

"Jim, darling," she cried, "don't look at me that way. I had my hair cut off and sold because I couldn't have lived through Christmas without giving you a present. It'll grow out again—you won't mind, will you? I just had to do it. My hair grows awfully fast. Say 'Merry Christmas!' Jim, and let's be happy. You don't know what a nice—what a beautiful, nice gift I've got for you."

"You've cut off your hair?" asked Jim, laboriously, as if he had not arrived at that patent fact yet even after the hardest mental labor.

"Cut it off and sold it," said Della. "Don't you like me just as well, anyhow? I'm me without my hair, aren't I?"

Jim looked about the room curiously.

"You say your hair is gone?" he said, with an air almost of idiocy.

"You needn't look for it," said Della. "It's sold, I tell you—sold and gone, too. It's Christmas Eve, boy. Be good to me, for it went for you. Maybe the hairs of my head were numbered," she went on with sudden serious sweetness, "but nobody could ever count my love for you. Shall I put the chops on, Jim?"

Out of his trance Jim seemed quickly to wake. He enfolded his Della. For ten seconds let us regard with discreet scrutiny some inconsequential object in the other direction. Eight dollars a week or a million a year—what is the difference? A mathematician or a wit would give you the wrong answer. The magi brought valuable gifts, but that was not among them. This dark assertion will be illuminated later on.

Jim drew a package from his overcoat pocket and threw it upon the table.

"Don't make any mistake, Dell, about me," he said. "I don't think there's anything in the way of a haircut or a shave or a shampoo that could make me like my girl any less. But if you'll unwrap that package you may see why you had me going a while at first."

White fingers and nimble tore at the string and paper. And then an ecstatic scream of joy; and then—alas!—a quick feminine change to hysterical tears and wails, necessitating the immediate employment of all the comforting powers of the lord of the flat.

For there lay The Combs—the set of combs, side and back, that Della had worshipped long in a Broadway window. Beautiful combs, pure tortoise shell, with jeweled rims—just the shade to wear in the beautiful vanished hair. They were expensive combs, she knew, and her heart had simply craved and yearned over them without the least hope of possession. And now, they were hers, but the tresses that should have adorned the coveted adornments were gone.

Love is what's in the room
with you at CHRISTMAS
if you stop opening presents and listen.

~ Author unknown, attributed to a
seven-year-old named Bobby

But she hugged them to her bosom, and at length she was able to look up with dim eyes and a smile and say: "My hair grows so fast, Jim!"

And then Della leaped up like a little singed cat and cried, "Oh, oh!"

Jim had not yet seen his beautiful present. She held it out to him eagerly upon her open palm. The dull precious metal seemed to flash with a reflection of her bright and ardent spirit. "Isn't it a dandy, Jim? I hunted all over town to find it. You'll have to look at the time a hundred times a day now. Give me your watch. I want to see how it looks on it."

Instead of obeying, Jim tumbled down on the couch, put his hands under the back of his head, and smiled.

"Dell," said he, "let's put our Christmas presents away and keep 'em a while. They're too nice to use just at present. I sold the watch to get the money to buy your combs. And now suppose you put the chops on."

The magi, as you know, were wise men—wonderfully wise men—who brought gifts to the Babe in the manger. They invented the art of giving Christmas presents. Being wise, their gifts were no doubt wise ones, possibly bearing the privilege of exchange in case of duplication. And here I have lamely related to you the uneventful chronicle of two foolish children in a flat, who most unwisely sacrificed for each other the greatest treasures of their house. But in a last word to the wise of these days let it be said that of all who give gifts these two were the wisest. Of all who give and receive gifts, such as they are wisest. Everywhere they are wisest. They are the magi.

Christmas Candy Windows

The lights on Temple Square aren't the only unique Christmas tradition in Salt Lake City. Right across the street from the dazzling display of twinkling lights, you can find a different kind of decoration.

In the early 1970s, ZCMI, a now-defunct department store, began a tradition of celebrating the season with displays of candy ornaments in their store windows. The tradition has continued, now located in the store windows of the downtown Macy's. Typically, six local artists are chosen to each create a whimsical display entirely from candy. One year, the Macy's store manager revealed that they bought about one hundred pounds of assorted candy per window, including Ring Pops, lollipops, licorice, Hot Tamales, and jelly beans.

The Twelve Days of Christmas

On the first day of Christmas,
my true love sent to me
A partridge in a pear tree.

On the second day of Christmas,
my true love sent to me
Two turtle doves,
And a partridge in a pear tree.

On the third day of Christmas,
my true love sent to me
Three French hens,
Two turtle doves,
And a partridge in a pear tree.

On the fourth day of Christmas,
my true love sent to me
Four calling birds,
Three French hens,
Two turtle doves,
And a partridge in a pear tree.

On the fifth day of Christmas,
my true love sent to me
Five golden rings,
Four calling birds,
Three French hens,
Two turtle doves,
And a partridge in a pear tree.

On the sixth day of Christmas,
my true love sent to me
Six geese a-laying,
Five golden rings,
Four calling birds,
Three French hens,
Two turtle doves,
And a partridge in a pear tree.

On the seventh day of Christmas,
my true love sent to me
Seven swans a-swimming,
Six geese a-laying,
Five golden rings,
Four calling birds,
Three French hens,
Two turtle doves,
And a partridge in a pear tree.

On the eighth day of Christmas,
my true love sent to me
Eight maids a-milking,
Seven swans a-swimming,
Six geese a-laying,
Five golden rings,
Four calling birds,
Three French hens,
Two turtle doves,
And a partridge in a pear tree.

On the ninth day of Christmas,
my true love sent to me
Nine ladies dancing,
Eight maids a-milking,
Seven swans a-swimming,
Six geese a-laying,
Five golden rings,
Four calling birds,
Three French hens,
Two turtle doves,
And a partridge in a pear tree.

On the tenth day of Christmas,
my true love sent to me
Ten lords a-leaping,
Nine ladies dancing,
Eight maids a-milking,

Seven swans a-swimming,
Six geese a-laying,
Five golden rings,
Four calling birds,
Three French hens,
Two turtle doves,
And a partridge in a pear tree.

On the eleventh day of Christmas,
my true love sent to me
Eleven pipers piping,
Ten lords a-leaping,
Nine ladies dancing,
Eight maids a-milking,
Seven swans a-swimming,
Six geese a-laying,
Five golden rings,
Four calling birds,
Three French hens,
Two turtle doves,
And a partridge in a pear tree.

On the twelfth day of Christmas,
my true love sent to me

Twelve drummers drumming,
Eleven pipers piping,
Ten lords a-leaping,
Nine ladies dancing,
Eight maids a-milking,
Seven swans a-swimming,
Six geese a-laying,
Five golden rings,
Four calling birds,
Three French hens,
Two turtle doves,
And a partridge in a pear tree.

First published in England in 1780, this carol is actually French in origin and had been popular as a nursery rhyme since the sixteenth century. Evidence shows that it actually began as a Twelfth Night memory-and-forfeit game in which the leader recited increasing numbers of verses and the players had to repeat them; the first to make a mistake had to pay a "penalty," such as offering a kiss or a sweet. It was played every Twelfth Night before participants ate mince pies and twelfth cake. There is actually religious symbolism in each of the twelve "days" outlined in the song: Partridge to the true love of God; two turtle doves to the Old and New Testaments; three French hens to faith, hope, and charity; four calling birds to the four Gospels; five golden rings to the Pentateuch (the first five books of the Old Testament); six geese a-laying to the six days of creation; seven swans a-swimming to the seven gifts of the Holy Spirit; eight maids a-milking to the eight beatitudes; nine ladies dancing to the nine fruits of the Holy Spirit; ten lords a-leaping to the ten commandments; eleven pipers piping to the eleven faithful Apostles; and twelve drummers drumming to the twelve points of doctrine in the Apostle's Creed.

GREAT GIFTS FOR YOUR NEIGHBORS

Cookies in a Jar

Layer the following in a large Mason jar:

- 1⅓ cups all purpose flour, spooned into measuring cup & leveled
- 1 teaspoon baking powder
- 1 teaspoon baking soda
- ¼ teaspoon salt
- 1 cup cooking oats
- ¾ cup red and green M&Ms
- ¾ cup semi-sweet or milk chocolate chips
- ½ cup brown sugar, packed
- ½ cup white sugar

Then prepare instructions for adding the remaining ingredients:

- 1 slightly beaten egg
- ½ cup butter (melted slightly in the microwave)
- 1 teaspoon vanilla

Mix wet ingredients into dry ingredients. Use a large spoon to work it all together. You may need to use your hands to get everything incorporated. Bake at 350 degrees F for 12–15 minutes.

Snowman Kits

Assemble a variety of snowman accessories (hat, mittens, large buttons, scarf, etc.). Place the accessories in a box, and you have a cute gift for a young family.

Peppermint Play-Dough

A great gift for your children's friends!

1 cup flour
¼ cup salt
2 Tablespoons cream of tartar
1 Tablespoon Peppermint Oil Extract
1 Tablespoon vegetable oil
1 cup water
A few drops of red food coloring (optional)

1. Mix flour, salt, and cream of tartar in a medium cooking pot.
2. Add water, peppermint extract, and oil.
3. Stir regularly over medium heat for 3–5.
4. When mixture forms a ball, remove and place on wax paper.
5. Knead until smooth. (If you are feeling extra festive, you can add a handful of glitter to give it some sparkle!)
6. Put in a small Mason jar and add a decorative ribbon.

Homemade Honey Cinnamon Nutmeg Facial Mask

Mix together about a cup of honey, 1 Tablespoon of cinnamon, and ½ Tablespoon of nutmeg. Stir until the spices are incorporated into the honey. For thicker mask, use less honey. Don't use cinnamon if you're giving this to someone with sensitive skin!

Probably the reason we all go so haywire at
Christmas time
with the endless unrestrained and often silly buying of gifts
is that we don't quite know how to put
our LOVE into words.

~ Harlan Miller

GIFTS of time and love are surely the basic ingredients of a truly *merry Christmas.*

~ Peg Bracken

Christmas gift suggestions:

To your enemy,
FORGIVENESS.

To an opponent,
TOLERANCE.

To a friend,
YOUR HEART.

To a customer,
SERVICE.

To all,
CHARITY.

To every child, a
GOOD EXAMPLE.

To yourself,
respect.

~ Oren Arnold

I THINK OF YOU IN KIND REGARDS AND FRIENDSHIP TRUE.

A LITTLE ESSAY

Christmas-Giving and Christmas-Living

By Henry Van Dyke

The custom of exchanging presents on a certain day in the year is very much older than Christmas and means very much less. It has obtained in almost all ages of the world and among many different nations. It is a fine thing or a foolish thing, as the case may be; an encouragement to friendliness or a tribute to fashion; an expression of good nature or a bid for favor; an outgoing of generosity or a disguise of greed; a cheerful old custom or a futile old farce, according to the spirit which animates it and the form which it takes.

But when this ancient and variously interpreted tradition of a day of gifts was transferred to the Christmas season, it was brought into vital contact with an idea which must transform it and with an example which must lift it up to a higher plane. The example is the life of Jesus. The idea is unselfish interest in the happiness of others.

The great gift of Jesus to the world was Himself. He lived with and for men. He kept back nothing. In every particular and personal gift that He made to certain people, there was something of Himself that made it precious.

For example, at the wedding in Cana of Galilee, it was His thought for the feelings of the giver of the feast and His wish that every guest should find due entertainment that lent the flavor of a heavenly hospitality to the wine which He provided.

When He gave bread and fish to the hungry multitude who had followed him out among the hills by the Lake of Gennesaret, the people were refreshed and strengthened by the sense of the personal care of Jesus for their welfare, as much as by the food which He bestowed upon them. It was another illustration of the sweetness of "a dinner of herbs, where love is."

The gifts of healing which He conferred upon many different kinds of sufferers were, in every case, evidences that Jesus was willing to give something of Himself—His thought, His sympathy, His vital power—to the men and women among whom He lived. Once, when a paralytic was brought to Jesus on a bed, He surprised everybody and offended many by giving the poor wretch the pardon of his sins, before He gave new life to his body. That was just because Jesus thought before He gave; because He desired to satisfy the deepest need; because, in fact, He gave something of Himself in every gift. All true Christmas-giving ought to be after this pattern.

Not that it must all be solemn and serious. For the most part it deals with little wants, little joys, little tokens of friendly feeling. But the feeling must be more than the token; else the gift does not really belong to Christmas.

It takes time and effort and unselfish expenditure of strength to make gifts in this way. But it is the only way that fits the season.

The finest Christmas gift is not the one that costs the most money, but the one that carries the most love.

II

But how seldom Christmas comes—only once a year—and how soon it is over—a night and a day! If that is the whole of it, it seems not much more durable than the little toys that one buys of a fakir on the street corner. They run for an hour and then the spring breaks and the legs come off, and nothing remains but a contribution to the dust heap.

But surely that need not and ought not to be the whole of Christmas—only a single day of generosity, ransomed from the dull servitude of a selfish year, only a single night of merry-making, celebrated in the slave-quarters of a selfish race! If every gift is the token of a personal thought, a friendly feeling, an unselfish interest in the joy of others, then the thought, the feeling, the interest, may remain after the gift is made.

The little present or the rare and long-wished-for gift (it matters not whether the vessel be of gold or silver or iron or wood or clay or just a small bit of birch bark folded into a cup), may carry a message something like this:

"I am thinking of you today, because it is Christmas, and I wish you happiness. And tomorrow, because it will be the day after Christmas, I shall still wish you happiness; and so on, clear through the year. I may not be able to tell you about it every day, because I may be far away or because both of us may be very busy or perhaps because I cannot even afford to pay the postage on so many letters or find the time to write them. But that makes no difference. The thought and the wish will be here just the same. In my work and in the business of life, I mean to try not to be unfair to you or injure you in any way. In my pleasure, if we can be together, I would like to share the fun with you. Whatever joy or success comes to you will make me glad. Without pretense, and in plain words, goodwill to you is what I mean, in the Spirit of Christmas."

It is not necessary to put a message like this into high-flown language, to swear absolute devotion and deathless consecration. In love and friendship, small, steady payments on a gold basis are better than immense promissory notes. Nor, indeed, is it always necessary to put the message into words at all, nor even to convey it by a tangible token. To feel it and to act it out—that is the main thing.

There are a great many people in the world whom we know, more or less, but to whom for various reasons we cannot very well send a Christmas gift. But there is hardly one, in all the circles of our acquaintance, with whom we may not exchange the touch of Christmas life.

In the outer circles, cheerful greetings, courtesy, consideration; in the inner circles, sympathetic interest, hearty congratulations, honest encouragement; in the inmost circle, comradeship, helpfulness, tenderness,—

"Beautiful friendship tried by sun and wind
Durable from the daily dust of life."

After all, Christmas-living is the best kind of Christmas-giving.

"Christmas is not just a time for festivity and merry making. It is more than that. It is a time for the contemplation of eternal things. The Christmas spirit is a spirit of giving and forgiving."

~ J. C. Penney

Mankind is a great, an immense family.
This is proved by what we feel in our *hearts*
at CHRISTMAS.

~ Pope John XXIII

May all the
Christmas Joys
be Yours

A Legend of the White Gifts

As Told by Phebe A. Curtiss

A great many years ago in a land far away from us, there was a certain king who was dearly beloved by all of his people. Men admired him because he was strong and just. In all of his dealings, they knew they could depend upon him. Every matter that came to his consideration was carefully weighed in his mind, and his decisions were always wise. Women trusted him because he was pure and true, with lofty thoughts and high ambitions, and the children loved him because of his gentleness and tenderness toward them. He was never so burdened with affairs of state that he could not stop to speak a pleasant word of greeting to the tiniest child, and the very poorest of his subjects knew they could count upon his interest in them.

This deep-seated love and reverence for their king made the people of this country wish very much for a way in which to give expression to it so that he would understand it. Many consultations were held, and one after another the plans suggested were rejected. But at last a most happy solution was found. It was rapidly circulated here and there, and it met with the most hearty approval everywhere.

It was a plan for celebrating the king's birthday.

Of course, that had been done in many lands before, but there were certain features about this celebration which differed from anything that had ever been tried. They decided that on the king's birthday the people should all bring him gifts, but they wanted in some way to let him know that these gifts were the expression of a love which was pure and true and unselfish, and in order to show that, it was decided that each gift should be a white gift.

The king heard about this beautiful plan, and it touched his heart in a wonderful way. He decided that he would do his part to carry out the idea and let his loving subjects know how much he appreciated their thoughtfulness.

You can just imagine the excitement there was all over the land as the king's birthday drew near. All sorts of loving sacrifices had been made, and everyone was anxious to make his gift the very best he had to offer. At last the day dawned, and eagerly the people came dressed in white and carrying their white gifts. To their surprise they were ushered into a great big room—the largest one in the palace. They stood in silence when they first entered it, for it was beautiful beyond all expression. It was a white room—the floor was white marble; the ceiling looked like a mass of soft, white, fluffy clouds; the walls were hung with beautiful white silken draperies; and all the furnishings were white. At one end of the room stood a stately white throne, and seated upon it was their beloved ruler clad in shining white robes. His attendants—all dressed in white—were grouped around him.

Then came the presentation of the gifts. What a wealth of them there was—and how different they were in value. In those days it was just as it is now—there were many people who had great wealth, and they brought gifts which were generous in proportion to their wealth.

One brought a handful of pearls, another a number of carved ivories. There

were beautiful laces and silks and embroideries, all in pure white. Even splendid white chargers were brought to his majesty.

But many of the people were poor—some of them very poor—and their gifts were quite different from those I have been telling about. Some of the women brought handfuls of white rice, some of the boys brought their favorite white pigeons, and one dear little girl smilingly gave him a pure white rose.

It was wonderful to watch the king as each one came and kneeled before him as he presented his gift. He never seemed to notice whether the gift was great or small; he regarded not one gift above another so long as all were white. Never had the king been so happy as he was that day, and never had such real joy filled the hearts of the people. They decided to use the same plan every year, and so it came to pass that year after year on the king's birthday, the people came from here and there and everywhere and brought their white gifts—the gifts which showed that their love was pure, strong, true, and without stain. And year after year, the king sat in his white robes on the white throne in the great white room, and it was always the same—he regarded not one gift above another so long as all were white.

Did You Know?

In the United States, there are more than 3 billion Christmas cards sent each year.

Christmas Party

Getting together with friends and family is the most beloved part of Christmas. It gives us the opportunity to remember what is truly important in a season that can sometimes overwhelm us with materialism. Here are a few suggestions for themes, games, recipes, and so on for your own Christmas party.

- Host your own "White Gifts" party. You can send the story out with the invitations or just let guests know to bring a white gift. Read the story and hold a gift exchange.
- Throw a cookie swap. Invite guests to make their favorite Christmas cookie (or other treat) and ask them to come prepared to supply enough copies of the recipe for each guest.
- Or do a variation on the cookie swap, and instead of desserts, ask guests to bring their favorite appetizer. Everyone will appreciate new ideas for foods to bring to another Christmas party.
- Sing Christmas carol karaoke or go caroling around your neighborhood. Make sure to provide refreshments to warm your guests up if you're going to be in the cold weather for a while!
- Host an international Christmas celebration. Invite your guests to learn about the Christmas traditions of another country and bring a dish appropriate to that culture. See, for example, the following Swedish Christmas Braid recipe. Allow guests time to share what they learned.
- Hold a breakfast-themed party. Many people have a traditional Christmas-morning breakfast. To get started, see the following Overnight Breakfast Casserole recipe. Ask guests to share their personal Christmas traditions.

SWEDISH CHRISTMAS BRAID

2¾ cup bread flour
1 package yeast (2¼ teaspoons)
1 teaspoon ground cardamom
¾ cup whole milk
⅓ cup sugar
¼ cup butter
½ teaspoon salt
1 egg

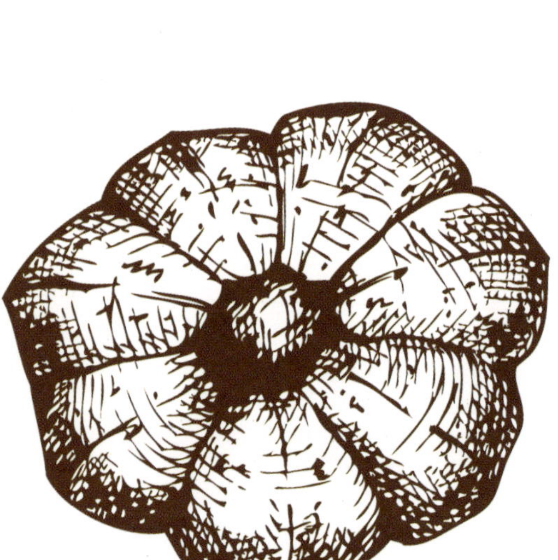

1. In a mixing bowl or stand mixer, combine yeast, ¾ cup flour, and cardamom.
2. In the microwave, heat the milk, butter, and sugar until warm. Stir together.
3. Add the milk mixture to the dry mixture, and mix on low for 30 seconds.
4. Add egg. Beat for 3 minutes at medium speed.
5. Slowly add flour to make a soft dough (use only what you need of the remaining flour). Mix between additions to make sure you don't add too much.
6. Using a dough hook, mix until the dough is smooth and pulls away from the side of the bowl.
7. Cover the mixing bowl and put in a warm place to rise until doubled. This takes almost an hour.
8. Punch down dough. Place it onto a floured surface, and cut into 3 sections. Let rest for 10 minutes.
9. Cover a cookie sheet with parchment paper.
10. Roll the 3 sections into 3 ropes (about 16 inches long) and braid loosely on the lined cookie sheet. When you're finished, tuck the ends under the braid.
11. Cover the braid with a towel and let rise again until double in size.
12. Bake at 375 degrees F for 18–20 minutes.

OVERNIGHT BREAKFAST CASSEROLE

10 eggs, whisked
¼ cup milk, whisked with the eggs
1 package pork breakfast sausage roll, uncooked (you can use a package of uncooked bacon, too)
½ bag shredded hash browns, frozen
½ cup shredded cheddar cheese
seasoning to taste (salt, pepper, garlic powder, etc.)

1. Before you go to bed, spray your Crock Pot with cooking spray. Line the bottom and all along the edges.
2. Place your sausage first, breaking it into small pieces.
3. Lay shredded hash browns on top, sprinkling evenly over the sausage.
4. Season the hash browns mixture.
5. Pour whisked eggs over top the potatoes and sausage, ensuring everything is covered in egg.
6. Season a little again on top and cover to cook on low overnight.
7. Before serving, sprinkle shredded cheese over top to melt.

Serves: 10

Christmas Group Games

Keep everyone entertained at your Christmas party with fun, lively games the whole family can take part in:

- Fill the stocking—Divide into teams. Each team receives a spoon, a bag of pre-wrapped candy, and a stocking. Race to see which team can get their stocking filled first. You can use the stockings as prizes for the winners of any games.

- Christmas carol charades—Divide into teams and take turns acting out carols. Or do a variation and act out classic Christmas movies.

- Holiday ABC's—Give each person or team a piece of paper with the alphabet written vertically from A to Z. Have them write a holiday word that starts with each letter. The first one to complete the list wins.

- Christmas dice gift exchange—Have everyone sit in a circle and start with a gift. Play a Christmas carol while 1, 2, or 3 dice are being passed around (space them out). Each person rolls and passes the dice. If they roll a six, they can trade packages with whomever they want. At the end of the song, everyone keeps the package in front of him or her.

- Snowball Toss—Set up a bucket on one side of the room. On the other side, place a bucket of large marshmallows. See how many "snowballs" make it into the empty bucket in 30 seconds.

Away in a Manger

Away in a manger, no crib for a bed,
The little Lord Jesus lay down His sweet head.
The stars in the bright sky looked down where He lay,
The little lord Jesus asleep on the hay.

The cattle are lowing, the baby awakes
But little Lord Jesus, no crying He makes.
I love Thee, Lord Jesus, look down from the sky.
And stay by my side till morning is nigh.

Be near me, Lord Jesus, I ask Thee to stay
Close by me for ever and love me, I pray.
Bless all the dear children in Thy tender care
And take us to Heaven to live with Thee there.

The author of "Away in a Manger" is actually unknown, but many throughout the world believe the words were written by Martin Luther; in Dainty Songs for Little Lads and Lasses, published in 1887, it is titled "Luther's Cradle Hymn" and bears the note, "Composed by Martin Luther for his children, and still sung by German mothers to their little ones." Some believe that the words of the text were written as a poem for the four hundredth anniversary of Luther's birth and were credited to him as a marketing gimmick. In actuality, it was a poem of unknown origin published in a Sunday school book in Philadelphia. The music, while written by William J. Kirkpatrick, is based on a waltz Johann Strauss Jr. wrote nineteen years earlier.

HOW MUCH DO YOU KNOW ABOUT *Christmas on Temple Square?*

How long do the lights take to put up?

The grounds crews get started on the Christmas display in August, preparing power sources and cables. The first lights begin to go up in September. The crews work through February or March to remove the lights once the season is over.

Why don't they leave the lights up year-round?

Because the trees on Temple Square grow every year, if the crews left the lights up, by the time Christmas came around again, there could be anywhere from eighteen inches to six feet of growth. The lights wouldn't fit anymore!

When did the Church start hanging lights at temple square?

In 1965, President David O. McKay approached the Temple Square gardener and asked him to put lights in the trees. That year 40,000 lights were illuminated at a lighting ceremony in front of a crowd of almost 15,000 people. For more than thirty years, there was a ceremony featuring speakers and music, but soon the crowds became too large and the ceremony was discontinued.

How many lights are used?

The number of lights increases through the years. In 1986, around 250,000 lights went up. By 1999, that number had increased to more than 750,000. Today, the crew believes there are more than one million lights adorning Temple Square. There are so many lights, in fact, that additional trees are brought in to decorate. These are called stand-in trees. Each year the grounds crew harvests about one hundred trees from the mountains from state school trust lands, so the payment for those trees goes to helping Utah schools.

Has there ever been a time when they didn't turn the lights on?

In 1973, U.S. president Richard Nixon called for conserving energy. In response to that request, the Church refrained from lighting up Temple Square.

Are there other temples that decorate the grounds for Christmas?

A few other temples around the world have taken up the tradition of putting up lights at Christmastime. At the Hamilton New Zealand Temple, civic leaders are invited to turn on the lights, building bridges in the community. Volunteers from fifty-six stakes help decorate the Los Angeles California Temple. In Manila, Philippines, the temple displays 360,000 lights, and the lighting ceremony typically draws a crowd of 10,000 people, increasing the Church's exposure in that country. In addition to lights, many temples are known for their nativity scenes, or crèches. In Washington, D.C., you can see an international exhibit of more than one hundred crèches. The Mesa Arizona Temple features a life-size reproduction of Mary and Joseph on the road to Bethlehem.

Did You Know?

The first recorded instance we have of lights used on an evergreen tree was in the sixteenth century, when Christian reformer Martin Luther added candles after being inspired by the stars shining through the evergreens as he walked home.

The first known electrically illuminated Christmas tree was the creation of Edward H. Johnson. He had light bulbs made especially for him, hand-wired with eighty red, white and blue electric incandescent bulbs the size of walnuts, which he used to decorate his Christmas tree in 1882.

Christmas
Greetings

The Little Match Girl

By Hans Christian Anderson

It was dreadfully cold; it was snowing fast and was almost dark, as evening came on—the last evening of the year. In the cold and the darkness, there went along the street a poor little girl, bareheaded and with naked feet. When she left home, she had slippers on, it is true; but they were much too large for her feet—slippers that her mother had used until then—and the poor little girl lost them in running across the street when two carriages were passing terribly fast. When she looked for them, one was not to be found, and a boy seized the other and ran away with it, saying he would use it for a cradle someday when he had children of his own.

So on the little girl went with her bare feet, which were red and blue with cold. In an old apron that she wore were bundles of matches, and she carried a bundle also in her hand. No one had bought so much as a bunch all the long day, and no one had given her even a penny.

Poor little girl! Shivering with cold and hunger she crept along, a perfect picture of misery!

The snowflakes fell on her long flaxen hair, which hung in pretty curls about her throat; but she thought not of her beauty nor of the cold. Lights gleamed in every window, and there came to her the savory smell of roast goose, for it was New Year's Eve. And it was of this which she thought.

In a corner formed by two houses, one of which projected beyond the other, she sat cowering down. She had drawn under her little feet, but still she grew colder and colder; yet she dared not go home, for she had sold no matches and could not bring a penny of money. Her father would certainly beat her; and, besides, it was cold enough at home, for they had only the houseroof above them; and, though the largest holes had been stopped with straw and rags, there were left many through which the cold wind whistled.

And now her little hands were nearly frozen with cold. Alas! A single match might do her good if she might only draw it from the bundle, rub it against the wall, and warm her fingers by it. So at last she drew one out. *Whischt*! How it blazed and burned! It gave out a warm, bright flame like a little candle as she held her hands over it. A wonderful little light it was. It really seemed to the little girl as if she sat before a great iron stove, with polished brass feet and brass shovel and tongs. So blessedly it burned that the little maiden stretched out her feet to warm them also. How comfortable she was! But lo! The flame went out, the stove vanished, and nothing remained but the little burned match in her hand.

She rubbed another match against the wall. It burned brightly, and where the light fell upon the wall it became transparent like a veil, so that she could see through it into the room. A snow-white cloth was spread upon the table, on which was a beautiful china dinner service, while a roast goose, stuffed with apples and prunes, steamed famously and sent forth a most savory smell. And what was more delightful still, and wonderful, the goose jumped from the dish, with knife and fork still in its breast, and waddled along the floor straight to the little girl.

But the match went out then, and nothing was left to her but the thick, damp wall.

She lighted another match. And now she was under a most beautiful Christmas tree, larger and far more prettily trimmed than the one she had seen through the glass doors at the rich merchant's. Hundreds of wax tapers were burning on the green branches, and gay figures, such as she had seen in the shop windows, looked down upon her. The child stretched out her hands to them; then the match went out.

Still the lights of the Christmas tree rose higher and higher. She saw them as stars in heaven, and one of them fell, forming a long trail of fire.

"Now someone is dying," murmured the child softly; for her grandmother, the only person who had loved her and who was now dead, had told her that whenever a star falls, a soul mounts up to God.

She struck yet another match against the wall, and again it was light; and in the brightness there appeared before her the dear old grandmother, bright and radiant, yet sweet and mild and happy as she had never looked on earth.

"Oh, Grandmother," cried the child, "take me with you. I know you will go away when the match burns out. You, too, will vanish, like the warm stove, the splendid New Year's feast, the beautiful Christmas tree." And lest her grandmother should disappear, she rubbed the whole bundle of matches against the wall.

And the matches burned with such a brilliant light that it became brighter than noonday. Her grandmother had never looked so grand and beautiful. She took the little girl in her arms, and both flew together, joyously and gloriously, mounting higher and higher, far above the earth; and for them there was neither hunger, nor cold, nor care—they were with God.

But in the corner, at the dawn of day, sat the poor girl, leaning against the wall, with red cheeks and smiling mouth—frozen to death on the last evening of the old year. Stiff and cold she sat with the matches, one bundle of which was burned.

"She wanted to warm herself, poor little thing," people said. No one imagined what sweet visions she had had or how gloriously she had gone with her grandmother to enter upon the joys of a new year.

Symbolism of the Wreath:

Wreaths are used to remind us of the eternal nature of Christ and His Atonement. Their shape, a circle, is never-ending.

What is Christmas?
It is TENDERNESS for the past,
courage for the present, HOPE for the future.
It is a fervent wish that every cup may overflow
with *blessings rich and eternal,*
and that every path may lead to peace.

-Agnes M. Pharo

How the Fir Tree Became the Christmas Tree

By Aunt Hede

This is the story of how the fir tree became the Christmas tree.

At the time when the Christ Child was born, all the people, the animals, and the trees and plants were very happy. The Child was born to bring peace and happiness to the whole world. People came daily to see the little One, and they always brought gifts with them.

There were three trees, which saw the people, standing near the crypt, and they wished that they, too, might give presents to the Christ Child.

The Palm said: "I will choose my most beautiful leaf and place it as a fan over the Child."

"And I," said the Olive, "will sprinkle sweet-smelling oil upon His head."

"What can I give to the Child?" asked the Fir, who stood near.

"You!" cried the others. "You have nothing to offer Him. Your needles would prick Him, and your tears are sticky."

So the poor little Fir tree was very unhappy, and it said: "Yes, you are right. I have nothing to offer the Christ Child."

Now, quite near the trees stood the Christmas Angel, who had heard all that the trees had said. The Angel was sorry for the Fir tree, who was so lowly and without envy of the other trees. So, when it was dark, and the stars came out, he begged a few of the little stars to come down and rest upon the branches of the Fir tree. They did as the Christmas Angel asked, and the Fir tree shone suddenly with a beautiful light.

And, at that very moment, the Christ Child opened His eyes—for He had been asleep—and as the lovely light fell upon Him, He smiled.

Every year people keep the dear Christmas Child's birthday by giving gifts to each other, and every year, in remembrance of His first birthday, the Christmas Angel places in every house a fir tree. Covered with starry candles, it shines for the children as the stars shone for the Christ Child. The Fir tree was rewarded for its meekness, for to no other tree is it given to shine upon so many happy faces.

Symbolism of the Christmas Tree:

Christmas trees remind us of the true meaning of Christmas in multiple ways. Unlike other trees, fir trees stay green and living throughout the winter, representing the eternal nature of God. The triangle shape of a Christmas tree can also serve to remind us of the three members of the Godhead.

Christmas Trees

DID YOU KNOW?

- There are about 25–30 million real Christmas trees sold in the United States every year.
- Currently, there are about 350 million Christmas trees growing on Christmas tree farms in the United States.
- For every Christmas tree harvested from a tree farm, there are three seedlings planted the following spring.
- A Christmas tree takes between four and fifteen years to grow to full height, but the average is seven years.
- The states that produce the most Christmas trees are Oregon, North Carolina, Michigan, Pennsylvania, Wisconsin, and Washington.
- The record for the most Christmas trees chopped down in two minutes is twenty-seven and belongs to Erin Lavoie. She set the record in 2008.
- The largest human Christmas tree consisted of 2,945 participants in Honduras on 1 December 2014. The tree included people dressed in yellow to form a star, in red for the tree's ornaments, and in green for the tree branches.

O Christmas Tree

O Christmas tree, O Christmas tree,
How lovely are your branches!
In beauty green will always grow
Through summer sun and winter snow.
O Christmas tree, O Christmas tree,
How lovely are your branches!

O Christmas tree, O Christmas tree,
You are the tree most loved!
How often you give us delight
In brightly shining Christmas light!
O Christmas tree, O Christmas tree,
You are the tree most loved!

O Christmas tree, O Christmas tree,
Your beauty green will teach me
That hope and love will ever be
The way to joy and peace for me.
O Christmas tree, O Christmas tree,
Your beauty green will teach me.

No one knows who wrote the original music or lyrics to "O Christmas Tree"—also known as "O Tannenbaum"—but we do know it's a carol of German origin whose lyrics date back to 1550. Music for the arrangement we now sing, which is based on an old folk tune, was written in 1824 by Ernst Anschütz, a Leipzig composer and organist. The tannenbaum, a fir tree, has inspired a number of songs, but this carol is the best known among them; it celebrates the tradition that began in the nineteenth century of bringing a tree inside at Christmas and decorating it with bells and ornaments. It was also inspired by the legend that on the night Jesus was born, all the trees in all the forests throughout the world bore their most delicate fruit.

MERRY
CHRISTMAS

The Three Kings

By Henry Wadsworth Longfellow

Three Kings came riding from far away,
Melchior and Gaspar and Baltasar;
Three Wise Men out of the East were they,
And they travelled by night and they slept by day,
For their guide was a beautiful, wonderful star.

The star was so beautiful, large, and clear,
That all the other stars of the sky
Became a white mist in the atmosphere,
And by this they know that the coming was near
Of the Prince foretold in the prophecy.

Three caskets they bore on their saddle-bows,
Three caskets of gold with golden keys;
Their robes were of crimson silk with rows
Of bells and pomegranates and furbelows,
Their turbans like blossoming almond-trees.

And so the Three Kings rode into the West,
Through the dusk of night, over hill and dell,
And sometimes they nodded with beard on breast,
And sometimes talked, as they paused to rest,
With the people they met at some wayside well.

"Of the child that is born," said Baltasar,
"Good people, I pray you, tell us the news;
For we in the East have seen his star,
And have ridden fast, and have ridden far,
To find and worship the King of the Jews."

And the people answered, "You ask in vain;
We know of no king but Herod the Great!"
They thought the Wise Men were men insane,
As they spurred their horses across the plain,
Like riders in haste, and who cannot wait.

And when they came to Jerusalem,
Herod the Great, who had heard this thing,
Sent for the Wise Men and questioned them;

And said, "Go down unto Bethlehem,
And bring me tidings of this new king."

So they rode away; and the star stood still,
The only one in the gray of morn;
Yes, it stopped, it stood still of its own free will,
Right over Bethlehem on the hill,
The city of David where Christ was born.

And the Three Kings rode through the gate and the guard,
Through the silent street, till their horses turned
And neighed as they entered the great inn-yard;
But the windows were closed, and the doors were barred,
And only a light in the stable burned.

And cradled there in the scented hay,
In the air made sweet by the breath of kine,
The little child in the manger lay,
The child, that would be king one day
Of a kingdom not human but divine.

His mother Mary of Nazareth
Sat watching beside his place of rest,
Watching the even flow of his breath,
For the joy of life and the terror of death
Were mingled together in her breast.

They laid their offerings at his feet:
The gold was a tribute to the King,
The frankincense, with its odor sweet,
Was for the Priest, the Paraclete,
The myrrh for the body's burying.

And the mother wondered and bowed her head,
And sat as still as a statue of stone;
Her heart was troubled yet comforted,
Remembering what the Angel had said
Of an endless reign and of David's throne.

Then the Kings rode out of the city gate,
With a clatter of hoofs in proud array;
But they went not back to Herod the Great,
For they knew his malice and feared his hate,
And returned to their homes by another way.

We Three Kings of Orient Are

We three kings of Orient are,
Bearing gifts we traverse afar,
Field and fountain, moor and mountain,
Following yonder star.

Chorus
O Star of wonder, Star of light,
Star with royal beauty bright,
Westward leading, still proceeding,
Guide us to Thy perfect light.

Born a King on Bethlehem's plain,
Gold I bring, to crown Him again,
King forever, ceasing never,
Over us all to rein.

Chorus

Frankincense to offer have I,
Incense owns a Deity nigh.
Pray'r and praising, all men raising
Worship Him, God most high.

Chorus

Myrrh have I, its bitter perfume
Breathes a life of gathering gloom;
Sorr'wing, sighing, bleeding, dying,
Sealed in the stone cold tomb.

Chorus

Glorious now behold Him arise,
King and God and Sacrifice.
Alleluia, Alleluia,
Earth to the heav'ns replies.

Chorus

The Reverend John Henry Hopkins Jr. wrote both the lyrics and the music to this carol when, as an ordained Episcopal deacon, he was asked in 1857 to organize an holiday pageant for the students of the General Theological Seminary in New York City. "We Three Kings of Orient Are" comprised the part of the pageant in which Melchior, Caspar, and Balthazar brought their gifts of gold, frankincense, and myrrh to the Christ child to signify His kingship.

What Child Is This?

What child is this, who, laid to rest,
On Mary's lap is sleeping?
Whom angels greet with anthems sweet,
While shepherds watch are keeping?
This, this is Christ the King,
Whom shepherds guard and angels sing:
Haste, haste to bring Him laud,
The babe, the son of Mary.

Why lies He in such mean estate,
Where ox and donkeys are feeding?
Good Christians, fear, for sinners here
The silent Word is pleading.
Nails, spears shall pierce him through,
the cross He bore for me, for you.
Hail, hail the Word made flesh,
the Babe, the Son of Mary.

So bring him incense, gold, and myrrh,
Come, peasant, king, to own Him.
The King of kings salvation brings,
Let loving hearts enthrone Him.
Raise, raise a song on high,
The virgin sings her lullaby
Joy, joy for Christ is born,
The babe, the Son of Mary.

This, this is Christ the King,
Whom shepherds guard and angels sing:
Haste, haste to bring Him laud,
The babe, the son of Mary.

At the age of twenty-nine, lyricist William Chatterton Dix was suddenly struck with a near-fatal illness and was confined to bed for several months; during the resulting deep depression that followed his near-death experience, he wrote the words to a number of hymns, among them "What Child Is This?" The carol is actually three stanzas of a longer piece, "The Manger Throne." The words were later set to the traditional English tune "Greensleeves," which was first licensed in 1580 to Richard Jones, though many believe it even older than that.

Once in Royal David's City

Once in royal David's city,
Stood a lowly cattle shed,
Where a mother laid her Baby,
In a manger for His bed:
Mary was that mother mild,
Jesus Christ, her little Child.

He came down to earth from heaven,
Who is God and Lord of all,
And His shelter was a stable,
And His cradle was a stall:
With the poor, and mean, and lowly,
Lived on earth our Saviour holy.

For He is our childhood's pattern;
Day by day, like us, He grew;
He was little, weak, and helpless,
Tears and smiles, like us He knew;
And He cares when we are sad,
And He shares when we are glad.

And our eyes at last shall see Him,
Through His own redeeming love;
For that Child so dear and gentle,
Is our Lord in heaven above:
And He leads His children on,
To the place where He is gone.

Painting a rich picture of the events of the Nativity, the words of this carol were written in the mid-1800s as a poem by Cecil Frances Alexander, the wife of an Anglican clergyman. A hymn writer and poet born in Dublin, she began writing while still a child. Her compositions were featured in the Church of Ireland hymnbooks; by the close of the nineteenth century, her book—*Hymns for Little Children*—which contained this carol, was in its sixty-ninth edition, and all profits from its sales were donated to the Derry and Raphoe Diocesan Institution for the Deaf and Dumb. Among her other hymns are such well-known pieces as "All Things Bright and Beautiful" and "There Is a Green Hill Far Away." "Once in Royal David's City" was put to music by English organist Henry John Gauntlett a year after the poem was written.

Babouscka

Russian Legend

It was the night the dear Christ Child came to Bethlehem. In a country far away from Him, an old, old woman named Babouscka sat in her snug little house by her warm fire. The wind was drifting the snow outside and howling down the chimney, but it only made Babouscka's fire burn more brightly.

"How glad I am that I may stay indoors!" said Babouscka, holding her hands out to the bright blaze. But suddenly she heard a loud rap at her door. She opened it, and her candle shone on three old men standing outside in the snow. Their beards were as white as the snow and so long that they reached the ground. Their eyes shone kindly in the light of Babouscka's candle, and their arms were full of precious things—boxes of jewels, sweet-smelling oils, and ointments.

"We have traveled far, Babouscka," said they, "and we stop to tell you of the Baby Prince born this night in Bethlehem. He comes to rule the world and teach all men to be loving and true. We carry Him gifts. Come with us, Babouscka!"

Babouscka looked at the driving snow, and then inside at her cozy room and the crackling fire. "It is too late for me to go with you, good sirs," she said. "The weather is too cold." She went inside again and shut the door, and the old men journeyed on to Bethlehem without her. But as Babouscka sat rocking by her fire, she began to think about the little Christ Child, for she loved all babies.

"Tomorrow I will go to find Him," she said. "Tomorrow, when it is light, I will carry Him some toys."

So when it was morning, Babouscka put on her long cloak, took her staff, and filled a basket with the pretty things a baby would like—gold balls, wooden toys, and strings of silver cobwebs—and she set out to find the Christ Child.

But, oh! Babouscka had forgotten to ask the three old men the road to Bethlehem, and they had traveled so far through the night that she could not overtake them. Up and down the roads she hurried, through woods and fields and towns, saying to whomsoever she met: "I go to find the Christ Child. Where does He lie? I bring some pretty toys for His sake."

But no one could tell her the way to go, and they all said: "Farther on, Babouscka. Farther on." So she traveled on and on and on for years and years—but she never found the little Christ Child.

They say that old Babouscka is traveling still, looking for Him. When Christmas Eve comes and the children are lying fast asleep, Babouscka comes softly through the snowy fields and towns, wrapped in her long cloak and carrying her basket. With her staff she raps gently at the doors, goes inside, and holds her candle close to the little children's faces.

"Is He here?" she asks. "Is the little Christ Child here?" And then she turns sorrowfully away again, crying: "Farther on, farther on." But before she leaves, she takes a toy from her basket and lays it beside the pillow for a Christmas gift. "For His sake," she says softly and then hurries on forever in search of the little Christ Child.

May every goodly gift combine your Christmas hours to bless

The Wooden Shoes of Little Wolff

By François Coppée [Adapted]

Once upon a time—so long ago that the world has forgotten the date—in a city in the north of Europe—the name of which is so hard to pronounce that no one remembers it—there was a little boy, just seven years old, whose name was Wolff. He was an orphan and lived with his aunt, a hard-hearted, avaricious old woman, who never kissed him but once a year, on New Year's Day, and who sighed with regret every time she gave him a bowlful of soup. The poor little boy was so sweet-tempered that he loved the old woman in spite of her bad treatment.

As Wolff's aunt was known to have a house of her own and a woolen stocking full of gold, she did not dare to send her nephew to the school for the poor. But she wrangled so that the schoolmaster of the rich boys' school was forced to lower his price and admit little Wolff among his pupils. The bad schoolmaster was vexed to have a boy so meanly clad and who paid so little, and so he punished little Wolff severely without cause, ridiculed him, and even incited against him his comrades, who were the sons of rich citizens. They made the orphan their drudge and mocked him so much that the little boy was as miserable as the stones in the street and hid himself away in corners to cry when the Christmas season came.

On the eve of the great day, the schoolmaster was to take all his pupils to the midnight mass and then to conduct them home again to their parents' houses.

Now as the winter was very severe and a quantity of snow had fallen within the past few days, the boys came to the place of meeting warmly wrapped up, fur-lined caps drawn down over their ears, padded jackets, knitted gloves and mittens, and good strong shoes with thick soles. Only little Wolff presented himself shivering in thin, everyday clothes and wearing on his feet socks and wooden shoes.

His naughty comrades tried to annoy him in every possible way, but the orphan was so busy warming his hands by blowing on them that he paid no heed to the taunts of the others. Then the band of boys, marching two by two, started for the parish church.

It was comfortable inside the church, which was brilliant with lighted tapers. The pupils, made lively by the gentle warmth, the sound of the organ, and the singing of the choir, began to chatter in low tones. They boasted of the midnight treats awaiting them at home. The son of the mayor had seen, before leaving the house, a monstrous goose larded with truffles so that it looked like a black-spotted leopard. Another boy told of the fir tree waiting for him, on the branches of which hung oranges, sugarplums, and punchinellos. Then they talked about what the Christ Child would bring them, or what He would leave in their shoes, which they would be certain to place before the fire when they went to bed. And the eyes of the little rogues, lively as a crowd of mice, sparkled with delight as they thought of the many gifts they would find on waking—the pink bags of burnt almonds, the bonbons, lead soldiers standing in rows, menageries, and magnificent jumping-jacks dressed in purple and gold.

Little Wolff—alas!—knew well that his miserly old aunt would send him to bed without any supper; but as he had been good and industrious all the year, he trusted that the Christ Child would not forget him, so he meant that night to set his wooden shoes on the hearth.

The midnight mass was ended. The worshipers hurried away, anxious to enjoy the treats awaiting them in their homes. The band of pupils, two by two, followed the schoolmaster out of the church.

Now, under the porch on a stone bench was a child asleep—a little child dressed in a white garment with bare feet exposed to the cold. He was not a beggar, for his dress was clean and new, and beside him upon the ground, tied in a cloth, were the tools of a carpenter's apprentice.

Under the light of the stars, his face, with its closed eyes, shone with an expression of divine sweetness, and his soft, curling, blond hair seemed to form an aureole of light about his forehead. But his tender feet, blue with the cold on this cruel night of December, were pitiful to see!

The pupils so warmly clad and shod, passed with indifference before the unknown child. Some, the sons of the greatest men in the city, cast looks of scorn on the barefooted one. But deeply moved, little Wolff stopped before the beautiful, sleeping child.

"Alas!" said the orphan to himself. "How dreadful! This poor little one goes without stockings in weather so cold! And, what is worse, he has no shoe to leave beside him while he sleeps, so that the Christ Child may place something in it to comfort him in all his misery."

Carried away by his tender heart, little Wolff drew off the wooden shoe from his right foot, placed it before the sleeping child, and as best as he was able—now hopping, now limping, and wetting his sock in the snow—he returned to his aunt.

"You good-for-nothing!" cried the old woman, full of rage as she saw that one of his shoes was gone. "What have you done with your shoe, little beggar?"

Little Wolff did not know how to lie, and, though shivering with terror, he tried, stammering, to tell his adventure.

But the old woman burst into frightful laughter. "Ah! The sweet young master takes off his shoe for a beggar! Ah! Master spoils a pair of shoes for a barefoot! This is something new, indeed! Ah! Well, since things are so, I will place the shoe that is left in the fireplace, and tonight the Christ Child will put in a rod to whip you when you wake. And tomorrow you shall have nothing to eat but water and dry bread, and we shall see if the next time you will give away your shoe to the first vagabond that comes along."

Saying this, the wicked woman gave him a box on each ear and made him climb to his wretched room in the loft. There the heartbroken little one lay down in the darkness, and, drenching his pillow with tears, fell asleep.

In the morning, when the old woman, awakened by the cold and shaken by her cough, descended to the kitchen, oh, wonder of wonders! She saw the great fireplace filled with bright toys, magnificent boxes of sugarplums, riches of all sorts. In front of all this treasure, the wooden shoe which her nephew had given to the vagabond, stood beside the other shoe which she herself had placed there the night before.

And as little Wolff, who had come running at the cries of his aunt, stood in speechless delight before all the splendid Christmas gifts, there came great shouts of laughter from the street.

The old woman and the little boy went out to learn what it was all about. The gossips gathered around the public fountain. What could have happened? Oh, a most amusing and extraordinary thing! The children of all the rich men of the city, whose parents wished to surprise them with the most beautiful gifts, had found nothing but switches in their shoes!

The old woman and little Wolff remembered all the riches that were in their own fireplace, but just then they saw the pastor of the parish church arriving with his face full of perplexity.

Above the bench near the church door, in the very spot where the night before a child, dressed in white, with bare feet exposed to the great cold, had rested his sleeping head, the pastor had seen a golden circle wrought into the old stones. Then all the people knew that the beautiful, sleeping child, beside whom had lain the carpenter's tools, was the Christ Child himself and that He had rewarded the faith and charity of little Wolff.

As we seek
Christ,
as we find Him,
as we follow Him,
we shall have the
CHRISTMAS
SPIRIT,
not for one fleeting day
each year, but as a
COMPANION
always.

~ Thomas S. Monson

"Are you willing to believe that love is the strongest thing in the world—stronger than hate, stronger than evil, stronger than death—and that the blessed life which began in Bethlehem nineteen hundred years ago is the image and brightness of the Eternal Love? Then you can keep Christmas."

~ Henry Van Dyke

CHRISTMAS AROUND THE WORLD

Christmas in Africa

Christmas day begins with groups of carolers walking through the village, singing the lovely carols known the world around. People may be awakened by a group of carolers beginning to converge on the house of worship. Later on there is a feast of rice and yam paste called fufu with stew or okra soup, porridge, and meats. In the evening, people flock to churches which have been decorated with Christmas evergreens or palm trees massed with candles.

On the west coast of Africa, in Liberia, most homes have an oil palm for a Christmas tree, which is decorated with bells.

Christmas in Australia

In the Australian gold rushes, Christmas puddings often contained a gold nugget. Today a small favor is baked inside. Whoever finds this knows he or she will enjoy good luck.

"Carols by Candlelight" is held every year on Christmas Eve, where tens of thousands of people gather in the city of Melbourne to sing their favorite Christmas songs. The evening is lit by many candles as the people sing under the night sky.

At many beaches Santa Claus arrives on a surfboard or even on a lifesaving boat.

Christmas in Bangladesh

In Bangladesh, formerly known as East Pakistan, the Christian village men cut down scores of banana trees and replant them along the paths to churches and outside their homes. They then bend the huge leaves of the banana trees over to form an arch. Finally they make small holes in bamboo poles, fill them with oil, and tie them across the arches. When the oil is lit, the way to the church is bright enough for all to see.

Christmas in Bulgaria

Christmas Eve is as important as Christmas Day in Bulgaria. A special dinner, consisting of at least twelve dishes is prepared. All of them are without meat, and each of them represents a separate month of the year. The dishes consist of beans, different kinds of nuts, dried plums, cakes, and the traditional Banitza.

Christmas in France

On Christmas Eve, children leave their shoes by the fireplace to be filled with gifts from Pere Noel.

Traditionally, families had a Three Kings Cake with a bean hidden in it. Whoever found the bean in their slice was made king or queen for the day.

Christmas in Greece

On almost every table are loaves of christopsomo or "Christ Bread." This bread is made in large sweet loaves of various shapes, and the crusts are engraved and decorated in some way that reflects the family's profession.

Christmas trees are not commonly used. In almost every home the main symbol of the season is a shallow wooden bowl with a piece of wire suspended across the rim; from that hangs a sprig of basil wrapped around a wooden cross. A small amount of water is kept in the bowl to keep the basil alive and fresh. Once a day, a family member, usually the mother, dips the cross and basil into some holy water and uses it to sprinkle water in each room of the house.

Christmas in the Netherlands

St. Nicholas arrives early, December 5, in Holland with his gifts. He is dressed in a bishop's robes and journeys in a boat with his helper, Black Peter, who wears Spanish clothes. It is said that the pair live most of the year preparing lists of presents and writing every child's behavior in a very large book. Many people go to the Amsterdam docks to greet him. He mounts a snow horse and rides through the streets in a great parade, amid many festivities.

December 25 is First Christmas, when the Kerstman visits, and December 26 is called Second Christmas.

Christmas in Mexico

The main Christmas celebration is called La Posada, which is a religious procession that reenacts the search for shelter by Joseph and Mary before the birth of Jesus. During the procession, the celebrants go from house to house carrying the images of Mary and Joseph looking for shelter.

The Mexican Christmas season is joyously extended up to February 2—when the nativity scene is put away, and another family dinner of delicious tamales and hot chocolate is served.

Christmas in Ukraine

Sviata Vechera, or "Holy Supper," is the central tradition of the beautiful Christmas Eve celebrations in Ukrainian homes. The dinner table sometimes has a few wisps of hay on the embroidered tablecloth as a reminder of the manger in Bethlehem.

Father Frost visits all the children in a sleigh pulled by only three reindeer. He brings along a little girl named Snowflake Girl. She wears a silver-blue costume trimmed with white fur and a crown shaped like a snowflake.

Christmas means giving.
The Father gave HIS SON, and the Son gave His life.
Without giving there is no
TRUE CHRISTMAS
and without sacrifice there is no true worship.

~Gordon B. Hinckley

A
Merry
Christmas

Piccola

By Cella Laighton Thaxter

Poor, sweet Piccola! Did you hear
What happened to Piccola, children dear?
'Tis seldom Fortune such favor grants
As fell to this little maid of France.
'Twas Christmastime, and her parents poor
Could hardly drive the wolf from the door,
Striving with poverty's patient pain
Only to live till summer again.
No gift for Piccola! Sad were they
When dawned the morning of Christmas day!
Their little darling no joy might stir;
St. Nicholas nothing would bring to her!
But Piccola never doubted at all
That something beautiful must befall
Every child upon Christmas day,
And so she slept till the dawn was gray.
And full of faith, when at last she woke,
She stole to her shoe as the morning broke;
Such sounds of gladness filled all the air,
'Twas plain St. Nicholas had been there.
In rushed Piccola, sweet, half wild—
Never was seen such a joyful child—
"See what the good saint brought!" she cried,
And mother and father must peep inside.
Now such a story I never heard!
There was a little shivering bird!
A sparrow, that in at the window flew,
Had crept into Piccola's tiny shoe!
"How good poor Piccola must have been!"
She cried, as happy as any queen,
While the starving sparrow she fed and warmed,
And danced with rapture, she was so charmed.
Children, this story I tell to you
Of Piccola sweet and her bird, is true.
In the far-off land of France, they say,
Still do they live to this very day.

The Elves and the Shoemaker

By Horace E. Scudder

There was once a shoemaker who worked very hard and was honest. Still, he could not earn enough to live on. At last, all he had in the world was gone except just enough leather to make one pair of shoes. He cut these out at night and meant to rise early the next morning to make them up.

His heart was light in spite of his troubles, for his conscience was clear. So he went quietly to bed, left all his cares to God, and fell asleep. In the morning he said his prayers and sat down to work, when, to his great wonder, there stood the shoes, already made, upon the table.

The good man knew not what to say or think. He looked at the work. There was not one false stitch in the whole job. All was neat and true.

That same day a customer came in, and the shoes pleased him so well that he readily paid a price higher than usual for them. The shoemaker took the money and bought leather enough to make two pairs more. He cut out the work in the evening and went to bed early. He wished to be up with the sun and get to work.

He was saved all trouble, for when he got up in the morning, the work was done. Pretty soon buyers came in, who paid him well for his goods. So he bought leather enough for four pairs more.

He cut out the work again overnight and found it finished in the morning, as before. So it went on for some time. What was got ready at night was always done by daybreak, and the good man soon was well-to-do.

One evening, at Christmastime, he and his wife sat over the fire, chatting, and he said: "I should like to sit up and watch tonight, that we may see who it is that comes and does my work for me." So they left the light burning and hid themselves behind a curtain to see what would happen.

As soon as it was midnight, there came two little elves. They sat upon the shoemaker's bench, took up all the work that was cut out, and began to ply their little fingers. They stitched and rapped and tapped at such a rate that the shoemaker was amazed and could not take his eyes off them for a moment.

On they went till the job was done, and the shoes stood, ready for use, upon the table. Then they ran away as quick as lightning.

The next day the wife said to the shoemaker: "These little elves have made us rich, and we ought to be thankful to them and do them some good in return. I am vexed to see them run about as they do. They have nothing upon their backs to keep off the cold. I'll tell you what we must do. I will make each of them a shirt and a coat and waistcoat and a pair of pantaloons. You make each of them a little pair of shoes."

The good shoemaker liked the thought very well. And one evening, he and his wife had the clothes ready and laid them on the table instead of the work. Then they went and hid behind the curtain to watch what the little elves would do.

At midnight, the elves came in and were going to sit down at their work as usual. But when they saw the clothes lying there for them, they laughed in glee. They dressed themselves in the twinkling of an eye and danced and capered and sprang about as merry as could be, till at last they danced out of the door and over the green.

The shoemaker saw them no more, but everything went well with him as long as he lived.

"Christmas is not a time or a season but a state of mind. To cherish peace and good will, to be plenteous in mercy, is to have the real spirit of Christmas."

~ Calvin Coolidge

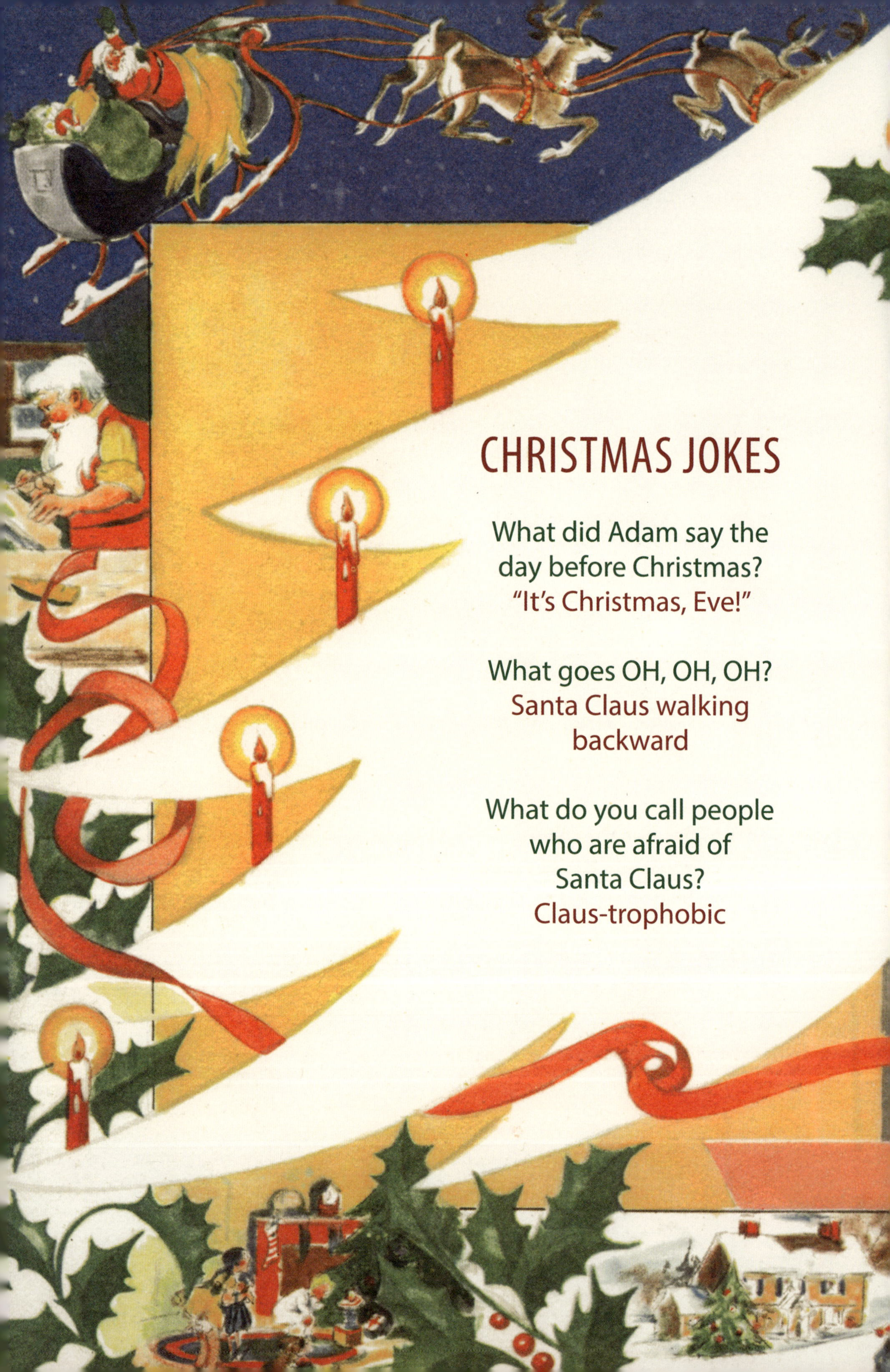

CHRISTMAS JOKES

What did Adam say the day before Christmas?
"It's Christmas, Eve!"

What goes OH, OH, OH?
Santa Claus walking backward

What do you call people who are afraid of Santa Claus?
Claus-trophobic

What do snowmen eat
for breakfast?
Snowflakes

Why did the gingerbread
man go to the doctor?
He was feeling crummy.

What did one snowman
say to the other?
Can you smell carrot?

What did the gingerbread
man put on his bed?
A cookie sheet

The Mansion

By Henry Van Dyke [Adapted]

John Weightman was like the house into which he had built himself thirty years ago, and in which his ideals and ambitions were incrusted. He was a self-made man. But in making himself he had chosen a highly esteemed pattern and worked according to the approved rules. There was nothing irregular, questionable, flamboyant about him. He was solid, correct, and justly successful. . . .

He went to his chair at the library table. A strange weight of weariness rested upon him, but he opened the book at a familiar place, and his eyes fell upon the verse at the bottom of the page: "Lay not up for yourselves treasures upon earth."

That had been the text of the sermon a few weeks before. Sleepily, heavily, he tried to fix his mind upon it and recall it. What was it that Dr. Snodgrass had said? Ah, yes—that it was a mistake to pause here in reading the verse. We must read on without a pause—"Lay not up treasures upon earth where moth and rust do corrupt and where thieves break through and steal"—that was the true doctrine. We may have treasures upon earth, but they must not be put into unsafe places, but into safe places. A most comforting doctrine! He had always followed it. Moths and rust and thieves had done no harm to his investments.

John Weightman's drooping eyes turned to the next verse, at the top of the second column: "But lay up for yourselves treasures in heaven."

Now what had the doctor said about that? How was it to be understood—in what sense—treasures—in heaven? . . .

How long afterward conscious life returned to him he did not know. The blank might have been an hour or a century. He knew only that something had happened in the interval. What it was he could not tell. He found great difficulty in catching the thread of his identity again. He felt that he was himself; but the trouble was to make his connections, to verify and place himself, to know who and where he was.

At last it grew clear. John Weightman was sitting on a stone, not far from a road in a strange land. . . . From the edge of the hill, where John Weightman sat, he could see travelers, in little groups or larger companies, gathering from time to time by the different paths, and making the ascent. They were all clothed in white, and the form of their garments was strange to him; it was like some old picture. They passed him, group after group, talking quietly together or singing; not moving in haste but with a certain air of eagerness and joy as if they were glad to be on their way to an appointed place. They did not stay to speak to him, but they looked at him often and spoke to one another as they looked; and now and then one of them would smile and beckon him a friendly greeting, so that he felt they would like him to be with them. . . .

For a long time he sat there watching and wondering. It was a very different world from that in which his mansion on the Avenue was built; and it looked strange to him but most real—as real as anything he had ever seen. Presently he felt a strong desire to know what country it was and where the people were going. He had a faint premonition of what it must be, but he wished to be sure. So he rose from the stone where he was sitting and came down through the short grass and the lavender flowers, toward a passing group of people. One of them turned to meet him and held out his hand. It was an old man, under whose white beard and brows John Weightman thought he saw a suggestion of the face of the village doctor who had cared for him years ago, when he was a boy in the country.

"Welcome," said the old man. "Will you come with us?"

"Where are you going?"

"To the heavenly city, to see our mansions there."

"And who are these with you?"

"Strangers to me, until a little while ago; I know them better now. But you I have known for a long time, John Weightman. Don't you remember your old doctor?"

"Yes," he cried. "Yes; your voice has not changed at all. I'm glad indeed to see you, Dr. McLean, especially now. All this seems very strange to me, almost oppressive. I wonder if—but may I go with you, do you suppose?"

"Surely," answered the doctor, with his familiar smile. "It will do you good. And you also must have a mansion in the city waiting for you—a fine one, too—are you not looking forward to it?"

"Yes," replied the other, hesitating a moment. "Yes—I believe it must be so, although I had not expected to see it so soon. But I will go with you, and we can talk by the way."

The two men quickly caught up with the other people, and all went forward together along the road. The doctor had little to tell of his experience, for it had been a plain, hard life, uneventfully spent for others, and the story of the village was very simple. John Weightman's adventures and triumphs would have made a far richer, more imposing history, full of contacts with the great events and personages of the time. But somehow or other he did not care to speak much about it. . . .

There was only one person besides the doctor in that little company whom John Weightman had known before—an old bookkeeper who had spent his life over a desk, carefully keeping accounts—a rusty, dull little man, patient and narrow, whose wife had been in the insane asylum for twenty years and whose only child was a crippled daughter for whose comfort and happiness he had toiled and sacrificed himself without stint. It was a surprise to find him here, as carefree and joyful as the rest.

The lives of others in the company were revealed in brief glimpses as they talked together—a mother, early widowed, who had kept her little flock of children together and labored through hard and heavy years to bring them up in purity and knowledge; a Sister of Charity who had devoted herself to the nursing of poor folk who were being eaten to death by cancer; a schoolmaster whose heart and life had been poured into his quiet work of training boys for a clean and thoughtful manhood; . . . a paralyzed woman who had lain for thirty years upon her bed, helpless but not hopeless, succeeding by a miracle of courage in her single aim, never to complain, but always to impart a bit of her joy and peace to everyone who came near her. All these, and other persons like them, were in the company that passed along the road, talking together of things past and things to come, and singing now and then with clear voices from which the veil of age and sorrow was lifted.

John Weightman joined in some of the songs—which were familiar to him from their use in the church—at first with a touch of hesitation and then more confidently. For as they went on, his sense of strangeness and fear at his new experience diminished, and his thoughts began to take on their habitual assurance and complacency. Were not these people going to the Celestial City? And was not he in his right place among them? He had always looked forward to this journey. If they were sure, each one, of finding a mansion there, could not he be far more sure? His life had been more fruitful than theirs. He had been a leader, a founder of new enterprises, a pillar of church and state, a prince of the House of Israel. Ten talents had been given him, and he had made them twenty. His reward would be proportionate. He was glad that his companions were going to find fit dwellings prepared for them; but he thought also with a certain pleasure of the surprise that some of them would feel when they saw his appointed mansion. . . .

The wall of the city was very low, a child could see over it, for it was made only of precious stones, which are never large. The gate of the city was not like a gate at all, for it was not barred with iron or wood, but only a single pearl, softly gleaming, marked the place where the wall ended and the entrance lay open.

A person stood there whose face was bright and grave, and whose robe was like the flower of the lily, not a woven fabric, but a living texture. "Come in," he said to the company of travelers. "You are at your journey's end, and your mansions are ready for you." . . .

They passed from street to street among fair and spacious dwellings, set in amaranthine gardens and adorned with an infinitely varied beauty of divine simplicity. The mansions differed in size, in shape, in charm: each one seemed to have its own personal look of loveliness; yet all were alike in fitness to their place, in harmony with one another, in the addition which each made to the singular and tranquil splendor of the city.

As the little company came, one by one, to the mansions which were prepared for them, and their guide beckoned to the happy inhabitant to enter in and take possession. There was a soft murmur of joy, half wonder and half recognition, as if the new and immortal dwelling were crowned with the beauty of surprise, lovelier and nobler than all the dreams of it had been; and yet also as if it were touched with the beauty of the familiar, the remembered, the long-loved. One after another the travelers were led to their own mansions and went in gladly; and from within, through the open doorways, came sweet voices of welcome and low laughter and song.

At last there was no one left with the guide but the two old friends, Dr. McLean and John Weightman. They were standing in front of one of the largest and fairest of the houses, whose garden glowed softly with radiant flowers. The guide laid his hand upon the doctor's shoulder.

"This is for you," he said. "Go in; there is no more pain here, no more death, nor sorrow, nor tears; for your old enemies are all conquered. But all the good that you have done for others, all the help that you have given, all the comfort that you have brought, all the strength and love that you have bestowed upon the suffering, are here; for we have built them all into this mansion for you."

A Merry
Christmas

The good man's face was lighted with a still joy. He clasped his old friend's hand closely and whispered: "How wonderful it is! Go on, you will come to your mansion next—it is not far away—and we shall see each other again soon, very soon." So he went through the garden and into the music within.

The keeper of the gate turned to John Weightman with level, quiet, searching eyes. Then he asked, gravely, "Where do you wish me to lead you now?"

"To see my own mansion," answered the man, with half-concealed excitement. "Is there not one here for me? You may not let me enter it yet, perhaps, for I must confess to you that I am only—"

"I know," said the keeper of the gate. "I know it all. You are John Weightman."

"Yes," said the man, more firmly than he had spoken at first, for it gratified him that his name was known. "Yes, I am John Weightman Sr., warden of St. Petronius's Church. I wish very much to see my mansion here, if only for a moment. I believe that you have one for me. Will you take me to it?"

The keeper of the gate drew a little book from the breast of his robe and turned over the pages. "Certainly," he said, with a curious look at the man, "your name is here; you shall see your mansion if you will follow me."

It seemed as if they must have walked miles and miles, through the vast city, passing street after street of houses larger and smaller, of gardens richer and poorer, but all full of beauty and delight. They came into a kind of suburb, where there were many small cottages, with plots of flowers, very lowly, but bright and fragrant. Finally they reached an open field, bare and lonely-looking. There were two or three little bushes in it, without flowers, and the grass was sparse and thin. In the center of the field was a tiny hut, hardly big enough for a shepherd's shelter. It looked as if it had been built of discarded things, scraps and fragments of other buildings, put together with care and pains, by someone who had tried to make the most of cast-off material. There was something pitiful and shamefaced about the hut. It shrank and drooped and faded in its barren field and seemed to cling only by sufferance to the edge of the splendid city.

"This," said the keeper of the gate, standing still and speaking with a low, distinct voice, "this is your mansion, John Weightman."

An almost intolerable shock of grieved wonder and indignation choked the man for a moment so that he could not say a word. Then he turned his face away from the poor little hut and began to remonstrate eagerly with his companion. "Surely, sir," he stammered, "you must be in error about this. There is something wrong—some other John Weightman—a confusion of names—the book must be mistaken."

"There is no mistake," said the keeper of the gate, very calmly. "Here is your name, the record of your title and your possessions in this place."

"But how could such a house be prepared for me," cried the man, with a resentful tremor in his voice. "For me, after my long and faithful service? Is this a suitable mansion for one so well known and devoted? Why is it so pitifully small and mean? Why have you not built it large and fair, like the others?"

"That is all the material you sent us."

"What?"

"We have used all the material that you sent us," repeated the keeper of the gate.

"Now I know that you are mistaken," cried the man, with growing earnestness, "for all my life long I have been doing things that must have supplied you with material. Have you not heard that I have built a schoolhouse; the wing of a hospital; two—three—small churches, and the greater part of a large one; the spire of St. Petro—"

The keeper of the gate lifted his hand. "Wait," he said. "We know all these things. They were not ill done. But they were all marked and used as foundation for the name and mansion of John Weightman in the world. Did you not plan them for that?"

"Yes," answered the man, confused and taken aback, "I confess that I thought often of them in that way. Perhaps my heart was set upon that too much. But there are other things—my endowment for the college, my steady and liberal contributions to all the established charities, my support of every respectable—"

"Wait," said the keeper of the gate again. "Were not all these carefully recorded on earth where they would add to your credit? They were not foolishly done. Verily, you have had your reward for them. Would you be paid twice?"

"No," cried the man, with deepening dismay, "I dare not claim that. I acknowledge that I considered my own interest too much. But surely not altogether. You have said that these things were not foolishly done. They accomplished some good in the world. Does not that count for something?"

"Yes," answered the keeper of the gate. "It counts in the world—where you counted it. But it does not belong to you here. We have saved and used everything that you sent us. This is the mansion prepared for you."

As he spoke, his look grew deeper and more searching, like a flame of fire. John Weightman could not endure it. It seemed to strip him naked and wither him. He sank to the ground under a crushing weight of shame, covering his eyes with his hands and cowering face downward upon the stones. Dimly through the trouble of his mind he felt their hardness and coldness.

"Tell me, then," he cried, brokenly, "since my life has been so little worth, how came I here at all?"

"Through the mercy of the King"—the answer was like the soft tolling of a bell.

"And how have I earned it?" he murmured.

"It is never earned; it is only given," came the clear, low reply.

"But how have I failed so wretchedly," he asked, "in all the purpose of my life? What could I have done better? What is it that counts here?"

"Only that which is truly given," answered the bell-like voice. "Only that good which is done for the love of doing it. Only those plans in which the welfare of others is the master thought. Only those labors in which the sacrifice is greater than the reward. Only those gifts in which the giver forgets himself."

The man lay silent. A great weakness, an unspeakable despondency and humiliation were upon him. But the face of the keeper of the gate was infinitely tender as he bent over him.

"Think again, John Weightman. Has there been nothing like that in your life?"

"Nothing," he sighed. "If there ever were such things, it must have been long ago—they were all crowded out—I have forgotten them."

There was an ineffable smile on the face of the keeper of the gate, and his hand made the sign of the cross over the bowed head as he spoke gently: "These are the things that the King never forgets; and because there were a few of them in your life, you have a little place here." . . .

The chimney clock on the mantel had just ended the last stroke of seven as he lifted his head from the table. Thin, pale strips of the city morning were falling into the room through the narrow partings of the heavy curtains.

What was it that had happened to him? Had he been ill? Had he died and come to life again? Or had he only slept, and had his soul gone visiting in dreams? He sat for some time, motionless, not lost, but finding himself in thought. Then he took a narrow book from the table drawer, wrote a check, and tore it out.

He went slowly up the stairs, knocked very softly at his son's door, and, hearing no answer, entered without noise. Harold was asleep, his bare arm thrown above his head, and his eager face relaxed in peace. His father looked at him a moment with strangely shining eyes, and then tiptoed quietly to the writing-desk, found a pencil and a sheet of paper, and wrote rapidly:

"My dear boy, here is what you asked me for; do what you like with it, and ask for more if you need it. If you are still thinking of that work with Grenfell, we'll talk it over today after church. I want to know your heart better; and if I have made mistakes—"

A slight noise made him turn his head. Harold was sitting up in bed with wide-open eyes. "Father!" he cried, "is that you?"

"Yes, my son," answered John Weightman; "I've come back--I mean I've come up--no, I mean come in--well, here I am, and God give us a good Christmas together."

THE END

"At the focal point of all human history, a point illuminated by a new star in the heavens revealed for just such a purpose, probably no other mortal watched--none but a poor young carpenter, a beautiful virgin mother, and silent stabled animals who had not the power to utter the sacredness they had seen. Shepherds would soon arrive and later, wise men from the East. Later yet the memory of that night would bring Santa Claus and Frosty and Rudolph—and all would be welcome. But first and forever there was just a little family, without toys or trees or tinsel. With a baby—that's how Christmas began. It is for this baby that we shout in chorus: "Hark! the herald angels sing Glory to the newborn King! . . . Mild he lays his glory by, Born that man no more may die; Born to raise the sons of earth, Born to give them second birth"

~ Jeffrey R. Holland

GINGERBREAD HOUSE

½ cup sugar
½ cup molasses
1½ teaspoons ginger
1 teaspoon allspice
1 teaspoon cinnamon
1 teaspoon clove
2 teaspoons baking soda
½ cup margarine
1 egg, beaten
3½ cups all-purpose flour

1. In a medium saucepan, heat sugar, molasses, ginger, allspice, cinnamon, and cloves, stirring occasionally.
2. When it begins to boil, remove from heat, and stir in baking soda.
3. Stir in margarine till melted.
4. With a fork, stir in egg, then flour.
5. On a floured surface, knead dough till mixed.
6. It is easier not to work with all the dough at once, so you can divide dough in half, wrap half with plastic wrap, and set it aside.
7. Roll out the other half of the dough, with a rolling pin, slightly thinner than ¼ inch.
8. Cut with cutters.
9. Bake at 325 degrees F on a cookie sheet for about 12 minutes; cool on a wire rack.

GINGERBREAD HOUSE ICING

3 large egg whites
4¾ cups powdered sugar
½ teaspoon cream of tartar

1. In a large clean bowl, beat egg whites and cream of tartar with electric mixer at medium speed.
2. Add powdered sugar in small amounts, mixing well on high after each addition.
3. Beat for 4–5 minutes or until mixture thickens.
4. Cover and refrigerate until ready to use.
5. Stir the icing to soften before use.

Did You Know?

The largest gingerbread village consisted of 1,003 buildings. It was constructed by Jon Lovitch (USA) and displayed at the New York Hall of Science on 12 December 2014.

The largest gingerbread man weighed 1,435 lb 3 oz—a little heavier than a horse—and was made by IKEA Furuset (Norway) in Oslo, Norway, on 9 November 2009. The giant gingerbread man was baked in one piece.

A MERRY CHRISTMAS
TO YOU

Papa Panov's Special Christmas

By Leo Tolstoy

It was Christmas Eve, and although it was still afternoon, lights had begun to appear in the shops and houses of the little Russian village, for the short winter day was nearly over. Excited children scurried indoors, and now only muffled sounds of chatter and laughter escaped from closed shutters.

Old Papa Panov, the village shoemaker, stepped outside his shop to take one last look around. The sounds of happiness, the bright lights and the faint but delicious smells of Christmas cooking reminded him of past Christmas times when his wife had still been alive and his own children little. Now they had gone. His usually cheerful face, with the little laughter wrinkles behind the round steel spectacles, looked sad now. But he went back indoors with a firm step, put up the shutters, and set a pot of coffee to heat on the charcoal stove. Then, with a sigh, he settled in his big armchair.

Papa Panov did not often read, but tonight he pulled down the big old family Bible, and slowly tracing the lines with one forefinger, he read again the Christmas story. He read how Mary and Joseph, tired by their journey to Bethlehem, found no room for them at the inn, so that Mary's little baby was born in the cowshed.

"Oh, dear, oh, dear!" exclaimed Papa Panov. "If only they had come here! I would have given them my bed, and I could have covered the baby with my patchwork quilt to keep Him warm."

He read on about the wise men who had come to see the baby Jesus, bringing Him splendid gifts. Papa Panov's face fell. *I have no gift that I could give Him*, he thought sadly.

Then his face brightened. He put down the Bible, got up, and stretched his long arms to the shelf high up in his little room. He took down a small, dusty box and opened it. Inside was a perfect pair of tiny leather shoes. Papa Panov smiled with satisfaction. Yes, they were as good as he had remembered—the best shoes he had ever made. *I should give Him those*, he decided, as he gently put them away and sat down again.

He was feeling tired now, and the farther he read, the sleeper he became. The print began to dance before his eyes so that he closed them, just for a minute. In no time at all, Papa Panov was fast asleep.

And as he slept he dreamed. He dreamed that someone was in his room, and he knew at once, as one does in dreams, who the person was. It was Jesus.

"You have been wishing that you could see me, Papa Panov," He said kindly. "Then look for me tomorrow. It will be Christmas Day, and I will visit you. But look carefully, for I shall not tell you who I am."

When at last Papa Panov awoke, the bells were ringing out, and a thin light was filtering through the shutters. "Bless my soul!" said Papa Panov. "It's Christmas Day!"

He stood up and stretched himself, for he was rather stiff. Then his face filled with happiness as he remembered his dream. This would be a very special Christmas after all, for Jesus was coming to visit him. How would He look? Would He be a little baby, as at that first Christmas? Would

He be a grown man, a carpenter—or the great King that He is, God's Son? He must watch carefully the whole day through so that he recognized Him however He came.

Papa Panov put on a special pot of coffee for his Christmas breakfast, took down the shutters, and looked out of the window. The street was deserted; no one was stirring yet. No one except the road sweeper. He looked as miserable and dirty as ever, and well he might! Whoever wanted to work on Christmas Day—and in the raw cold and bitter freezing mist of such a morning?

Papa Panov opened the shop door, letting in a thin stream of cold air. "Come in!" he shouted across the street cheerily. "Come in, and have some hot coffee to keep out the cold!"

The sweeper looked up, scarcely able to believe his ears. He was only too glad to put down his broom and come into the warm room. His old clothes steamed gently in the heat of the stove, and he clasped both red hands round the comforting warm mug as he drank.

Papa Panov watched him with satisfaction, but every now and then his eyes strayed to the window. It would never do to miss his special visitor.

"Expecting someone?" the sweeper asked at last. So Papa Panov told him about his dream.

"Well, I hope He comes," the sweeper said. "You've given me a bit of Christmas cheer I never expected to have. I'd say you deserve to have your dream come true." And he actually smiled.

When he had gone, Papa Panov put on cabbage soup for his dinner, then went to the door again, scanning the street. He saw no one. But he was mistaken. Someone was coming.

The girl walked so slowly and quietly, hugging the walls of shops and houses, that it was a while before he noticed her.

She looked very tired, and she was carrying something. As she drew nearer he could see that it was a baby, wrapped in a thin shawl. There was such sadness in her face and in the pinched little face of the baby that Papa Panov's heart went out to them.

"Won't you come in," he called, stepping outside to meet them. "You both need a warm by the fire and a rest."

The young mother let him shepherd her indoors to the comfort of the armchair. She gave a big sigh of relief.

"I'll warm some milk for the baby," Papa Panov said. "I've had children of my own—I can feed her for you." He took the milk from the stove and carefully fed the baby from a spoon, warming her tiny feet by the stove at the same time.

"She needs shoes," the cobbler said.

But the girl replied, "I can't afford shoes; I've got no husband to bring home money. I'm on my way to the next village to get work."

Sudden thought flashed through Papa Panov's mind. He remembered the little shoes he had looked at last night. But he had been keeping those for Jesus. He looked again at the cold little feet and made up his mind.

"Try these on her," he said, handing the baby and the shoes to the mother.

The beautiful little shoes were a perfect fit. The girl smiled happily, and the baby gurgled with pleasure.

"You have been so kind to us," the girl said, when she got up with her baby to go. "May all your Christmas wishes come true!"

But Papa Panov was beginning to wonder if his very special Christmas wish would come true. Perhaps he had missed his visitor? He looked anxiously up and down the street. There were plenty of people about, but they were all faces that he recognized. There were neighbors going to call on their families. They nodded and smiled and wished him Happy Christmas! Or beggars—and Papa Panov hurried indoors to fetch them hot soup and a generous hunk of bread, hurrying out again in case he missed the Important Stranger.

All too soon, the winter dusk fell. When Papa Panov next went to the door and strained his eyes, he could no longer make out the passersby. Most were home and indoors by now anyway. He walked slowly back into his room at last, put up the shutters, and sat down wearily in his armchair.

So it had been just a dream after all. Jesus had not come.

Then all at once he knew that he was no longer alone in the room.

This was not a dream, for he was wide awake. At first he seemed to see before his eyes the long stream of people who had come to him that day. He saw again the old road sweeper, the young mother and her baby, and the beggars he had fed. As they passed, each whispered, "Didn't you see me, Papa Panov?"

"Who are you?" he called out, bewildered.

Then another voice answered him. It was the voice from his dream—the voice of Jesus.

"I was hungry and you fed me," He said. "I was naked and you clothed me. I was cold and you warmed me. I came to you today in everyone of those you helped and welcomed."

Then all was quiet and still, only the sound of the big clock ticking. A great peace and happiness seemed to fill the room, overflowing Papa Panov's heart until he wanted to burst out singing and laughing and dancing with joy.

"So He did come after all!" was all that he said.

Symbolism of the Christmas Gift:

Gifts are a Christmas tradition that began with the Wise Men bringing gifts to the Christ Child. Now these gifts should remind us of the greatest gift of all—the gift of a Savior.

PAPER CHAIN SERVICE
Advent Countdown

Decide how long you want your countdown chain to be. You could do twenty-four links, one for each day of the month leading up to Christmas. You could do the twelve days before. Or, make the entire month dedicated to service, and continue the chain even after Christmas!

Cut out 1½-inch strips of red and green construction paper. You'll want to cut the paper so that your strips are long enough to write a service activity on.

On each strip, write a service activity to be done on the day that link is removed.

To start the chain, loop one strip, with the writing on the inside, and staple the ends. Continue the chain, alternating colors, by inserting the strip into the previous loop before stapling.

Here are some ideas of service activities to include in your chain:

- Make Christmas cards to send to relatives who don't live nearby.
- Write Christmas cards and deliver to a local hospital.
- Make salt dough ornaments for friends and neighbors.
- Make a bird feeder.
- Make and deliver Christmas cookies.
- Donate canned food to a pantry.
- Choose three of your toys and give them away to a charity.
- Help wrap presents.
- Donate unwanted gifts or used clothes.
- Give gifts to Toys for Tots.
- Give blood through the American Red Cross.
- Volunteer at an animal shelter with the Humane Society.
- Volunteer at a St. Jude's Children's Hospital event in your community.
- Volunteer with Meals on Wheels to provide holiday dinners to the elderly, sick and disabled.
- Visit the elderly at a retirement home and play games or do a craft with them.
- Take holiday treats to the local police station or fire station to say thank you for keeping your community safe.
- Buy and decorate a Christmas tree to deliver to a family in need.
- Babysit for someone who needs to go Christmas shopping.

Jolly Old St. Nicholas

Jolly old St. Nicholas,
Lean your ear this way!
Don't you tell a single soul,
What I'm going to say;
Christmas Eve is coming soon,
Now, you dear old man,
Whisper what you'll bring to me:
Tell me if you can.

When the clock is striking twelve,
When I'm fast asleep,
Down the chimney broad and black,
With your pack you'll creep.
All the stockings you will find
Hanging in a row;
Mine will be the shortest one,
You'll be sure to know.

Johnny wants a pair of skates,
Susie wants a sled
Nellie wants a picture book,
yellow, blue, and red.
Now I think I'll leave to you
what to give the rest.
Choose for me dear Santa Claus
what you think is best.

There isn't a lot known about the origins of the song "Jolly Old St. Nicholas." It is commonly believed to have been written by Benjamin Hanby, who is credited with writing approximately eighty songs, including "Darling Nelly Gray," and Christmas songs "Up on the Housetop" and "Who Is He in Yonder Stall." "Jolly Old St. Nicholas" was first published in the mid-1800s. Hanby was also a pastor and schoolteacher.

A Merry Christmas

Christmas Conversion.

By Jean Blewett

I can see her in the kitchen,
Apron on and sleeves rolled up,
Measurin' spices in a teaspoon,
Figs and raisins in a cup.

Now she's throwin' apple quarters
In that wooden bowl of hers,
Long with lemon peel and orange,
An' she stirs, an' stirs, an' stirs.

Then she takes her knife an' chops it,
Chops so fast her hand jest flies.
Now I know what ma is up to—
Makin' mincemeat for the pies.

I smell Christmas in our kitchen,
An' my heart gets big an' glad,
An' I, somehow, fall to wishin',
That I wasn't quite so bad.

An' I tell myself I'll never
Cheat at marbles anymore,
Nor make faces at my teacher,
Nor hang 'round the corner store

'Stead of goin' on my errands;
Never touch the cookie pail,
Nor play hooky an' go skatin',
Nor tie cans on Rover's tail;

Never let ma think it's spellings
When it's only Robin Hood.
With the gladness comes the wishin'
To be, oh, just awful good!

'Bout this time of year it takes me—
Pa, he doesn't understand,
Always says: "You sly young codger,
You know Christmas is at hand."
But it isn't that, it's something—
Can't explain it very well—
Takes me when ma fills the kitchen
With this juicy Christmas smell.

When she chops the spice an' raisins,
With the peels an' Northern Spies,
Sleeves rolled up above her elbows,
Makin' mincemeat for the pies.

"Instead of being a time of unusual behavior,
Christmas is perhaps the only time in the year when people
can obey their natural impulses and express their true
sentiments without feeling self-conscious and, perhaps,
foolish. Christmas, in short, is about
the only chance a man has to be himself."

~ Francis C. Farley

A Happy
CHRISTMAS
to You

Feliz Navidad

By Fred C. Rowley

There was a chill in the air just before the Christmas sun rose in Sonora, Mexico, so Maria Sanchez lit a little fire in her *chiminea* before she began her morning routine. She sat on a small wooden stool by the crackling fire to brush her hair and wind it into a bun. Her full, black hair had always been her glory. When loosed, it spilled the length of her back. Now, in her later years, it was shot through with gray, but still it was her pride and joy.

How her Francisco had loved her hair! How many Christmases had she been without him now—seventeen? At least he had never seen the gray. She was grateful for that. Instinctively, she reached to the side table and touched the black-and-white photograph of Francisco and her on their wedding day. How handsome and strong he had looked in that fine dark suit and those shiny black boots! Then she picked up the other photo, the little one tucked into the corner of the frame, tattered and creased from years of wear. It was a Polaroid of two Americans in front of the Cananea Hospital holding a tiny bundle—her little Christmas baby.

Before the Christmas baby was born, Maria and Francisco had already had fifteen sons and daughters together. How happy their family had been! But then came that hot, horrible day in July when her son Miguel had come running to tell her that Francisco had been tangled in the farm machinery. Francisco lived through the accident, but he had been so badly injured he could never work again. From that day on, a darkness began to lurk over their tiny *casita* as though good fortune had gotten on a little burro and ridden out of their village.

Just one month later, Maria, then five months pregnant with the Christmas baby, was sweeping behind the stove with a little hand broom and tangled a black widow's web into the bristles. The spider bit her hand, and her hand began to swell. The swelling was followed by nausea. For the final four months of her pregnancy, she threw up almost everything she ate as she worked and cared for her injured husband.

In the middle of October, while churning butter in the mild autumn air, Maria began to think of the life her new baby would have. The copper mines were closing down, and work was scarce. Her older sons helped Francisco and her as much as they could, but it still wasn't enough. She could see that this baby would have a very hard life. She thought of the blessed Virgin Maria and how there was no room for *her* baby when *He* was born, and she began to cry as she worried—would there be no room for her baby either? What could she do? For days she brooded over the question. Finally, one afternoon as she was changing the dressings on Francisco's wounds, she said the words she thought she never would, or could, say.

"Francisco . . . there's a woman named Dolores . . . she knows the Americans. She arranges adoptions for Mexican babies in the United States. I think there is no other hope for this baby . . ." She could go no further and began to weep. Francisco stroked her long hair with his bandaged hand and whispered, "You speak the truth, my Maria. It's what is best." And so it was done. They contacted Dolores and made the arrangements.

When the baby's time came on that Christmas Day those many years ago, her eldest son Gilberto put her on the handlebars of his bicycle and pedaled her

two miles to the hospital in Cananea. Every rock and rut jolted her with pain. When she arrived at the hospital, she was delivered of a three-pound, malnourished, little Christmas angel. Maria became very weak herself and was not even able to see the Americans when they came.

She had taken only one thing with her to the hospital that day. It was a tiny silver hairbrush that her grandmother had given to her when she was a baby. She asked the nurse to give it to the Americans as a keepsake when they came for her little angel. In return, the Americans took a Polaroid snapshot of themselves holding the baby and gave it to the nurse to pass along.

Today, this *navidad,* that baby would have been twenty-one years old—if she had lived. But after the Americans left and Maria had recovered some of her strength, the nurse had confided to her that the baby was too tiny and sick to live more than a week.

Maria and Francisco had been tormented with grief for weeks after that day but knew that this thing that had left such a wound in their hearts was the only choice they'd had.

As time went on, Maria felt sure that the baby had died. She never heard from the Americans again.

Then, a few years later, her Francisco's broken body could carry on no longer. He left her to be with the baby in heaven, and now she was a widow. Her children were all grown with families of their own, and although each one lived nearby, she was alone in her house on this Christmas morning.

With a sigh, she got up and went to her little wooden table. She opened a bag of *masa harina* and began preparing tamales for the evening's Christmas fiesta.

❄

With the tamales wrapped and steaming on the stove, Maria lay down for a short rest. *Making tamales certainly isn't as easy as it was when I was younger,* she thought. She had only dozed for a few minutes when she was suddenly awakened from her siesta by the sound of a car door closing outside in her yard. She sat up and looked out the window. It was an American car with Arizona plates. A young woman was standing at the side of the car looking like she was lost. An older man and a woman waited in the car.

Maria walked out into the yard. "*Buenos dias.* May I help you?"

"Yes," said the young woman in Spanish, "I'm looking for Maria Sanchez. Is that you?"

"Yes, that is me."

Timidly the young woman approached. "My name is Navida Maria Murphey . . ."

"Yes?" said Maria.

The girl opened her extended hand. In it was a tiny silver hairbrush. "You are my mother."

Maria stared at the angel in front of her—this angel with dark eyes and a long, ebony train of hair flowing down her back. How could it be?

She stood transfixed for a moment and then cried, "*Mi bebé! Mi bebé!* I thought you had died!"

The two women fell sobbing into one another's arms.

"No, no, it's me; it's me, my beloved mama. I've come to meet you at last," the angel whispered in her ear. "I've come to meet my family."

The commotion had attracted the attention of little Carlos, the neighbor boy, who was playing in his yard. With wide eyes he had watched as the two women sobbed and hugged and kissed each other's cheeks. In a flash he had spread the word throughout the village. Soon a noisy, happy crowd gathered—many of them related to Navida Murphey—brothers and sisters, nephews and nieces. Navida's American parents had been coaxed from the car, and there was loud and happy chattering and introductions in two different languages.

After things had settled down a bit, Navida announced to everyone that their duty was to take care of her American mom and dad while she spent time alone with Maria.

A neighbor, Miguel, was drafted to act as translator for the Americans, and the whole mob moved noisily toward the village center. Navida and Maria went quietly into the little *casita.* They sat on stools next to the cheery *chiminea.* After holding hands and looking silently into one another's eyes for a long, long time, Navida finally handed Maria a silver-wrapped package. "It's for you, Mama." Again, Maria's tears began to flow. Never had she held such a beautifully wrapped gift. She carefully unwrapped it, and inside she found a vanity set made of sterling silver, with delicate twining roses engraved on the back of the mirror and the brush.

"It's so beautiful, Navida," Maria whispered as she stroked them with her gnarled hands. "Thank you."

Navida then produced shampoo and conditioner—the finest Maria had ever seen. Navida heated a bucket of water on the stove and then gently lathered and conditioned her mother's long, magnificent hair. For the next two hours as Navida dried and brushed Maria's hair, they talked quietly of the past twenty-one years.

Navida told her she had been given two names—Navida because she had been born on Christmas, and Maria so she would never forget her mama. She told of how her parents had found the finest doctors available in Phoenix to care for her in those first few weeks. She had been so tiny and so sick, but with love and care she had grown healthy and strong. Often as she grew, her mother would brush her hair with the tiny silver hairbrush and tell her of what Dolores the adoption agent had said of Maria's magnificent black hair and how Navida's hair was growing to be the same. She told Maria how she had learned hairdressing in high school to pay her way through college and how she had polished her high school Spanish by talking to her Mexican customers in the beauty shop.

She apologized that her family had never contacted Maria. Time, language, and border constraints had somehow all tangled together to keep it from happening. But in September of that year, Navida had sat her adoptive parents down and informed them that for her twenty-first birthday, she wanted to meet her birth mother. They had wholeheartedly agreed.

Maria's hair had now been brushed to a glowing sheen, and her face was glowing with happiness. She felt radiant. Together she and Navida packed the warm tamales into a basket and walked arm in arm to the Christmas fiesta in the plaza.

That night, as the mariachi trumpets played, Navida Maria Murphey sang and danced and celebrated with her fifteen brothers and sisters and her *two* dear, dear mothers.

Author's note: This story is based on the true story of my niece Marisa Rowley Rasmussen. Her adoption from Mexico, the spider bite, the bicycle ride, the number of siblings, and the family's belief that the baby had died are all fact, as is the mother-daughter reunion. My setting of the story at Christmastime and other descriptive details are all artistic license.

"I am not alone at all, I thought. I was never alone at all. And that, of course, is the message of Christmas. We are never alone. Not when the night is darkest, the wind coldest, the world seemingly most indifferent. For this is still the time God chooses."

~ Taylor Caldwell

How is Christmas regarded today? The legend of Santa Claus, the Christmas tree, the decorations of tinsel and mistletoe, and the giving of gifts all express to us the spirit of the day we celebrate; but the true spirit of Christmas lies much deeper than these. It is found in the LIFE OF THE SAVIOR, in the principles He taught, in His atoning sacrifice—which become our great heritage.

-Howard W. Hunter

Poinsettias

DID YOU KNOW?

Besides the Christmas tree, the poinsettia is one of the most recognizable Christmas decorations. However, as common as these plants are, there are a lot of things you probably didn't know about them!

- There is a common misconception that poinsettia plants are very poisonous. However, numerous studies have concluded that the majority of poinsettia exposures do not result in any form of medical treatment. While it's not a good idea to eat the plant, even a fifty-pound child would have to eat nearly 500 leaves before experiencing any seriously dangerous effects. In fact, long before poinsettias were brought to North America, the ancient Aztecs used the plant's milky white sap to treat fevers.

- Poinsettias are not actually flowers. They are typically classified as a shrub or small tree. The brightly colored parts that resemble flowers are actually called bracts—which basically means a modified or special type of leaf.

- December 12 is National Poinsettia Day.

- While the poinsettia plant didn't come to the United States until about 1828, the plant's association with Christmas began in sixteenth-century Mexico. The most popular legend holds that there was a poor Mexican girl called Pepita, who had no present to give the baby Jesus at the Christmas Eve Services. As Pepita walked to the chapel, her cousin Pedro tried to cheer her up, saying that even the smallest gift, given by someone who loves Him would make the Savior happy. Pepita picked a small handful of weeds and made them into a small bouquet. Though she felt embarrassed, she walked through the chapel to the altar, knelt down, and laid the bouquet at the foot of the nativity scene. Suddenly, the weeds burst into bright red flowers, and everyone who saw them was sure they had seen a miracle.

- One reason these plants are so popular at Christmastime is their symbolism. The shape of the poinsettia symbolizes the Star of Bethlehem, which led the wise men to Jesus. The red-colored leaves symbolize the blood of Christ. White leaves represent His purity.

- Poinsettias are known by many names in different cultures. In Mexico and Guatemala, it is called *Flor de Noche Buena*, or "Christmas Eve Flower." In Chile and Peru, the plant became known as Crown of the Andes. And in Spain, the poinsettia is associated with another Christian holiday; there, poinsettias are known as *Flor de Pascua* or *Pascua*, meaning "Easter Flower."

The message of this season that is applicable throughout the year lies NOT IN THE RECEIVING of earthly presents and treasures but in the forsaking of selfishness and greed and in going forward, seeking and ENJOYING the gifts of the *Spirit*, which Paul said are "love, joy, peace, longsuffering, gentleness, goodness, faith, meekness, temperance: against such there is no law."

~James E. Faust

Best Christmas Wishes.

The Burglar's Christmas

By Elizabeth L. Seymour

Two very shabby-looking young men stood at the corner of Prairie Avenue and Eightieth Street, looking despondently at the carriages that whirled by. It was Christmas Eve, and the streets were full of vehicles; florists' wagons, grocers' carts, and carriages. The streets were in that half-liquid, half-congealed condition peculiar to the streets of Chicago at that season of the year. The swift wheels that spun by sometimes threw the slush of mud and snow over the two young men who were talking on the corner.

"Well," remarked the elder of the two, "I guess we are at our rope's end, sure enough. How do you feel?"

"Pretty shaky. The wind's sharp tonight. If I had had anything to eat, I mightn't mind it so much. There is simply no show. I'm sick of the whole business. Looks like there's nothing for it but the lake."

"Oh, nonsense, I thought you had more grit. Got anything left you can hoc?"

"Nothing but my beard, and I am afraid they wouldn't find it worth a pawn ticket," said the younger man ruefully, rubbing the week's growth of stubble on his face.

"Got any folks anywhere? Now's your time to strike 'em if you have."

"Never mind if I have, they're out of the question."

"Well, you'll be out of it before many hours if you don't make a move of some sort. A man's got to eat. See here, I am going down to Longtin's saloon. I used to play the banjo in there with a couple of coons, and I'll bone him for some of his free lunch stuff. You'd better come along, perhaps they'll fill an order for two."

"How far down is it?"

"Well, it's clear downtown, of course, way down on Michigan Avenue."

"Thanks. I guess I'll loaf around here. I don't feel equal to the walk, and the cars—well, the cars are crowded." His features drew themselves into what might have been a smile under happier circumstances.

"No, you never did like street cars; you're too aristocratic. See here, Crawford, I don't like leaving you here. You ain't good company for yourself tonight."

"Crawford? Oh, yes, that's the last one. There have been so many I forget them."

"Have you got a real name, anyway?"

"Oh, yes, but it's one of the ones I've forgotten. Don't you worry about me. You go along and get your free lunch. I think I had a row in Longtin's place once. I'd better not show myself there again." As he spoke the young man nodded and turned slowly up the avenue.

He was miserable enough to want to be quite alone. Even the crowd that jostled by him annoyed him. He wanted to think about himself. He had avoided this final reckoning with himself for a year now. He had laughed it off and drunk it off. But now, when all those artificial devices which are employed to turn our thoughts into other channels and shield us from ourselves had failed him, it must come. Hunger is a powerful incentive to introspection. . . .

It was not the first time he had been hungry and desperate and alone. But always before there had been some outlook, some chance ahead, some pleasure yet untasted that seemed worth the effort, some face that he fancied was, or would be, dear. But it was not so tonight. The unyielding conviction was upon him that he had failed in everything, had outlived everything. . . .

Yet he was but four and twenty, this man—he looked even younger—and he had a father some place down East who had been very proud of him once. Well, he had taken his life into his own hands, and this was what he had made of it. That was all there was to be said. He could remember the hopeful things they used to say about him at college in the old days, before he had cut away and begun to live by his wits. . . .

His last venture had been with some ten-cent specialty company, a little lower than all the others, that had gone to pieces in Buffalo, and he had worked his way to Chicago by boat. When the boat made up its crew for the outward voyage, he was dispensed with as usual. He was used to that. . . .

Tonight was his birthday, too. There seemed something particularly amusing in that. He turned up a limp little coat collar to try to keep a little of the wet chill from his throat, and instinctively began to remember all the birthday parties he used to have. He was so cold and empty that his mind seemed unable to grapple with any serious question. He kept thinking about gingerbread and frosted cakes like a child. He could remember the splendid birthday parties his mother used to give him, when all the other little boys in the block came in their Sunday clothes and creaking shoes, with their ears still red from their mother's towel, and the pink-and-white birthday cake, and the stuffed olives, and all the dishes of which he had been particularly fond, and how he would eat and eat and then go to bed and dream of Santa Claus. . . .

Whichever way his mind now turned there was one thought that it could not escape, and that was the idea of food. He caught the scent of a cigar suddenly, and felt a sharp pain in the pit of his abdomen and a sudden moisture in his mouth. . . . In all his straits he had never stolen anything, his tastes were above it. But tonight there would be no tomorrow. . . .

A girl hastened by him with her arms full of packages. She walked quickly and nervously, keeping well within the shadow, as if she were not accustomed to carrying bundles and did not care to meet any of her friends. As she crossed the muddy street, she made an effort to lift her skirt a little, and as she did so one of the packages slipped unnoticed from beneath her arm. He caught it up and overtook her. "Excuse me, but I think you dropped something."

She started. "Oh, yes, thank you! I would rather have lost anything than that."

The young man turned angrily upon himself. The package must have contained something of value. Why had he not kept it? Was this the sort of thief he would make? He ground his teeth together. There is nothing more maddening than to have morally consented to crime and then lack the nerve force to carry it out.

A carriage drove up to the house before which he stood. Several richly dressed women alighted and went in. It was a new house and must have been built since he was in Chicago last. The front door was open, and he could see down the hallway and up the staircase. The servant had left the door and gone with the guests. The first floor was brilliantly lighted, but the windows upstairs were dark. It looked very easy, just to slip upstairs to the darkened chambers where the jewels and trinkets of the fashionable occupants were kept.

Still burning with impatience against himself, he entered quickly. Instinctively he removed his mud-stained hat as he passed quickly and quietly up the staircase. It struck him as being a rather superfluous courtesy in a burglar, but he had done it before he had thought. His way was clear enough, he met no one on the stairway or in the upper hall. The gas was lit in the upper hall. He passed the first chamber door through sheer cowardice. The second he entered quickly, thinking of something else lest his courage should fail him, and closed the door behind him. The light from the hall shone into the room through the transom. The apartment was furnished richly enough to justify his expectations. He went at once to the dressing case. A number of rings and small trinkets lay in a silver tray. These he put hastily in his pocket. He opened the upper drawer and found, as he expected, several leather cases. In the first he opened was a lady's watch, in the second a pair of old-fashioned bracelets; he seemed to dimly remember having seen bracelets like them before, somewhere. The third case was heavier, the spring was much worn, and it opened easily. It held a cup of some kind. He held it up to the light, and then his strained nerves gave way, and he uttered a sharp exclamation. It was the silver mug he used to drink from when he was a little boy.

The door opened, and a woman stood in the doorway facing him. She was a tall, with white hair, in evening dress. The light from the hall streamed in upon him, but she was not afraid. She stood looking at him a moment, then she threw out her hand and went quickly toward him. "Willie, Willie! Is it you!"

He struggled to loose her arms from him, to keep her lips from his cheek. "Mother—you must not! You do not understand!" Hunger, weakness, cold, shame, all came back to him and shook his self-control completely. Physically he was too weak to stand a shock like this. Why could it not have been an ordinary discovery, arrest, the station house, and all the rest of it. Anything but this! A hard, dry sob broke from him. Again he strove to disengage himself.

"Who is it says I shall not kiss my son? Oh, my boy, we have waited so long for this! You have been so long in coming, even I almost gave you up."

Her lips upon his cheek burnt him like fire. He put his hand to his throat and spoke thickly and incoherently: "You do not understand. I did not know you were here. I came here to rob—it is the first time—I swear it—but I am a common thief. My pockets are full of your jewels now. Can't you hear me? I am a common thief!"

"Hush, my boy, those are ugly words. How could you rob your own house? How could you take what is your own? They are all yours, my son, as wholly yours as my great love—and you can't doubt that, Will, do you?"

That soft voice, the warmth and fragrance of her person stole through his chill, empty veins like a gentle stimulant.

He felt as though all his strength were leaving him and even consciousness. He held fast to her, bowed his head on her strong shoulder, and groaned aloud. "Oh, Mother, life is hard, hard!"

She said nothing, but held him closer. And, oh, the strength of those white arms that held him! Oh, the assurance of safety in that warm bosom that rose and fell under his cheek! For a moment they stood so, silently. Then they heard a heavy step upon the stair. She led him to a chair and went out and closed the door. At the top of the staircase she met a tall, broad-shouldered man, with iron-gray hair, and a face alert and stern. Her eyes were shining and her cheeks on fire; her whole face was one expression of intense determination.

"James, it is William in there, come home. You must keep him at any cost. If he goes this time, I go with him. Oh, James, be easy with him; he has suffered so." She broke from a command to an entreaty and laid her hand on his shoulder. He looked questioningly at her a moment, then went in the room and quietly shut the door.

She stood leaning against the wall, clasping her temples with her hands and listening to the low indistinct sound of the voices within. Her own lips moved silently. She waited a long time, scarcely breathing.

"Each of us is an innkeeper who decides if there is room for Jesus!"

~ Neal A. Maxwell

At last the door opened, and her husband came out. He stopped to say in a shaken voice, "You go to him now, he will stay. I will go to my room. I will see him again in the morning."

She put her arm about his neck, "Oh, James, I thank you, I thank you! This is the night he came so long ago, you remember? I gave him to you then, and now you give him back to me!"

"Don't, Helen," he muttered. "He is my son, I have never forgotten that. I failed with him. I don't like to fail, it cuts my pride. Take him and make a man of him." He passed on down the hall.

She flew into the room where the young man sat with his head bowed upon his knee. She dropped upon her knees beside him. Ah, it was so good to him to feel those arms again!

"He is so glad, Willie, so glad! He may not show it, but he is as happy as I. He never was demonstrative with either of us, you know."

"I told him everything, and he was good enough. I don't see how either of you can look at me, speak to me, touch me." He shivered under her clasp again as when she had first touched him and tried weakly to throw her off.

But she whispered softly, "This is my right, my son."

Presently, when he was calmer, she rose. "Now, come with me into the library, and I will have your dinner brought there."

As they went downstairs, she remarked apologetically, "I will not call Ellen tonight; she has a number of guests to attend to. She is a big girl now, you know, and came out last winter. Besides, I want you all to myself tonight."

When the dinner came, and it came very soon, he fell upon it savagely. As he ate she told him all that had transpired during the years of his absence, and how his father's business had brought them there. “I was glad when we came. I thought you would drift west. I seemed a good deal nearer to you here.” There was a gentle unobtrusive sadness in her tone that was too soft for a reproach. “Have you everything you want? It is a comfort to see you eat.”

He smiled grimly. “It is certainly a comfort to me. I have not indulged in this frivolous habit for some thirty-five hours.”

She caught his hand and pressed it sharply, uttering a quick remonstrance. “Don’t say that! I know, but I can’t hear you say it—it’s too terrible! My boy, food has choked me many a time when I have thought of the possibility of that. Now take the old lounging chair by the fire, and if you are too tired to talk, we will just sit and rest together.”

He sat looking up at the magnificent woman beside him. . . . He sighed restlessly and laid his hand on hers. There seemed refuge and protection in the touch of her, as in the old days when he was afraid of the dark. He had been in the dark so long now, his confidence was so thoroughly shaken, and he was bitterly afraid of the night and of himself. “Ah, Mother, you make other things seem so false. You must feel that I owe you an explanation, but I can’t make any, even to myself. Ah, but we make poor exchanges in life. I can’t make out the riddle of it all. Yet there are things I ought to tell you before I accept your confidence like this.”

“I’d rather you wouldn’t, Will. Listen: Between you and me there can be no secrets. We are more alike than other people. Dear boy, I know all about it. I am a woman, and circumstances were different with me, but we are of one blood. I have lived all your life before you. You have never had an impulse that I have not known, you have never touched a brink that my feet have not trod. This is your birthday night. Twenty-four years ago I foresaw all this. I was a young woman then, and I had hot battles of my own, and I felt your likeness to me. You were not like other babies. From the hour you were born you were restless and discontented, as I had been before you. You used to brace your strong little limbs against mine and try to throw me off as you did tonight. Tonight you have come back to me, just as you always did after you ran away to swim in the river that was forbidden you, the river you loved because it was forbidden. You are tired and sleepy, just as you used to be then, only a little older and a little paler and a little more foolish. I never asked you where you had been then, nor will I now. You have come back to me, that’s all in all to me. I know your every possibility and limitation, as a composer knows his instrument.”

He found no answer that was worthy to give to talk like this. . . .

He drew a long sigh of rich content. . . . And as the chimes rang joyfully outside and sleep pressed heavily upon his eyelids, he wondered dimly if the Author of this sad little riddle of ours were not able to solve it after all, and if the Potter would not finally mete out his all comprehensive justice, such as none but he could have, to his things of clay, which are made in his own patterns, weak or strong, for his own ends; and if some day we will not awaken and find that all evil is a dream, a mental distortion that will pass when the dawn shall break.

GREETINGS

Christmas Wishes

By Juliana Horatia Ewing

A CAROL.

Oh, happy Christmas, full of blessings, come!
Now bid our discords cease;
Here give the weary ease;
Let the long-parted meet again in peace;
Bring back the far-away;
Grant us a holiday;
And by the hopes of Christmas-tide we pray—
Let love restore the fallen to his Home;
Whilst up and down the snowy streets the Christmas minstrels sing;
And through the frost from countless towers the bells of
Christmas ring.

Ah, Christ! and yet a happier day shall come!
Then bid our discords cease;
There give the weary ease;
Let the long-parted meet again in peace;
Bring back the far-away;
Grant us a holiday;
And by the hopes of Christmas-tide we pray—
Let love restore the fallen to his Home;
Whilst up and down the golden streets the blessed angels sing,
And evermore the heavenly chimes in heavenly cadence ring.

The Nutcracker and the Mouse King

By E. T. A. Hoffmann [adapted]

On the twenty-fourth of December, Dr. Stahlbaum's children were not allowed to set foot in the family parlor. Fritz and Marie sat together in the back room and waited. In whispers, Fritz told his younger sister that he had seen Godfather Drosselmeier. At that, Marie clapped her little hands for joy and cried out, "Oh, what do you think Godfather Drosselmeier has made for us?"

Fritz said it was a fortress, with all kinds of soldiers marching up and down.

"No, no," Marie interrupted. "Mr. Drosselmeier said something to me about a beautiful garden with a big lake in it and lovely swans swimming all around on it."

"Mr. Drosselmeier can't make a whole garden," said Fritz rather rudely.

Then the children tried to guess what their parents would give them. Marie sat deep in thought, while Fritz muttered, "I'd like a chestnut horse and some soldiers."

At that moment, a bell rang, the doors flew open, and a flood of light streamed in from the big parlor. "Come in, dear children," said Papa and Mama.

The children stood silently with shining eyes. Then Marie cried out, "Oh, how lovely!" And Fritz took two rather spectacular jumps into the air.

Marie discovered a silk dress hanging on the tree. "What a lovely dress!" she cried.

Meanwhile, Fritz galloped around the table, trying out the new horse he had found. Then he reviewed his new squadron of soldiers, who were admirably outfitted in red-and-gold uniforms.

Just then, the bell rang again. Knowing that Godfather Drosselmeier would be unveiling his present, the children ran to the table that had been set up beside the wall. The screen that had hidden it was taken away. The children saw a magnificent castle with dozens of sparkling windows and golden towers. Chimes played as tiny ladies and gentlemen strolled around the rooms, and children in little skirts danced to the music of the chimes.

Fritz looked at the beautiful castle, then said, "Godfather Drosselmeier, let me go inside your castle."

"Impossible," said Mr. Drosselmeier.

"Then make the children come out," cried Fritz.

"No," said their godfather crossly. "That, too, is impossible. This is how the mechanism works, and it cannot be changed."

"Then I don't really care for it," said Fritz. "My soldiers march as I command, and they're not shut up in a house." Fritz marched away to play with his soldiers.

Marie did not leave the Christmas table, for she was well-behaved.

The real reason why Marie did not want to leave the Christmas table was that she had just caught sight of something. When Fritz marched away, an excellent little man came into view.

The distinction of his dress showed him to be a man of taste and breeding. Oddly enough, though, he wore a skimpy cloak that was made of wood. His light green eyes were full of kindness, and his white-cotton beard was most becoming.

"Oh, Father dear," Marie cried out, "who does the dear little man belong to?"

"Dear child," said Dr. Stahlbaum, "our friend here will serve you all well. He will crack hard nuts for all of you with his teeth."

Carefully picking him up from the table, Dr. Stahlbaum lifted his wooden cloak, and the little man opened his mouth wide, revealing two rows of sharp white teeth. At her father's bidding, Marie put in a nut, and—crack. The little man bit it in two, the shell fell down, and Marie found the sweet kernel in her hand.

Fritz ran over to his sister. He chose the biggest nut, and all of a sudden—crack, crack—three little teeth fell out of the nutcracker's mouth.

"Oh, my poor little Nutcracker!" Marie cried, taking him out of Fritz's hands.

"He's just a stupid fool," said Fritz. "He calls himself a nutcracker, and his teeth are no good. Give him to me, Marie."

Marie was in tears. "No, no!" she cried. "He's my dear Nutcracker, and you can't have him." Sobbing, Marie wrapped the Nutcracker in her little handkerchief. She bandaged his wounded mouth. Then she rocked him in her arms like a baby.

It was getting late, and Mother urged her children to turn in for the night. But Marie pleaded, "Just a little while longer, Mother dear."

Marie's mother put out all of the candles, leaving on only one lamp. "Go to bed soon," she said, "or you won't be able to get up tomorrow."

As soon as Marie was alone, she set the nutcracker carefully on the table, unwrapped the handkerchief ever so slowly, and examined his wounds. "Dear Nutcracker," she said softly, "don't be angry at my brother, Fritz. He meant no harm. I'm going to take care of you until you're well and happy again."

Marie picked up the nutcracker and placed him next to the other toys in a glass cabinet in the parlor. She shut the door and was going to her bedroom, when she heard whispering and shuffling. The clock whirred twelve times. Then she heard giggling and squeaking all around her, followed by the sound of a thousand little feet scampering behind the walls. Soon Marie saw mice all over the room, and they formed ranks, just as Fritz's soldiers did.

Crushed stone flew out of the floor as though driven by some underground force, and seven mouse heads with seven sparkling crowns rose up, squeaking and squealing hideously. This enormous mouse was hailed by the entire army, cheering with three loud squeaks. And then the army set itself in motion—hop, hop, trot, trot—heading straight for the toy cabinet.

At the same time, Marie saw a strange glow inside the toy cabinet. All at once, Nutcracker jumped from the cabinet, and the squeaking and squealing started again.

"Trusty Vassal-Drummer," cried the nutcracker, "sound the advance!" The drummer played so loudly that the windows of the toy cabinet rattled. A clattering was heard from inside, and all the boxes containing Fritz's army burst open. Soldiers climbed out and jumped to the bottom shelf. Then they formed ranks on the floor. The nutcracker ran back and forth, shouting words of encouragement to the troops.

A few moments later, guns were going *boom! boom!* The mice advanced and overran some of the artillery positions. Such was the confusion, and such were the smoke and dust, that Marie could hardly see what was going on. But this much was certain—both sides fought with grim determination, and for a long while, victory hung in the balance. Then the mice brought up more troops.

Did You Know?

The world's largest nutcracker measures 33 feet 1 inch high and is fully functional. It was made in Germany.

The nutcracker found himself trapped against the toy cabinet. "Bring up the reserves!" he cried. And true enough, a few men came out, but they wielded their swords so clumsily that they knocked off General Nutcracker's cap.

The nutcracker was in dire peril. He tried to jump over the ledge of the toy cabinet, but his legs were too short. In wild despair he shouted, "A horse, a horse! My kingdom for a horse!"

At that moment, the king of mice charged the nutcracker. Without quite knowing what she was doing, Marie took off her left shoe and flung it with all her might, hoping to hit the mouse king. At that moment, everything vanished from Marie's sight. She felt a sharp pain in her left arm and fell to the floor in a faint.

When Marie awoke from her deep sleep, she was lying in her own little bed. The sun shining into the room sparkled on the ice-coated windowpanes. A strange gentleman was sitting beside her, but she soon recognized him as Dr. Wendelstern. "She's awake," he said softly to Marie's mother. She came over and gave Marie an anxious look.

"Oh, Mother dear," Marie whispered. "Have all the nasty mice gone away? Was Nutcracker saved?"

"Don't talk such nonsense, child," said her mother. "What have mice got to do with the nutcracker? Oh, we've been so worried about you. Last night, I went into the living room and found you lying beside the glass toy cabinet in a faint, bleeding. The nutcracker was lying on your arm, and your left shoe was lying on the floor nearby—"

"Oh, Mother," Marie broke in. "There had just been a big battle between the dolls and the mice. The mice were going to capture the poor nutcracker. So I threw my shoe at the mice, and after that I don't know what happened."

Marie's father came in and had a long talk with Dr. Wendelstern. Marie had to stay in bed and take medicine for a week.

Then Godfather Drosselmeier came to visit. "I've brought you something that will give you pleasure," he told Marie. With that, he reached into his pocket and took out the nutcracker, whose lost teeth he had put back in very neatly and firmly, and whose broken jaw he had fixed as good as new. Marie cried out for joy!

That night, Marie was awakened in the moonlight by a strange rumbling. "Oh, dear, the mice are here again!" Marie cried out in fright.

Then she saw the king of mice squeeze through the hole in the wall. He scurried across the floor and jumped onto the table beside Marie's bed. "Give me your candy," he said, "or I'll bite your nutcracker to pieces." Then he slipped back into the hole.

Marie was so frightened she could hardly say a word. That night she put her whole supply of delicacies at the foot of the toy cabinet. The next morning the candy was gone.

Marie was happy because she had saved the nutcracker, but that night the mouse king returned. “Give me your beautiful dress and all your picture books,” he hissed.

Marie was beside herself with anguish. The next morning she went to the toy cabinet sobbing and said to the nutcracker, “Oh, dear, what can I do? If I give that horrid mouse king all my books and my dress, he’ll just keep asking for more.”

The nutcracker said in a strained whisper, “Just get me a sword . . .” At that his words ebbed away, and his eyes became fixed.

Marie asked Fritz for a sword, and Fritz slung it around the nutcracker’s waist.

The next night, fear and dread kept Marie awake. At the stroke of twelve she heard clanging and crashing in the parlor. And then suddenly, “Squeak!”

Soon Marie heard a soft knocking at the door and a faint little voice, “Miss Stahlbaum, open the door and have no fear. I bring good news!” Marie swiftly opened the door and found that the nutcracker had turned into a prince!

The prince took Marie’s hand and told her how he was really Godfather Drosselmeier’s nephew, and an evil spell had turned him into a nutcracker. When he defeated the mouse king, the spell was broken and he was turned back into a prince.

“Oh, Miss Stahlbaum,” said the prince, “what splendid things I can show you in this hour of victory over my enemy, if you will follow me a little way.”

Marie agreed and followed the prince to the big clothes cupboard in the entrance hall. The door of the cupboard was wide open. The prince stepped inside, pulled a tassel, and a little ladder came down through the sleeve of a traveling coat.

Marie climbed the ladder and soon passed through the sleeve. When she looked out through the neck hole, she found herself in a fragrant meadow.

“This is Candy Meadow,” said the prince.

Looking up, Marie saw a beautiful arch as they were passing through it. “Oh, it’s so wonderful here,” she sighed.

The prince clapped his hands, and several little shepherds appeared. They brought up a golden chair and asked Marie to sit down. Then the shepherds danced a charming ballet. Suddenly, as if at a signal, they all vanished into the woods.

The prince took Marie’s hand and led her down Honey River. Downstream there was a sweet little village. “This is Gingerbread City,” said the prince. “The people who live here are beautiful, but most are dreadfully cranky because they have awful toothaches. But instead of worrying our heads over that, let’s sail across the lake to the capital.”

The prince clapped his hands. The gondola appeared in the distance and quickly came closer. Marie and the prince stepped onto the gondola, which quickly started off again.

Soon Marie found herself near a marvelous city.

“This,” said Nutcracker, “is the capital.” The city was so beautiful and splendorous. Not only were the walls and towers of the most magnificent colors, but the shapes of the buildings were like nothing else on earth.

Suddenly, Marie saw a castle with a hundred lofty towers.

“This,” said the prince, “is Marzipan Castle.” At that moment soft music was heard, the gates of the castle opened, and out stepped four ladies so richly and splendidly attired that Marie knew they could only be princesses. One by one, they embraced their brother.

The ladies led Marie and the prince to an inner room, whose walls were made of sparkling colored crystal. The princesses planned to prepare a meal for Marie and the prince. They brought in the most wonderful fruit and candy Marie had ever seen and began to squeeze the fruit and grate the sugared almonds.

The most beautiful of the prince's sisters handed her a little golden mortar and said, "Dear sweet friend, would you care to pound some rock candy?"

While Marie pounded away, the prince told the history of the cruel war between the mouse king's army and his own.

As Marie listened to his story, she began to feel very dizzy. Soon Marie felt as though she were falling.

When she opened her eyes, she was lying in her little bed, and her mother was standing there.

"How can anyone sleep so long!" her mother exclaimed.

"Oh, Mother," said Marie, "you cannot imagine all of the places that young Mr. Drosselmeier took me to last night."

Marie's mother looked at her in amazement. "You've had a long, beautiful dream, but now you must forget all that nonsense," she said.

"But, Mother dear," said Marie, "I know that the nutcracker is really young Mr. Drosselmeier from Nuremberg, Godfather Drosselmeier's nephew."

Mrs. Stahlbaum burst out laughing. Marie was on the verge of tears. Her mother sternly said, "You're to forget about this foolishness once and for all." So she did.

One day Marie's mother came into her room and said, "Your godfather's nephew from Nuremberg is here. So be on your good behavior."

Marie turned as red as a beet when she saw the young man, and she turned even redder when young Drosselmeier asked her to go with him to the cabinet in the parlor.

He went down on one knee and said, "Miss Stahlbaum, you see at your feet the happiest of men, whose life you saved on this very spot. Please come and reign with me over Marzipan Castle."

Marie said softly, "Of course I will come with you."

Marie left in a golden carriage. And she is still the queen of a country where the most wonderful things can be seen if you have the right sort of eyes for it.

Happy, happy
CHRISTMAS,
that can win us back
to the delusions of your
CHILDHOOD
DAYS,
recall to the old man the
PLEASURES
of his
YOUTH.
and transport the
traveler back
to his own fireside and
QUIET *home*.

~Charles Dickens

He who has no Christmas
in his *heart*
will never find
CHRISTMAS
under a tree.

~ Charlotte Carpenter

SWEET CANDIED NUTS

½ cup water
1 cup white sugar
1 Tablespoon ground cinnamon
2 cups whole almonds or other nut of your choice. (Walnuts, pecans, etc.)

1. Combine the water, sugar, and cinnamon in a saucepan over medium heat; bring to a boil; add in the almonds. Cook and stir the mixture constantly, until all the liquid evaporates and leaves a syrup-like coating on the almonds. (This process will take about 30 minutes. The water should be completely gone.)
2. Pour the almonds onto a baking sheet lined with waxed paper. Separate almonds using two forks.
3. Allow to cool 15–20 minutes.

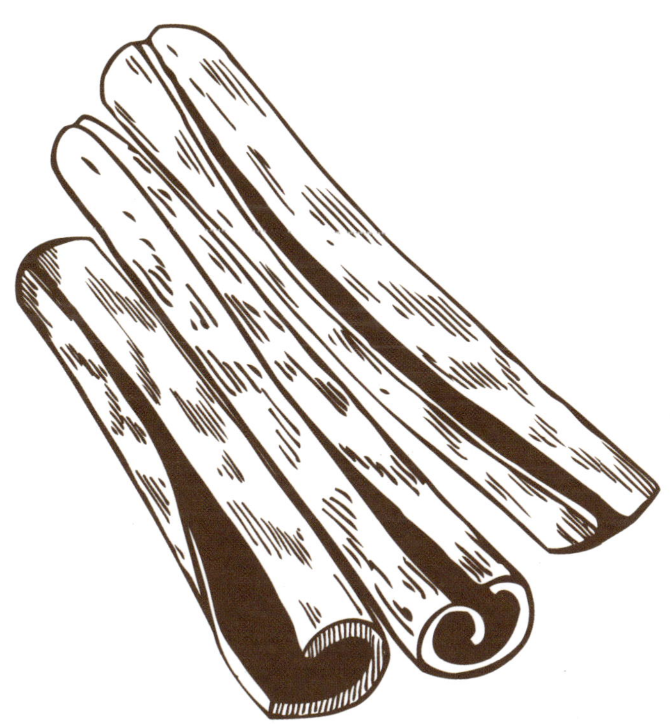

CHRISTMAS
GREETINGS

Candle in the Window

By Michele Ashman Bell

Nothing was the same for John after Molly died.

She passed away that spring of 1909, just as the earth was awakening from its winter solace. Somehow it didn't seem right, during that time of rebirth and renewal of life, to lay the love of his life into a cold, lonely grave. It was cruel irony and John doubted he would ever be able to fill the emptiness inside of him.

But it wasn't enough that his own heart had broken when his wife died. The sorrowful expressions on his children's faces drove his agony even deeper into his soul. The older two, Sarah and Catherine, seemed to be coping with the loss of their mother. Sarah, at fifteen, had been forced to assume the role of cook and housekeeper, with the help of twelve-year-old Catherine. Instead of playing with friends after school, they came home and took care of household duties and also helped their father around the farm.

John worried for all his daughters, but it was eight-year-old Emily who concerned him the most, especially as the first Christmas without Molly approached. Emily knew her mother was gone but somehow hadn't seemed to grasp the concept of the finality of death. Emily was convinced that Heavenly Father was going to let her mother come to visit her at Christmas. His daughter was so convinced that sometimes even John found himself believing it. Or at least, wanting to.

Emily had always been a sensitive, delicate child, and she had the spiritual depth of someone much older and wiser. At times her comments were so simple, yet so profound, that John was aware of how very close she was to Heavenly Father's spirit, and to Molly's.

"Mama visited me in my dream last night, Papa," Emily told him one morning.

Trying to be patient and understanding, John asked his blonde-haired, blue-eyed little angel about the dream.

"Oh, Papa, she looked ever so beautiful." Emily spoke with breathless wonder. "Her hair was long and shiny, and she laughed and played with me. We went to the meadow and picked flowers and laid on our backs and watched the clouds."

"That's very nice, Emily," John said, cradling his daughter on his lap. The fire in the fireplace crackled merrily on that chilly winter morning. Fresh snow had fallen and the windows had delicate patterns of ice crystals on them.

"Sometimes I'm sad that Mama had to leave, but then, when I see her, she's laughing and happy, and I'm not sad anymore," Emily told him. "She promised she would visit me on Christmas. Isn't that wonderful, Papa?"

John didn't know what to say. Emily's faith didn't waver—she was convinced it was true. How could he dash his young daughter's hopes and break her tiny heart? Instead, he held her close and rocked her, wishing in his own heart that Molly would indeed come home.

As Christmas approached, John tried to make the season as joyful for his daughters as he could. He knew that no matter what else happened, he had one surprise for his daughters so they would still feel their mother's love, although she was no longer with them.

In the past, Molly had made the girls matching Christmas dresses every year.

Before her death, she had managed to make their dresses and order shoes for each of them from the Sears Roebuck catalogue. John had been saving these gifts for months. He planned to give them to his daughters on Christmas Eve, just before they went to the town's Christmas celebration. This, he hoped, would help the girls make it through their first Christmas without their mother. Seeing them happy would, in turn, help him through the holiday.

The first Saturday in December, John and the girls bundled up and went into the hills above their town to select a tree, just as they'd done every year. Excitement shone in the girls' eyes as they anticipated bringing the tree home and decorating it for Christmas.

"What about this one?" John suggested when he spotted a nicely shaped evergreen.

"Papa," Sarah said indignantly. "We need a bigger tree. That one's no bigger than Emily."

"All right," John replied. "Suit yourselves, but remember, we have to haul the bloomin' thing home."

The girls ran around the hillside examining each tree until, finally, they located a beautiful blue spruce they proclaimed to be "perfect." In no time, they were dragging the evergreen behind them on the old wooden sled, and even though the girls were chilled to the bone, they were beside themselves with excitement to start decorating the tree.

While John went to the barn to do the evening chores, the girls began stringing fluffy white popcorn and bright red cranberries. Then they pasted colorful paper chains together using homemade paste made from flour, water, and a little bit of sugar.

Just as their mother had always done, Catherine lit a candle and put it in the window to help her father find his way back to the house through the darkness.

The decorations were strung about the fragrant limbs of the tree, and when their father returned from doing the chores, he helped the girls fasten candles to the branches, which would be lit on Christmas Eve.

"It's lovely," Emily said as she softly touched one of the candles. "Mama is going to like it very much."

John gave each of his daughters a hug and blinked back the tears that stung his eyes. Yes, Molly would love it.

Saturday was baking day, so they made Christmas cookies in the shapes of stars and gingerbread men. Some were to be hung on the tree, others were tightly packaged and stored to keep for their Christmas dinner at their grandmother's house. Each year Grandma made a huge turkey with stuffing, delicious-smelling breads and rolls, and tasty mincemeat and pumpkin pies.

In addition to Grandma's goodies, the girls also looked forward each year to the candy made by their Aunt Alice, who was Molly's sister and a wonderful candymaker. She made fudge and toffee and marshmallows that melted in their mouths. She also made divinity, Emily's favorite.

Every year, at the beginning of December, the girls would go to the city mercantile and browse for hours trying to find just the right gifts for each other and for their papa. Using their allowance, they made their purchases, keeping their gifts secret, and took them home. There they wrapped them in butcher paper or pieces of cloth and hid them in their trunks. On Christmas Eve, they would place all the gifts under the tree and light the candles.

Christmas had always been their mother's favorite time of year, and she had had a way of making it extra special. That first year after her death, when the girls started to feel sad that their mother was no longer with them, the secrets and busyness of the season helped them feel a little better. They tried to duplicate the things their mother had done, like hanging tinsel around the windows, or cutting paper snowflakes and hanging them with thread from the ceiling. And they kept a candle burning in the window to welcome guests and visitors during the holiday season.

But it just wasn't the same.

Christmas Eve morning, after chores were done, John entered the house to find his three daughters placing steaming bowls of oatmeal on the table. To make the meal special, they had sweet raisins for the cereal and maple syrup to drizzle on top. Sarah placed a platter of sizzling ham on the table, and they sat down to eat.

"Don't forget to bless Mama," Emily reminded him. John smiled at his daughter and bowed his head.

After breakfast, John made an announcement. "I have a special surprise for you after you've cleared up the dishes."

Hearing this, the girls quickly cleaned the kitchen and did the dishes, then gathered at the Christmas tree. Emily couldn't help bouncing on her chair, wondering what kind of surprise her father had for them. Moments later John returned from his bedroom, his arms loaded with a large bundle wrapped in an old muslin sheet.

"What is it, Papa?" Catherine asked, wide-eyed.

"You'll see." He placed the bundle on the settee and began unwrapping it.

The girls giggled with excitement, but when he exposed the contents, they stopped and stared.

"Your mother made these for you," he said. "She wanted me to save them for you until Christmas."

Tears welling up in their eyes, the girls stared speechless at the matching dresses. Lifting the dresses, one by one, John handed one to each daughter. The dresses were of rich, red wool plaid, with belts, cuffs, and collars out of black velvet. Even the buttons going up the back of each dress were covered with black velvet material.

With tears and smiles, the girls hugged their papa, who couldn't stop tears from streaming down his own face. As sweet as the gift was, it was still a painful reminder of Molly's absence. He felt it and he knew his daughters felt it. Hoping to dry their tears, John cleared his throat. "Well, now, that's not quite all of it."

The three girls stared at their father in disbelief as they wondered what else there could be. Surely these exquisite handmade dresses from their mother were all they could ever dream of.

"Shut your eyes and hold out your hands," John instructed.

Each girl closed her eyes and waited. Emily held her eyes shut tightly and felt excitement bubble up inside of her. "Hurry, Papa," she said anxiously. "I think I'm going to pop."

John laughed and placed something in each girl's hands. "Okay," he said. "You can open your eyes."

Each girl opened her eyes and looked down to see a pair of patent leather slippers. Beautiful, shiny, patent leather slippers. Black with little bows and a delicate strap that buckled on the side. Pretty enough for a princess. These were special shoes, to be worn on special occasions, Emily knew. Not like her brown everyday shoes, that sounded loud and clunky on the wooden floor when she walked.

"Ohhh," she said breathlessly. "They are the most beautiful shoes I've ever seen."

She admired the fancy shoes for a long time before she finally tried them on. They were a little big for her, but that's how her mother had always purchased shoes for each of them—so they'd have room to grow. Still they felt delicate and dainty on Emily's feet. Light enough that she felt like she was walking on air.

"Can we wear them to the celebration tonight?" she asked anxiously.

"I don't think you would want to wear them out in the snow," he said. "That would ruin them for sure."

At the look of disappointment on Emily's face, John thought quickly. "I have an idea, though. You can carry them to the church with you and wear your winter boots. Then you can change there."

Emily threw her arms around her father's neck and squeezed tightly. "Thank you, Papa," she said softly. She held onto her father just a moment longer before she stepped back and looked at him with smiling eyes. Eyes that reminded him of Molly's.

"I wish we could tell Mama how much we love the dresses and shoes," Catherine said.

John smiled. "I think she knows," he told her.

Emily smiled knowingly at her papa. "Of course she does, Papa. Just because we can't see her doesn't mean she isn't here."

John contemplated his sweet daughter for a moment, marveling at the insight and faith of such a young child. Yes, he believed Emily was right. Perhaps Molly was often with them; they just couldn't see her when she was.

The sisters helped each other get ready for the Christmas Eve celebration and dance, which had been a town tradition as long as anyone could remember. The girls curled their hair and pulled it back with ribbons. Then they put on their fluffy, stiff petticoats and buttoned up each other's dresses. After putting on their winter boots, they carried their new slippers downstairs and put on their hats, coats, and gloves. Emily didn't mind wearing her old, heavy boots since she would be able to put on her beautiful new shoes when they got to the party.

Tingling with excitement, Emily placed one slipper deep inside each coat pocket. Now she was ready to go to the party. She couldn't wait to show her grandparents her new dress and shoes.

Walking gingerly in the snow, they traipsed the five blocks to the town's center, where the church was brightly lit up and beckoned to them through the darkness. Even from a distance, John and his daughters could hear Christmas carols being sung and peals of laughter floating on the night air. Goose bumps prickled Emily's flesh as the magic of the night filled her entire body.

It seemed like forever, but finally they arrived at the church. They greeted their friends and neighbors, then hurried toward Grandma and Grandpa, who pulled the girls into big bear hugs.

"How lovely you look," Grandma said, blinking quickly to clear the tears from her eyes. "It made Molly so happy to make clothes for you beautiful girls."

"Here now," Grandfather said to the girls in his gruff voice. "Your cousins are waiting for you around the Christmas tree. Why don't you go find them?"

Emily saw her Grandma wipe her eyes as Grandpa slipped a loving arm around her shoulders. It was odd, she thought, that their family could be so happy and excited one minute, and so sad and tearful the next.

Emily's sisters took her by the hand and started to pull her toward the festivities, but she dug in her heels and cried, "Wait!"

Her sisters looked at her with surprise.

"I want to put on my new slippers first," she explained.

Her sisters had almost forgotten that they had also brought their new shoes in their coat pockets, and they all rushed back to the coat room to change their shoes. Grabbing a shoe out of her right pocket,

Emily reached into the other pocket, but to her horror, her shoe was gone.

Frantically she looked on the floor all around the coats to see if it had dropped out, but the shoe was nowhere to be seen.

"Emily, what's wrong?" Catherine asked her.

"My slipper," she cried. "It's gone." She held up one shoe, then burst into tears. Sarah ran to find her father and soon the whole family was searching for the missing shoe.

"It's not here," John told his heartbroken daughter.

Emily looked at him with the saddest eyes he'd ever seen. He knew what he had to do.

"You go have fun at the party. I'll find your shoe," he told her confidently. "I'm sure it's just outside the church." But in his heart he worried that he wouldn't find it. It was dark outside and fresh snow was falling. The shoe could easily sink into the snow.

"Come on, Em," Sarah coaxed her. "It's almost time for presents."

Reluctantly Emily went with her sisters, although she would have rather been out helping her papa look for her shoe. But she gathered with her cousins and neighborhood friends around the Christmas tree, and they all sang "Silent Night" and "Joy to the World."

After the songs the children were given bags that contained an orange, a whistle, nuts, and horehound candy bits. Even though the children received the same thing every year, it was still a greatly anticipated treat.

But even the candy didn't take Emily's mind off her shoe. As soon as she got her bag of goodies, she left the group to find her father—surely he was back with her shoe by now. But he was nowhere to be found.

A small five-piece band on the stage struck up a happy tune, and couples took to the dance floor, sashaying and whirling about. Emily kept one eye on the door and one eye on the dance floor. She remembered last year, watching her mother and father dancing happily, looking into each other's eyes. A twinge of sadness pinched her heart, but she remembered her mother's promise to come and visit. For Emily, that was enough to brighten her spirits again.

A table heavily laden with fruitcake, nut breads, cookies, candies, and finger sandwiches fed the festive crowd. Women bustled back and forth from the kitchen replacing empty platters with fresh Christmas goodies.

"Well, well," a deep voice said behind her. "I don't believe we've had a chance to dance yet this evening."

Emily turned to find her grandfather standing behind her. "Hi, Grandpa," she said sadly.

"Don't you worry, child," her grandfather said, hugging her close to him. "Your papa will find your shoe. How about we take a turn out on the dance floor, then fetch something to wet our whistles?"

Grandfather took Emily by the hands and guided her to the dance floor. He swung her around, her feet flying out from under her, making her feel light and airy. Soon she was laughing and breathless, and for a moment she forgot about her lost shoe.

Several dances later, Emily caught a glimpse of her father standing in the coat

Symbolism of Candles:

Candles bring light into dark places the same way Jesus Christ brings light into our lives.

room. Like a shot, she sped from the dance floor toward him.

"Emily," her grandfather called after her. But she didn't stop, anxious as she was to see if her father had found her shoe. As she got closer, she slowed to a walk. By the look on his face, she knew he hadn't found it.

"Papa?" she asked hopefully, noticing the thick layer of snow on his hat and coat.

He shook his head sadly, then said in an encouraging tone, "But I'm going to go back out and look again. I just came inside to ask your grandfather to take you girls home for me."

They found Grandpa and made arrangements for him to get the girls home, then her father wrapped his scarf around his neck twice and was off again.

The celebration continued on awhile longer with dancing and singing and eating. Again, Emily couldn't help wishing she could be outside, helping her papa look for her shoe. Maybe, with both of them looking, they'd find it.

When the party ended, the sisters bundled up and stepped outside into the thickly falling snow. Emily could feel her heart grow heavy, knowing that the new snow would cover any trace of her shoe. If her father hadn't found it by now, there wasn't much hope that he would.

As her grandfather walked the three sisters home, Emily couldn't stop the tears that rolled down her cheeks and froze onto her woolen scarf. How disappointed Mama would be in her, that she'd lost one of her brand-new shoes before she'd even had a chance to wear it once. It was the last gift from her mother, and she'd lost it.

They arrived home to find the house empty. "Papa must still be out looking," Catherine said.

"I'll stoke up the fire," Grandpa said. "You girls go change into your nightclothes. I'm sure your papa will be home by then."

Dragging her feet, Emily trudged to the room she shared with her sisters.

"Don't be sad," Sarah told her youngest sister. "Papa can order you a new pair from the catalogue."

"But I want the shoes Mama got me." Emily sniffled as she fought back her tears.

Sarah and Catherine looked at each other, not knowing what to do or say. They knew there wasn't much chance of finding Emily's shoe. They didn't want to build up her hopes, but they wished they could make her feel better.

"How about some nice hot cider?" Sarah suggested.

"And a cookie," Catherine enticed, knowing gingerbread cookies were Emily's favorite.

Emily shrugged. "Okay," she said sadly.

"Hurry and change your clothes, and we'll go get it ready," Sarah said. "And don't worry, Em. Everything will work out."

After her sisters left, Emily sat on her bed and thought about her papa outside, looking for her shoe. Even though she hoped he would find it, deep in her heart she knew it would be impossible. There was only one thing she could do. Climbing off her bed, she knelt, clasping her tiny hands together.

Dear Heavenly Father,

It's me, Emily. I don't mean to bother you, but I lost a shoe. This isn't just any shoe. It's a special shoe, from my mama. She lives with you now, but she said she would come and visit me tonight. Could you please ask her if she would help find my shoe? Maybe from up there in heaven, she can see where it is.

Thank you. And thank you for Jesus. If it's not too much trouble, could you tell him "Happy Birthday" for me since it's Christmas?

She closed her prayer and changed her clothes, then went to the kitchen to join her sisters and grandfather, who were sipping mugs of hot cider and munching on gingerbread cookies.

Just as Emily sat down at the table, the door opened and her father stepped inside. His face was pink from the cold, and he was covered with snow. She could read his expression immediately—he hadn't found the shoe. Sarah poured a mug of hot cider for her father, who accepted it gratefully.

"I'm sorry sweetie," he told his youngest. "I looked every inch of the way from our house to the church. It's just not there." His voice was sad and desperate.

"Don't be sad, Papa," Emily said, rising to give her father a hug. "It's okay."

Her father smiled at her and hugged her tightly. "That's my brave girl," he said.

After their treat, they bid their grandfather farewell. Then each of the girls moved one of the kitchen chairs next to the Christmas tree and hung a stocking around one of the knobs on the chair back.

Before they went to bed, their father opened up the Bible and read to them the story of Christ's birth. Emily listened intently and imagined what it must have been like for Joseph and Mary not to have a place to rest, a place where Mary could have her baby. After the story, they knelt together as a family, and her father said a prayer.

When John scooted his three daughters off to bed, Catherine and Sarah quickly jumped underneath the warm covers on their beds. But Emily had one last thing she needed to do before she went to bed.

Walking quietly down the stairs, Emily found her father sitting in his rocker, staring at the fire with a lonely, faraway look in his eye. Emily knew he was thinking about her mother. Papa didn't say so very often, but Emily knew how much he missed her.

She almost turned and went back to bed, but he turned his head and saw her. Without a word, he held out his arms and Emily went to her father and sat on his lap, wrapped in his safe, strong arms. They rocked together for a while, listening as the chair squeaked on the wooden floorboards and the fire crackled and hissed, slowly burning down to glowing embers.

"Papa?" Emily asked in a soft voice. "Would it be okay if I put a candle in the window?"

Her father looked at her, surprised. "Why do you want to do that?"

"So Mama can find her way home," she explained, not telling her papa about her special prayer. John shut his eyes, swallowing hard, as if trying to halt the tears that threatened to fill his eyes.

"Papa?" Emily reached up with a tiny hand to stroke his cheek. "It's okay, isn't it? To put a candle in the window?"

He nodded his head slowly and finally found his voice. "Yes, angel, it is."

Together they lit the candle and placed it on the windowsill, where its flickering light reflected brightly in the glass.

Emily's face beamed as brightly as the candle. "There," she said with quiet satisfaction. "That's much better."

"Off to bed now," her father told her.

Giving her papa a kiss on the cheek, Emily scurried up the stairs and hurried under the covers, thankful to have a warm bed to sleep in.

She knew she was very blessed to have such a warm, cozy house, with food and clothes and her father and sisters. She was thankful for everything she had, and she was especially thankful that Jesus could be born. And somehow she felt a little guilty that she had made such a fuss about her shoe when she should be thinking about Jesus and his birth. Maybe they could look for it tomorrow when the sun was out.

She lay in bed for a long time, wondering about her mother's promised visit. She didn't want to fall asleep just in case she missed it. But the hour grew late, and Emily's eyelids grew weary, and before long, she was fast asleep.

The next morning Sarah and Catherine had to wake Emily from a deep sleep. She'd almost forgotten it was Christmas morning. When the girls scrambled down the stairs, they found a roaring fire in the fireplace and their father anxiously waiting for them.

Emily looked around the room. Was her mother there? Had she come during the night while Emily was asleep?

She couldn't help feeling disappointed. She knew her sisters hadn't really believed that their mother would come, or her father either, but Emily had felt it so strongly in her heart.

With some coaxing from her sisters, she turned her attention to the bulging stocking that hung from the back of the chair. But no present inside that stocking could take the place of seeing her mother one more time.

Her sisters squealed with delight as they looked in their Christmas stockings and found treasures and treats—beautiful fur-lined mittens, tiny bottles of vanilla-scented perfume, and delicious candies. At the bottom, tucked deep into the toe of each stocking, was a quarter.

"Come on, Emily," Sarah coaxed. "What's in your stocking?"

Finally, to pacify her sisters, Emily reached inside and pulled out a lovely rag doll, with shoe-button eyes, long golden hair made of yarn, and a dress made from the same material as her Christmas dress.

Emily couldn't speak. No one had to tell her that her mother had made this doll for her. She knew it instinctively. And when she held the doll close to her face, she could smell the faint lilac fragrance her mother always used to wear.

Her eyes full of tears, Emily looked up at her father, whose eyes were also moist. Rushing into his arms, she let him hold her for a long time.

She knew she would treasure this doll forever. Whenever she needed a hug from her mother, she would be able to hug her soft rag doll and remember how much she loved her mama and how much her mama loved her.

"Papa," Emily asked in her tiny voice. "Would it be okay if I named her Molly?"

Smiling through his tears, John answered, "Of course, sweetie. I think your mama would like that." He swallowed the knot of emotion that clogged his throat and felt his heart grow warm, knowing that this gift to his youngest had brought peace to her little soul. He had been wondering how he could ever explain why Molly couldn't come to visit her on Christmas. The rag doll, he had hoped, would help ease Emily's disappointment.

With the stockings and their contents carefully examined and admired, Sarah took charge and began handing out presents. Everyone opened the gifts slowly, to make the event last as long as possible.

After the gifts had all been opened, Sarah announced that she was going to make a special breakfast of hotcakes and sausage. Catherine's job was to set the table, and Emily's was to fetch wood off the back porch to build a fire in the cook stove. Holding Molly in one arm, Emily opened the back door, bracing herself for the cold morning air. Suddenly she let out a loud gasp.

A feeling of joy filled her entire body with warmth, and a smile grew on her face until her cheeks hurt. A giggle tickled her insides until she laughed out loud.

"What is it?" Catherine asked as she rushed over to Emily's side. "Oh, Papa!" she cried when she saw what Emily was looking at.

John and Sarah hurried over and gasped when they looked out onto the porch. There, looking as good as new, was Emily's lost shoe.

Catherine and Sarah looked at their father, who shook his head with complete astonishment. No one had any idea where the shoe had come from—except for Emily.

Slowly, she bent down and, picking up the shoe, lifted it for all of them to see.

"See," she announced joyfully, smiling at her sisters and father while clutching the shoe tightly in her hand. "Mama did come. She brought me my slipper, just like I knew she would."

John opened his mouth to say something, then closed it again. Catherine and Sarah looked at Emily. Then they looked up at their father, then at each other, and finally, at the shoe again. None of them could provide any other explanation. And none was necessary.

Whether or not the shoe had been returned by a neighbor, a stranger, or by Santa Claus himself, it didn't matter. They all agreed that something very special had happened that day. It was a small miracle, but it had a momentous effect on them all.

In the years that followed, none of them ever forgot how special that Christmas was nor how Emily's unwavering faith had helped their family feel closer to each other and to their mother.

Emily knew with all her heart and soul that her mother had seen the light in the window that night from heaven. On her way to visit her family, she had found Emily's new patent leather slipper in the snow and returned it to her daughter—as evidence of a mother's love and acknowledgment of a daughter's faith. And for Emily, that was all that mattered.

Little Snowflakes

By Ella M. Powers

(Six children may sing these words to the tune, "Tiny Little Snowflakes" in "Golden Robin," with the following finger-play.)

a. Hands waving up and down, fingers moving rapidly.
b. Imitate the waving with hands and heads to right and left.
c. Quickly shake head and hands.
d. Sweep the hand.
e. Right hand raised as high as head, fist closed.
f. Abruptly bring fist down.
g. Similar to (a).
h. Hands clasped and eyes upturned as if gazing with admiration at the tree.

We are little snowflakes, (a)
Falling gently down,
On the fields and mountains
In the busy town.

Now the waving (b) spruce trees
Shaking (c) gently say,
Brush away this light snow, (d)
It's nearly Christmas day.

Then a man comes gaily
With his axe so bright, (e)
He chops down the spruce tree (f)
Early one fair night.

Then on Christmas morning
Children dance to see, (g)
Many lovely presents
On that stately tree. (h)

Christmas!

The very word brings joy to our hearts. No matter how we may dread the rush, the long Christmas lists for gifts and cards to be bought and given–when Christmas Day comes there is still the same warm feeling we had as children, the same warmth that enfolds our hearts and our homes.

~ Joan Winmill Brown

The First Journey with the Reindeer

By L. Frank Baum

Those were happy days for Claus when he carried his accumulation of toys to the children who had awaited them so long. . . . After quickly supplying the little ones living nearby, he saw he must now extend his travels to wider fields. . . .

So he loaded a great sack with all kinds of toys, slung it upon his back that he might carry it more easily, and started off on a longer trip than he had yet undertaken.

Wherever he showed his merry face, in hamlet or in farmhouse, he received a cordial welcome, for his fame had spread into far lands. At each village the children swarmed about him, following his footsteps wherever he went; and the women thanked him gratefully for the joy he brought their little ones; and the men looked upon him curiously that he should devote his time to such a queer occupation as toy-making. But everyone smiled on him and gave him kindly words, and Claus felt amply repaid for his long journey.

When the sack was empty, he went back again to the Laughing Valley and once more filled it to the brim. This time he followed another road, into a different part of the country, and carried happiness to many children who never before had owned a toy or guessed that such a delightful plaything existed.

After a third journey, so far away that Claus was many days walking the distance, the store of toys became exhausted, and without delay he set about making a fresh supply.

From seeing so many children and studying their tastes, he had acquired several new ideas about toys.

The dollies were, he had found, the most delightful of all playthings for babies and little girls, and often those who could not say "dolly" would call for a "doll" in their sweet baby talk. So Claus resolved to make many dolls, of all sizes, and to dress them in bright-colored clothing. The older boys—and even some of the girls—loved the images of animals, so he still made cats and elephants and horses. And many of the little fellows had musical natures, and longed for drums and cymbals and whistles and horns. So he made a number of toy drums, with tiny sticks to beat them with; and he made whistles from the willow trees, and horns from the bog-reeds, and cymbals from bits of beaten metal.

All this kept him busily at work, and before he realized it the winter season came, with deeper snows than usual, and he knew he could not leave the valley with his heavy pack. Moreover, the next trip would take him farther from home than ever before, and Jack Frost was mischievous enough to nip his nose and ears if he undertook the long journey while the Frost King reigned. The Frost King was Jack's father and never reproved him for his pranks.

So Claus remained at his workbench; but he whistled and sang as merrily as ever, for he would allow no disappointment to sour his temper or make him unhappy.

One bright morning he looked from his window and saw two of the deer he had known in the forest walking toward his house.

Claus was surprised; not that the friendly deer should visit him, but that they walked on the surface of the snow as easily as if it were solid ground, notwithstanding the fact that throughout the valley the snow lay many feet deep. He had walked out of his house a day or two before and had sunk to his armpits in a drift.

So when the deer came near, he opened the door and called to them: "Good morning, Flossie! Tell me how you are able to walk on the snow so easily."

"It is frozen hard," answered Flossie.

"The Frost King has breathed on it," said Glossie, coming up, "and the surface is now as solid as ice."

"Perhaps," remarked Claus, thoughtfully, "I might now carry my pack of toys to the children."

"Is it a long journey?" asked Flossie.

"Yes; it will take me many days, for the pack is heavy," answered Claus.

"Then the snow would melt before you could get back," said the deer. "You must wait until spring, Claus."

Claus sighed. "Had I your fleet feet," said he, "I could make the journey in a day."

"But you have not," returned Glossie, looking at his own slender legs with pride.

"Perhaps I could ride upon your back," Claus ventured to remark, after a pause.

"Oh no; our backs are not strong enough to bear your weight," said Flossie, decidedly. "But if you had a sledge and could harness us to it, we might draw you easily, and your pack as well."

"I'll make a sledge!" exclaimed Claus. "Will you agree to draw me if I do?"

"Well," replied Flossie, "we must first go and ask the Knooks, who are our guardians, for permission; but if they consent and you can make a sledge and harness, we will gladly assist you."

"Then go at once!" cried Claus, eagerly. "I am sure the friendly Knooks will give their consent, and by

the time you are back I shall be ready to harness you to my sledge."

Flossie and Glossie, being deer of much intelligence, had long wished to see the great world, so they gladly ran over the frozen snow to ask the Knooks if they might carry Claus on his journey.

Meantime the toy-maker hurriedly began the construction of a sledge, using material from his woodpile. He made two long runners that turned upward at the front ends, and across these, he nailed short boards, to make a platform. It was soon completed but was as rude in appearance as it is possible for a sledge to be.

The harness was more difficult to prepare, but Claus twisted strong cords together and knotted them so they would fit around the necks of the deer, in the shape of a collar. From these ran other cords to fasten the deer to the front of the sledge.

Before the work was completed, Glossie and Flossie were back from the forest, having been granted permission by Will Knook to make the journey with Claus provided they would to Burzee by daybreak the next morning.

"That is not a very long time," said Flossie. "But we are swift and strong, and if we get started by this evening we can travel many miles during the night."

Claus decided to make the attempt, so he hurried on his preparations as fast as possible. After a time he fastened the collars around the necks of his steeds and harnessed them to his rude sledge. Then he placed a stool on the little platform, to serve as a seat, and filled a sack with his prettiest toys.

"How do you intend to guide us?" asked Glossie. "We have never been out of the forest before, except to visit your house, so we shall not know the way."

Claus thought about that for a moment. Then he brought more cords and fastened two of them to the spreading antlers of each deer, one on the right and the other on the left.

"Those will be my reins," said Claus, "and when I pull them to the right or to the left you must go in that direction. If I do not pull the reins at all you may go straight ahead."

"Very well," answered Glossie and Flossie; and then they asked: "Are you ready?"

Claus seated himself upon the stool, placed the sack of toys at his feet, and then gathered up the reins. "All ready!" he shouted. "Away we go!"

The deer leaned forward, lifting their slender limbs, and the next moment, away flew the sledge over the frozen snow. The swiftness of the motion surprised Claus, for in a few strides they were across the valley and gliding over the broad plain beyond.

The day had melted into evening by the time they started; for, swiftly as Claus had worked, many hours had been consumed in making his preparations. But the moon shone brightly to light their way, and Claus soon decided it was just as pleasant to travel by night as by day. . . .

Away and away they sped, on and on over the hills and through the valleys and across the plains until they reached a village where Claus had never been before.

Here he called on them to stop, and they immediately obeyed. But a new difficulty now presented itself, for the people had locked their doors when they went to bed, and Claus found he could not enter the houses to leave his toys.

"I am afraid, my friends, we have made our journey for nothing," said he, "for I

shall be obliged to carry my playthings back home again without giving them to the children of this village."

"What's the matter?" asked Flossie.

"The doors are locked," answered Claus, "and I cannot get in."

Glossie looked around at the houses. The snow was quite deep in that village, and just before them was a roof only a few feet above the sledge. A broad chimney, which seemed to Glossie big enough to admit Claus, was at the peak of the roof. "Why don't you climb down that chimney?" asked Glossie.

Claus looked at it. "That would be easy enough if I were on top of the roof," he answered.

"Then hold fast, and we will take you there," said the deer, and they gave one bound to the roof and landed beside the big chimney.

"Good!" cried Claus, well pleased, and he slung the pack of toys over his shoulder and got into the chimney.

There was plenty of soot on the bricks, but he did not mind that, and by placing his hands and knees against the sides, he crept downward until he had reached the fireplace. Leaping lightly over the smoldering coals, he found himself in a large sitting room, where a dim light was burning.

From this room two doorways led into smaller chambers. In one a woman lay asleep, with a baby beside her in a crib.

Claus laughed, but he did not laugh aloud for fear of waking the baby. Then he slipped a big doll from his pack and laid it in the crib. The little one smiled, as if it dreamed of the pretty plaything it was to find on the morrow, and Claus crept softly from the room and entered at the other doorway.

Here were two boys, fast asleep with their arms around each other's neck. Claus gazed at them lovingly a moment and then placed upon the bed a drum, two horns, and a wooden elephant.

He did not linger, now that his work in this house was done, but climbed the chimney again and seated himself on his sledge.

"Can you find another chimney?" he asked the reindeer.

"Easily enough," replied Glossie and Flossie. Down to the edge of the roof they raced, and then, without pausing, leaped through the air to the top of the next building, where a huge, old-fashioned chimney stood.

"Don't be so long, this time," called Flossie, "or we shall never get back to the forest by daybreak."

Claus made a trip down this chimney also and found five children sleeping in the house, all of whom were quickly supplied with toys. . . .

When he had climbed down the chimneys of all the houses in that village, and had left a toy for every sleeping child, Claus found that his great sack was not yet half emptied.

"Onward, friends!" he called to the deer. "We must seek another village."

So away they dashed, although it was long past midnight. In a surprisingly short time they came to a large city, the largest Claus had ever visited since he began to make toys. But, nothing daunted by the throng of houses, he set to work at once, and his beautiful steeds carried him rapidly from one roof to another, only the highest being beyond the leaps of the agile deer.

At last the supply of toys was exhausted, and Claus seated himself in the sledge, with the empty sack at his feet, and turned the heads of Glossie and Flossie toward home.

Presently Flossie asked: "What is that gray streak in the sky?"

"It is the coming dawn of day," answered Claus, surprised to find that it was so late.

"Good gracious!" exclaimed Glossie. "Then we shall not be home by daybreak, and the Knooks will punish us and never let us come again."

"We must race for the Laughing Valley and make our best speed," returned Flossie. "So hold fast, friend Claus!"

Claus held fast, and the next moment they were flying so swiftly over the snow that he could not see the trees as they whirled past. Up hill and down dale, swift as an arrow shot from a bow they dashed, and Claus shut his eyes to keep the wind out of them and left the deer to find their own way. . . .

Finally the sledge came to a sudden stop, and Claus, who was taken unawares, tumbled from his seat into a snowdrift. As he picked himself up, he heard the deer crying:

"Quick, friend, quick! Cut away our harness!"

He drew his knife and rapidly severed the cords, and then he wiped the moisture from his eyes and looked around him.

The sledge had come to a stop in the Laughing Valley, only a few feet, he found, from his own door. In the east the day was breaking, and turning to the edge of Burzee, he saw Glossie and Flossie just disappearing in the forest.

"Christmas waves a
magic wand over this world,
and behold, everything is softer
and more beautiful."
~ Norman Vincent Peale

Jingle Bells

Dashing through the snow
In a one horse open sleigh
O'er the fields we go
Laughing all the way.
Bells on bob tails ring,
Making spirits bright.
What fun it is to laugh and sing
A sleighing song tonight.

Chorus

Oh, jingle bells, jingle bells,
Jingle all the way.
Oh, what fun it is to ride
In a one horse open sleigh.
Jingle bells, jingle bells,
Jingle all the way.
Oh, what fun it is to ride
In a one horse open sleigh.

A day or two ago
I thought I'd take a ride,
And soon Miss Fanny Bright
Was seated by my side.
The horse was lean and lank.
Misfortune seemed his lot.
We got into a drifted bank,
And then we got upsot.

Chorus

One of the best-known and most commonly sung Christmas carols, "Jingle Bells" is not specifically a Christmas song; originally called "One Horse Open Sleigh," it was written by James Lord Pierpont in 1857 for a Thanksgiving program at the large Boston. The children who performed it that Thanksgiving were asked to repeat the performance at Christmas, launching it as a Christmas tradition.

Christmas is not as much about
opening our PRESENTS
as opening our
hearts.

~ Janice Maeditere

A Merry
Christmas

How the First Stockings Were Hung by the Chimneys

By L. Frank Baum

When another Christmas Eve drew near, there was a monster load of beautiful gifts for the children ready to be loaded upon the big sledge. Claus filled three sacks to the brim and tucked every corner of the sledge-box full of toys besides.

Then, at twilight, the ten reindeer appeared and Flossie introduced them all to Claus. They were Racer and Pacer, Reckless and Speckless, Fearless and Peerless, and Ready and Steady, who, with Glossie and Flossie, made up the ten who have traversed the world these hundreds of years with their generous master. They were all exceedingly beautiful, with slender limbs, spreading antlers, velvety dark eyes, and smooth coats of fawn color spotted with white. . . .

The new harness fitted them nicely and soon they were all fastened to the sledge by twos, with Glossie and Flossie in the lead. These wore the strings of sleigh-bells, and were so delighted with the music they made that they kept prancing up and down to make the bells ring.

Claus now seated himself in the sledge, drew a warm robe over his knees and his fur cap over his ears, and cracked his long whip as a signal to start.

Instantly the ten leaped forward and were away like the wind, while jolly Claus laughed gleefully to see them run and shouted a song in his big, hearty voice:

"With a ho, ho, ho!
And a ha, ha, ha!
And a ho, ho, ha, ha, hee!
Now away we go
O'er the frozen snow,
As merry as we can be!
There are many joys
In our load of toys,
As many a child will know;
We'll scatter them wide
On our wild night ride
O'er the crisp and sparkling snow!"

Now it was on this same Christmas Eve that little Margot and her brother Dick and her cousins Ned and Sara, who were visiting at Margot's house, came in from making a snowman, with their clothes damp, their mittens dripping, and their shoes and stockings wet through and through. They were not scolded, for Margot's mother knew the snow was melting, but they were sent early to bed that their clothes might be hung over chairs to dry. The shoes were placed on the red tiles of the hearth, where the heat from the hot embers would strike them, and the stockings were carefully hung in a row by the chimney, directly over the fireplace. That was the reason Santa Claus noticed them when he came down the chimney that night and all the household were fast asleep. He was in a tremendous hurry, and seeing the stockings all belonged to children, he quickly stuffed his toys into them and dashed up the chimney again, appearing on the roof so suddenly that the reindeer were astonished at his agility.

"I wish they would all hang up their stockings," he thought, as he drove to the next chimney. "It would save me a lot of time, and I could then visit more children before daybreak."

When Margot and Dick and Ned and Sara jumped out of bed next morning and ran downstairs to get their stockings from the fireplace they were filled with delight to find the toys from Santa Claus inside them. In fact, I think they found more presents in their stockings than any other children of that city had received, for Santa Claus was in a hurry and did not stop to count the toys.

Of course they told all their little friends about it, and of course every one of them decided to hang his own stockings by the fireplace the next Christmas Eve. Even Bessie Blithesome, who made a visit to that city with her father, the great Lord of Lerd, heard the story from the children and hung her own pretty stockings by the chimney when she returned home at Christmastime.

On his next trip Santa Claus found so many stockings hung up in anticipation of his visit that he could fill them in a jiffy and be away again in half the time required to hunt the children up and place the toys by their bedsides.

The custom grew year after year and has always been a great help to Santa Claus. And, with so many children to visit, he surely needs all the help we are able to give him.

Did you know?

According to Guinness Book of World Records, the largest Christmas stocking measured more than 168 feet in length. That's as long as the White House! The stocking was made by a volunteer emergency services in Italy in 2011. The event was organized to raise money to help the elderly. In order to meet the world-record criteria, volunteers filled the stocking with balloons containing sweets.

Deck the Halls

Deck the halls with boughs of holly,
Fa la la la la, la la la la.
'Tis the season to be jolly,
Fa la la la la, la la la la.
Don we now our gay apparel,
Fa la la, la la la, la la la.
Troll the ancient Yuletide carol,
Fa la la la la, la la la la.

See the blazing Yule before us,
Fa la la la la, la la la la.
Strike the harp and join the chorus.
Fa la la la la, la la la la.
Follow me in merry measure,
Fa la la, la la la, la la la.
While I tell of Yuletide treasure,
Fa la la la la, la la la la.

Fast away the old year passes,
Fa la la la la, la la la la.
Hail the new, ye lads and lasses,
Fa la la la la, la la la la.
Sing we joyous, all together,
Fa la la, la la la, la la la.
Heedless of the wind and weather,
Fa la la la la, la la la la.

The tune to "Deck the Halls" is that of an old air, dating to the sixteenth century. Originally popular as a dance tune in Wales, it was celebrated as a winter carol. It became widely known in the eighteenth century; Mozart used the tune for a violin and piano duet, and Haydn used it in his "New Year's Night." The repeated "fa la la la la" comes from medieval ballads and was originally played on the harp; the remaining lyrics are American in origin and were written during the nineteenth century. During the Victorian era, Christmas was "re-invented," and "Deck the Halls" became a traditional English Christmas song, celebrating the custom of lavishly decorating homes for the holidays. The first English version appeared in 1881 in The Franklin Square Song Collection.

Yes, Virgina, There Is a Santa Claus

By Francis P. Church

DEAR EDITOR: I am eight years old.
Some of my little friends say there is no Santa Claus.
Papa says, 'If you see it in the *Sun*, it's so.'
Please tell me the truth; is there a Santa Claus?
—Virginia O'Hanlon

Virginia, your little friends are wrong. They have been affected by the skepticism of a skeptical age. They do not believe except they see. They think that nothing can be which is not comprehensible by their little minds. All minds, Virginia, whether they be men's or children's, are little. In this great universe of ours, man is a mere insect, an ant, in his intellect, as compared with the boundless world about him, as measured by the intelligence capable of grasping the whole of truth and knowledge.

Yes, Virginia, there is a Santa Claus. He exists as certainly as love and generosity and devotion exist, and you know that they abound and give to your life its highest beauty and joy. Alas! How dreary would be the world if there were no Santa Claus. It would be as dreary as if there were no Virginias. There would be no childlike faith then, no poetry, no romance to make tolerable this existence. We should have no enjoyment, except in sense and sight. The eternal light with which childhood fills the world would be extinguished.

Not believe in Santa Claus! You might as well not believe in fairies! You might get your papa to hire men to watch in all the chimneys on Christmas Eve to catch Santa Claus, but even if they did not see Santa Claus coming down, what would that prove? Nobody sees Santa Claus, but that is no sign that there is no Santa Claus. The most real things in the world are those that neither children nor men can see. Did you ever see fairies dancing on the lawn? Of course not, but that's no proof that they are not there. Nobody can conceive or imagine all the wonders there are unseen and unseeable in the world.

You may tear apart the baby's rattle and see what makes the noise inside, but there is a veil covering the unseen world which not the strongest man, nor even the united strength of all the strongest men that ever lived, could tear apart. Only faith, fancy, poetry, love, romance, can push aside that curtain and view and picture the supernal beauty and glory beyond. Is it all real? Ah, Virginia, in all this world there is nothing else real and abiding.

No Santa Claus! Thank God he lives, and he lives forever. A thousand years from now, Virginia, nay, ten times ten thousand years from now, he will continue to make glad the heart of childhood.

FAVORITE FAMILY Christmas Movies

- *It's a Wonderful Life*
- *Miracle on 34th Street*
- *Mr. Krouger's Christmas*
- *The Bishop's Wife*
- *How the Grinch Stole Christmas*
- *Rudolph the Red-Nosed Reindeer*
- *White Christmas*
- *Joyeux Noel*
- *Polar Express*
- *The Little Drummer Boy*
- *Christmas Carol*
- *Babes in Toyland*
- *Charlie Brown Christmas*
- *Frosty the Snowman*
- *The Fourth Wise Man*
- *Home Alone*

SWEET CANDY POPCORN

16 cups aired popped popcorn (½ cup kernels)
⅓ cup unsalted butter
½ cup light corn syrup
1 cup granulated sugar
1 packet unsweetened Kool-Aid drink mix
½ teaspoon baking soda

1. Preheat oven to 225 degrees F. Spray baking sheet with non-stick cooking spray. Set aside.
2. Cut butter in a few pieces and place it in a medium-large pot over medium-low heat. Add corn syrup and sugar, and stir until butter is completely melted. Increase heat just long enough to bring mixture to a boil. Then reduce heat to keep mixture at a simmer stirring constantly, for 3 minutes.
3. Remove pot from heat and slowly stir in Kool-Aid and baking soda. (Be careful because this step causes the mixture to foam up.) Once mixed well, pour immediately over popcorn and stir until it's all coated. Spread popcorn onto prepared baking sheet and cook for 40 minutes, stirring every 10 minutes.
4. When you take the popcorn out of the oven, spread it on wax paper. Allow to cool completely and then break into chunks.

Optional: Add sprinkles or Chocolate candies right after the popcorn is out of the oven before it cools.

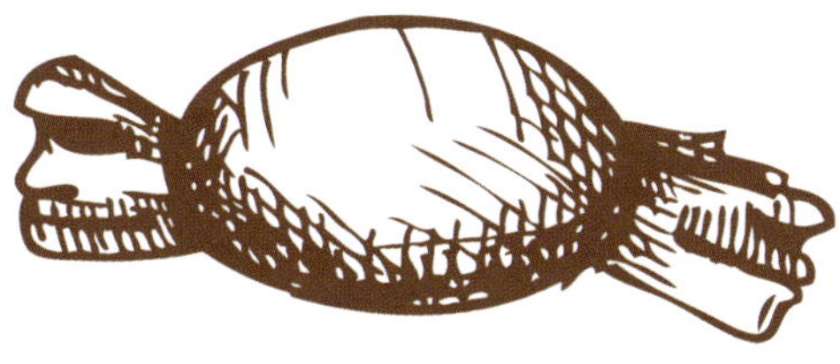

Greeting

Christmas Questions

By Wolstan Dixey

(At the three last words, the speaker raises her finger impressively.)

How old is Santa Claus? Where does he keep?

And why does he come when I am asleep?

His hair is so white in the pictures I know,

Guess he stands on his head all the time in the snow.

But if he does that, then why don't he catch cold?

He must be as much as—most twenty years old.

I'd just like to see him once stand on his head,

And dive down the chimney, as grandmother said.

Why don't his head get all covered with black?

And if he comes head first, how can he get back?

Mamma knows about it, but she won't tell me.

I shall keep awake Christmas Eve, then I can see.

I have teased her to tell me, but Mamma she won't,

So I'll find out myself now; see if I don't.

The Shepherd Maiden's Gift

By Eleanor L. Skinner

In the quiet midnight, peace brooded over the fields where the shepherds were watching their flocks. The tinkling of sheep bells, the bleating of lambs, and the barking of watchdogs had gradually ceased. Around a large campfire several shepherds lay resting, for they had had a long, hard day. Each had beside him a strong shepherd's crook and a stout club ready for use in case any lurking danger threatened the beloved flocks.

Not far away from the campfire, a shepherd maiden lay sleeping in the rude shelter of a rocky cave. All day long she had helped her father guard the sheep, and when darkness fell over the fields and hills, she was glad to lie down in her snug bed made of the fleecy skins of kids and lambs.

Suddenly a light filled the cave and wakened the maiden. Thinking it was daybreak, she sprang up, stepped to the rude doorway, and pushed aside the curtain of goatskin.

"What has happened?" she whispered.

The fields and hills were flooded with light. The group of shepherds were standing close together, gazing intently at the luminous eastern sky. A moment later she saw them fall on their knees in worship. There in the entrance of her rude shelter, she, too, knelt and prayed. Clearly she saw the shining angel appear, and in the peaceful stillness of the night she heard these words:

"Be not afraid; for, behold, I bring good tidings of great joy which shall be to all the people: for there is born to you this day, in the city of David, a Saviour, which is Christ the Lord. And this shall be the sign unto you: ye shall find a babe wrapped in swaddling clothes and lying in a manger."

And suddenly there was with the angel many, many others. Together they lifted up their voices in praise and sang,

"Glory to God in the highest! Peace on earth! Goodwill toward men!"

When the sweet music died away, the maiden rose to her feet and joined the shepherds. "I saw the angel, Father, and heard the singing," she whispered.

"Christ, the Lord, is born," answered her father.

"Let us hasten to Bethlehem and see the Heavenly Child who fulfills the promise of God," said one of the shepherds.

"Shall we leave our flocks?" asked another. But the question was not answered.

"Come, let us see what gifts we have to carry to the Christ-child," said the shepherd who first saw the light in the sky.

In a few moments these simple-hearted men were ready to start across the fields and over the low hills to Bethlehem. Very humble gifts they had to offer, but their hearts were filled with joy and wonder.

Standing near the entrance to the cave, the shepherd maiden could see the outline of the group of men making their way to the city of David. "They are going to see the Christ-child," she said to herself, "a babe wrapped in swaddling clothes and lying in a manger."

How she would love to see the Heavenly Child! A deep longing to behold the little newborn King seized her. She would follow the shepherds to

Bethlehem. One glimpse at the Christ-child would fill her heart with joy.

Away over the starlit fields and hills she started. Not once did she falter, although the way was long and some of the hillsides were hard to climb.

Finally, she saw the shepherds pass in the gate of the city of Bethlehem.

"I came to see the Christ-child," she said to a group of people who stood whispering together. They looked at her in astonishment.

"I am following the shepherds," she added.

"They have gone to the inn," was the answer.

When she reached the inn, she was directed to a cave nearby, which served as a stable.

There, through the entrance, she saw the shepherds lay their humble presents at Mary's feet and then kneel in solemn adoration.

"I have brought nothing to offer," whispered the maiden, looking wistfully into the rude shelter. "I cannot go in without a gift—a little gift for the Christ-child."

Tears of disappointment filled her eyes. Slowly she turned to leave the place. But after she had taken a few steps, she stopped and burst into sobs. How could she go away without a glimpse of the Heavenly Child? Then, as she stood weeping, a marvelous thing happened.

An angel appeared beside her and said: "Lo, here at thy feet is a gift for the Christ-child."

Then she saw growing near her, slender stems covered with delicate green leaves and bearing lovely flowers.

The maiden did not stop to wonder. Here was a gift fit to offer the little Saviour. With trembling joy she gathered the Christmas roses and stepped lightly into the humble house where the little babe lay smiling in his mother's arms. In Mary's lap the maiden laid her gift of flowers, and, with radiant face, she knelt and filled her heart with the glorious vision.

Symbolism of the Candy Cane:

Candy canes can be symbolic in many ways: The hard candy reminds us that Jesus Christ is our rock. The shape can either be a shepherd's staff—teaching us that Christ is the Good Shepherd—or, if turned upside down, a J, standing for Jesus. The color red reminds us of the Atonement Christ came to fulfill, and the color white signifies His purity and perfection.

Angels from the Realms of Glory

Angels from the realms of glory,
Wing your flight o'er all the earth;
Ye who sang creation's story,
Now proclaim Messiah's birth:
Come and worship,
Come and worship,
Worship Christ, the newborn King!

Shepherds, in the fields abiding,
Watching o'er your flocks by night,
God with man is now residing,
Yonder shines the infant Light;
Come and worship,
Come and worship,
Worship Christ, the newborn King!

Sages, leave your contemplations,
Brighter visions beam afar;
Seek the great desire of nations,
Ye have seen His natal star;
Come and worship,
Come and worship,
Worship Christ, the newborn King!

Saints before the altar bending,
Watching long in hope and fear,
Suddenly the Lord, descending,
In His temple shall appear:
Come and worship,
Come and worship,
Worship Christ, the newborn King!

James Montgomery began his career as a newspaper editor. While he ran the *Sheffield Iris*, Montgomery published numerous poems in the paper as well as in volumes of collected poems. He was recognized for his preferred themes of human interest, such as slavery and child labor. He himself, however, expected that if his name lived on, it would be not because of his poetry but because of his hymns. Besides "Angels from the Realms of Glory," Montgomery wrote "Prayer Is the Soul's Sincere Desire," "The Lord is My Shepherd," and "A Poor Wayfaring Man of Grief"—all of which are found in the LDS hymnbook.

"Angels from the Real of Glory" was first printed in Montgomery's paper in 1816 but didn't become popular until it was reprinted in a couple larger publications nearly ten years later. In the next hundred years, the hymn was sung to a number of different tunes. It is now most commonly sung to the tune "Regent Square," except in the United Kingdom, where it is often sung to the same tune as "Angles We Have Heard on High."

Hark the Herald Angels Sing

Hark the herald angels sing,
"Glory to the newborn King!
Peace on earth and mercy mild.
God and sinners reconciled."
Joyful, all ye nations rise,
Join the triumph of the skies
With th'angelic host proclaim:
"Christ is born in Bethlehem."
Hark! The herald angels sing,
"Glory to the newborn King!"

Christ by highest heav'n adored
Christ the everlasting Lord!
Late in time behold Him come,
Offspring of a Virgin's womb
Veiled in flesh the Godhead see.
Hail th'incarnate Deity
Pleased as man with man to dwell,
Jesus, our Emmanuel.
Hark! The herald angels sing,
"Glory to the newborn King!"

Hail the heav'n-born Prince of Peace!
Hail the Son of Righteousness!
Light and life to all He brings.
Ris'n with healing in His wings.
Mild He lays His glory by,
Born that man no more may die.
Born to raise the sons of earth,
Born to give them second birth.
Hark! The herald angels sing,
"Glory to the newborn King!"

Written by Charles Wesley, brother of Methodist founder John Wesley, "Hark! The Herald Angels Sing" was first published in 1739 in *Hymns and Sacred Poems*; Wesley was the Poet Laureate of the Methodist Church and published more than 6,500 hymns during his lifetime. The version we know today was altered by various people—most notably Wesley's coworker, George Whitefield, an itinerant Anglican minister who came up with the familiar opening couplet we now sing. When Whitefield—who did not have the ability to pay his college tuition—entered Oxford, he was assigned to work as a servant for other students in exchange for his tuition. He woke them in the morning, carried their books, polished their shoes, and even helped write their assignments. The melody of this carol is based on an energetic chorus composed by Felix Mendelssohn in 1840 as part of a cantata commemorating Bible printer Johann Gutenburg.

To
wish you
Christmas Happiness.

Christmas Angel

By Kaye Jacobs Volk

It was the official start of the Christmas season. All of the ornaments watched nervously as the good gentleman of the house, standing on a stepladder, his wife and two of their four children gathered on the floor below, carefully placed the new treetop angel on the uppermost branch of the family Christmas tree.

The kind lady of the house was especially anxious. "Careful. Careful," she coached softly, watching the procedure.

They all sighed in relief when the angel's position was secured and she stood royally in full view of everyone, ornaments and humans alike. Had it really been a year, they each thought, since disaster struck? The old, much-loved treetop angel, who had occupied that same place for more years than most of them could remember, had been accidentally dropped as the tree was being taken down and had broken into a dozen unmendable pieces. The kind lady of the house had wept. She had always taken such great care with everything, including the delicate handling of these, her precious Christmas tree ornaments.

Now, here stood the new angel, selected personally by the kind lady of the house herself.

"Oh, she's beautiful, Mama," her youngest daughter said, holding her mother's hand tightly.

"She's just as I remember," the kind lady said as if only speaking to herself.

"What did you say?" Her husband, the good gentleman of the house, asked as he set the stepladder aside.

"Oh, nothing." The kind lady smiled. "It's just something I remember from long ago." She paused. "I'll tell you all about it sometime . . . maybe very soon."

The kind lady's family looked at her and wondered. But her attention was purely fixed upon the tree. The ornaments, each now in precisely the right place, looked down upon this kind lady with loving devotion. They were once more complete, thanks to her and their new treetop angel.

For the ornaments, tucked away in boxes in the attic, it had been a long, sad, and anxious year. They had wondered over and over as to what the new treetop Christmas angel would be like; and at last, the waiting was over. For here she was, more beautiful than any of them had even imagined. She was dressed in a delicate, flowing gown of white and gold silk with a row of rhinestones at her throat. Atop her soft, white hair sat a wreathlike crown of shimmering gold and silver tinsel, and, at her back, a pair of gossamer wings glistened in the gentle light that seemed to surround her. Upon her porcelain face was painted the most beautiful rosebud mouth, and her eyes, downcast, were shadowed with the softest shade of blue, setting off her long, life-like lashes. In her outstretched arms, draped like a rich velvet ribbon, was a long golden scroll, which added a most important touch to one of such beauty. She was a wonder to behold, and the ornaments and the family alike remained still for a moment in silent admiration.

All the lights in the parlor were then turned off, leaving only the hundreds of tiny white ones that illuminated the entire tree. Their effect was magnificent, casting the room in a warm glow. This good family of humans lingered awhile and agreed that this was perhaps the most beautiful tree ever.

At last, the family gathered up all the empty storage boxes and took leave of the room. Only the kind lady paused, as she did every year, looking upward. But tonight she stood for even longer than usual, gazing upon the beautiful treetop angel. Then, with a sweet and grateful smile, she turned and exited the parlor.

It was only then that introductions upon the tree formally began. Taking charge, as he had done these twenty years, was the somewhat worn but very cherished Father Christmas ornament. He was allowed this authority because he had been with the man and his wife since their very first Christmas together as newlyweds.

"Fair Angel," he called her, for she was indeed something fairly extraordinary. "I would like you to meet all of us who adorn this Christmas tree with you, and bid you welcome." He spoke in his most official-sounding voice.

The treetop Christmas angel simply nodded her head in his direction, speaking not a word.

He hesitantly continued. "I am the Father Christmas ornament. I have been fortunate enough to last through four children, five cats, one dog, and a stray mouse that wandered in here one Christmastime and mistook me for a morsel of food." He paused, reliving the memory. "I was spared any real harm when one of those five cats saved the day—and me!—and had a lovely supper as well." Father Christmas chuckled softly to himself. He liked the thought of being clever, and so he repeated the entire story. All of the other ornaments appreciated his attempt at humor and laughed quietly along with him. All, that is, with the one great exception of the gray Christmas mouse ornament.

"Father Christmas," Gray Mouse said sharply. "Must you tell that story to every new ornament that is added to our tree—and especially to her?" He drew in a big sigh. "We must complete introductions quickly, remember?"

"Yes, of course," Father Christmas agreed halfheartedly, mumbling under his breath. "It was just once that I failed to properly introduce us all, and that was due to the weather . . . lights kept going out, as I recall. I couldn't find everyone in the dark." He adjusted himself as best he could; his white cotton beard and long red robe seemed more in the way this year than usual. Clearing his throat, he continued. "Ah, hmm . . . let's see . . . who have we here? Oh, well yes, you've practically met Gray Mouse already. He's been with us for ten years, if I'm not mistaken." Father Christmas glanced toward the mouse ornament, who looked back at him as if in shock.

"This, dear sir, is my twelfth year!" Gray Mouse announced with great indignation and then abruptly turned away to punctuate his distress at the immense miscalculation.

"Oh, yes . . . twelve, that's right. Sorry about that . . . the old memory bank isn't what it once was." Father Christmas glanced quickly at the new treetop Christmas angel, who seemed completely unaware of the exchange, standing serenely in her place as if nothing that was happening below mattered in the slightest. This bothered Father Christmas, but he didn't know exactly why.

Looking around the tree, he continued. "Let's see. May I introduce you to our Santa collection?" With that, five very different Santa ornaments turned and, speaking as one, bid her a "Me-e-e-e-erry Christmas!" tipping their caps affectionately. The other ornaments smiled; they so enjoyed these five Santas. Though "Merry Christmas" was about all they ever said, it was always spoken with such enthusiasm that it warmed them one and all. They had been purchased over a period of years for or by the good gentleman, and they were now loved equally by all of the other ornaments.

Hoping for at least a smile from the new angel, Father Christmas paused a long moment; but when none came, he continued. Eagerly waiting to be introduced were the several birds-of-a-feather ornaments. The kind lady had started collecting these for one of her children years earlier. Some were made of wood, others of silk, satin, or porcelain. Some were constructed with great detail, while others were plain and simple. They chirped—or honked, in the case of the satin swan and wooden goose—a cheery "hello" to the new angel. But as before, she made no reply.

Next came the dozen or so hand-crafted Black Forest ornaments. These were a grand assortment of little boys on sleds or skis, little girls on ice skates, a baby in a cradle, a woodcutter, a ballerina, a cuckoo in his clock, one delightful rocking horse, and two little children tucked safely into a blue, four-poster bed. They each greeted the new ornament in their own kind way, extending to her the friendliest feelings. Yet still she stood, seemingly unmoved by all this hospitality.

Puzzled by her coolness, Father Christmas asked, "Are you weary, Fair Angel? Would you like to pause for a while? I'm certain you've had a busy evening, and we can finish up with our introductions tomorrow if you would like."

The longest time went by, and finally, in nearly a whisper of a voice, the angel spoke. "That would be fine. I am a bit tired."

And that was it. No "thank you" and no indication whatsoever that she cared in the least to continue with introductions—tomorrow, or the next day, or ever.

The ornaments were stunned. Visibly disappointed, they all settled in for what was going to be a rather restless night. Oh, how they had hoped for a treetop angel like the old one, whose cheerfulness and caring had been felt by everyone. And now, this night, they longed for her more than ever. Father Christmas felt the worst of all. Things had started off badly, and he spent the night determined to begin tomorrow on a new note.

With morning came the happy sounds of music and children laughing throughout the house. The kind lady of the home was busily going about her day, humming and singing dozens of enchanting Christmas carols. Listening to her, the ornaments felt that the troubles of last night were somehow diminished. Father Christmas sensed that in some way, their kind lady could make all things right for them and their new treetop Christmas angel, who stood without so much as a downward glance at anyone.

Father Christmas spent most of the morning planning out the order of events. Perhaps if he started simply by pointing out to her the other decorations on the tree, it would put her in a more amiable mood. After all, their Christmas tree also wore a golden chain of beads; glimmering snowflakes; lights; Christmas balls of red, blue, pink, gold, and green; and bows and ribbons of red satin. And the bells! Bells of glass hung in three tiers—bells of hand-painted porcelain, old bells, and new bells. Each ornament dangled from a golden twine, and the entire tree reflected the beauty and gentleness that was, indeed, Christmas. That was good, he thought to himself.

Next, in his mind, he lined up the remaining ornaments for proper introductions. He would start with the porcelain figurines—the two lads carrying a Christmas tree; the miniature caroler, his hands warm inside a furry muff; the cheerful, brown skiing mouse with his extra-large ears popping out from slits in a fine green knit stocking cap. The bears would come next—a fun bunch, to be sure. Some were handmade by the kind lady and were little round balls of colored cotton in various sizes. Each wore two beads for eyes and a bow at its neck. Other bears were made of wood and grinned continually. One bear was even dressed like Santa himself and was encased in his own little crystal ball that would snow down tiny bits of glitter which floated in midair above his head and then alighted softly upon his nose, capped head, and brow.

"Oh, this is good!" Father Christmas assured himself. "No doubt she'll be impressed."

But there *was* doubt—a great deal of it—still buzzing around the entire tree as the time for introductions once more approached. The lights on the tree were finally lit, and the good family had retired to the dining room, while in the parlor the soft shades of evening filtered in through the large west window. The room was aglow. This was the hour; Father Christmas straightened himself and began.

"Fair Angel," he said, clearing his throat. "Ahem! Fair Angel? We wish to continue with our introductions, if that would please you." He waited. They all waited for her response.

Finally, a rather large and distinctly audible sigh escaped her lips. "Yes. I guess so," came her small, halfhearted reply.

This was going to be harder than yesterday, thought Father Christmas. But finding strength in the encouraging glances of the other ornaments, he began to recite his well-planned speech.

"Perhaps you would like me to mention a few of the additional adornments that share this beautiful tree with us?" Once again, she was totally silent. Nevertheless, this was the plan, and he was determined to carry it out. He quickly noted all the decorations, then introduced the porcelains and bear ornaments, and each one extended to her a most gracious welcome. Still, she was unmoved.

Finally, Father Christmas had only one group left to introduce. He had

purposely left these for last, for they were indeed special. His inclination was to rush through them so as to finish his task quickly, but he felt this would be inappropriate given their great importance to the tree, to the family, and to the other ornaments as well.

"And so, Fair Angel, this brings us to our last and very cherished group of ornaments—our angels." Once again he paused and then slowly began. "As you may have noticed—"

"Angels?" Her voice was shockingly loud, and she looked down at the others for the first time since she'd arrived. It startled everyone.

Alarmed by this unexpected response, Father Christmas could only mutter a most confused "Ah . . . y-yes . . . angels."

"No one told me there would be other angels on this tree," she protested. "I assumed I would be the only one! I don't understand!" She was now leaning out as far as she could, trying desperately to see for herself if it was true. *Could this be?* she wondered to herself. *Must I be required to share this Christmas tree—forever—with other angels?*

All of the ornaments were now astir at her unexpected expression of concern. Father Christmas knew he must restore peace.

"All right, everyone, let's quiet ourselves. Please."

His words were useless, for Fair Angel had spotted two or three of the other angels. Without so much as a moment's hesitation, she blurted out, "Those angels? Why, they are not even beautiful! I am much more beautiful than they are!"

Stunned, the entire assortment of ornaments drew in one long, audible gasp, then all was silent. Instantly realizing the impact of her words, Fair Angel glanced around cautiously. Each pair of eyes she met glared back for a moment; then, heads shaking in disbelief, they slowly turned their backs to her. Only the eyes of kind Father Christmas remained fixed upon her. At first she could not look at him, for a shame was beginning to grow within her, a feeling she had never known. These ornaments, and especially Father Christmas, had gone out of their way to make her feel welcome, and she had returned their goodness with thoughtlessness. Struck now by what she had said, she turned to Father Christmas. "I just didn't understand . . . I don't. I'm sorry, but I really thought—" She stopped there for fear of saying something that would sound even worse.

"Perhaps it is we . . . er, me, who should be apologizing." Father Christmas's words were gentle and sincere.

Amazed by his kindness, she looked pleadingly at him and finally asked in a whisper, "Will you help me to understand?"

"But of course," he said with a sigh and began. "There are, no doubt, Fair Angel, Christmas trees everywhere that have but one angel who sits on the top and reigns supreme above beautiful ornaments of every description. Yet, beyond their beauty, they are meaningless. But we are the fortunate ones. We are much more than just fancy decorations. We are the real ornaments, each one reminding our humans of something good and wonderful. Yet, as cherished as we all are, it is the angels who are the reminders of those things that are the most important." He could see the puzzled look on her face and knew a different approach was needed.

"You see, from their first Christmas together as man and wife, our good owners have exchanged Christmas tree ornaments. I was given to him by her. As *he* shopped, however, with so little in his pockets for her ornament, he became discouraged and was about to head for home, when he found Heart Angel. She is over there." He nodded toward a dainty little angel who wore a slightly faded gown of silken red. From her delicate hands dangled two golden hearts, forever intertwined.

"He thought of his young wife as he counted out the exact amount. He thought about her kind and giving heart, her unselfishness, about how she had not complained, not one word about their struggles, their meager surroundings, especially now that it was Christmas. And so he purchased Heart Angel as a reminder of the many qualities he so loved in his dear wife. And with that, a grand tradition began. Each year he adds one, sometimes two, sometimes three angels to our tree as symbols of her goodness. It is a secret that just the two of them share, which makes it ever so priceless."

Fair Angel looked longingly at Heart Angel, seeing her in the light of understanding. *Oh, she is beautiful,* she thought to herself. As her heart softened, she said, "Tell me, please, about the others."

Father Christmas felt her sincerity and continued. "There were twenty-nine angels at last year's count, and there are sure to be others added before this season's close. I gave up long ago remembering the order of their arrival, so I will simply tell you about each as we come to them."

Father Christmas stretched and moved to where he could take in the full view of the surrounding tree. By now, some of the other ornaments had turned toward Fair Angel and intently listened to Father Christmas recount the stories of the angels of the lower branches.

"Over there," he said, "you see those four, very close together. They are our baby angels. The good gentleman gave one to his dear wife after the birth of each of their children. Two in pink and two in blue. These are especially dear, since each one brought into their home a full measure of joy and love. They love one another, of that there is no doubt."

Fair Angel looked at the baby angels for the longest time without saying a word; then a smile shone on her face. "How grand," she whispered, "to know such love."

By now, most of the tree's ornaments were attentive and exchanged hopeful smiles. Unaware that she was fast becoming the center of attention once again, Fair Angel urged, "Please continue."

Eager to capture the moment, Father Christmas quickly moved on. "Let me see," he said thoughtfully, anxious to choose just the right one to introduce next. The satin swan caught his eye and motioned toward Grandmother Angel. "Good choice," Father Christmas said, knowing the sweet affection the swan had always held for the grandmother angel ornament.

"Over there," he said, pointing to his left, "is Grandmother Angel." She was a wonderful, winged angel, dressed in a sea-green gown. "She is dear indeed. You see, the kind lady's mother grew very ill before passing away, and she came to this house to live. It was a difficult and yet most wonderful time. She died on the Sunday before Christmas that year, and on Christmas Eve the good gentleman handed his wife our grandmother angel. Sea-green had been the dear old woman's favorite color, and that the good gentleman found an ornament so appropriate and so near Christmas—well, it was a miracle, to be sure. It was a very tender moment. We all cried, and the sense of love and devotion the kind lady had given to her mother gave us a most cherished memory."

Fair Angel's eyes had become fixed upon Grandmother Angel. "I had no idea such love even existed," she whispered.

"Oh, but there is more," Father Christmas replied softly.

It was now Gray Mouse's turn to indicate the next angel. He signaled to Father Christmas and urged him toward one of his own personal favorites. These angels, everyone thought, were perhaps the most unusual upon the entire tree. There were four of them, made of wood and connected by a silver circle. One was of dark walnut, another of a crimsoned mahogany. The third was of oak, and the fourth was of a golden-toned maple. Each piece was exquisitely formed and polished to a high gloss.

"Whatever do they represent?" Fair Angel asked.

"All of the people in the world," Father Christmas replied proudly. "For many years, and continuing until this very day, our kind lady has worked for understanding among all people. Her love for everyone knows few limitations. Her influence has been felt in many ways in this regard; and because of that, the good gentleman had these angels made just for her. She cherishes them dearly."

"They are lovely." Fair Angel felt as if she were running out of words to describe her feelings, and she settled back as Father Christmas continued.

For the next few hours, assisted tirelessly by the entire ornament family, Father Christmas told her long stories about each angel and its importance to the kind lady and, therefore, to all of the ornaments upon the tree. They were all recollections of love, caring, and deeds of goodness. As Fair Angel moved her gaze from one ornament to the next, these accounts became part of the most wonderful experience she had ever known. But the greatest, she would soon learn, was still ahead.

"So there you have them," Father Christmas concluded. "All but one."

"One more? Which is it?" she asked.

"Oh, it's the one," he said, choosing his words most carefully, "that is the most important angel upon this tree. The story of that angel is in fact the beginning to all the others."

Fair Angel was awestruck. "Really! Where? Which is it?" She looked eagerly about her. The watchful eyes of the other ornaments gave her no clue, and she looked again at Father Christmas.

"You must learn of this angel on Christmas Eve," he said. "I am sorry, you must wait until then. But know this now: that angel represents the grandest message of them all."

His words took her breath away. She wondered to herself how this could be possible. Was she yet to know the grandest of them all? Sensing to ask no further questions, Fair Angel simply settled back to ponder all she had learned.

Time and again, her gaze swept across the wonderful tree below and each time met the eager gaze of many of the other ornaments. She was moved by their concern, but most especially by thoughts of the goodness represented by each of the angels of the lower branches. This was a tree, a home, a family filled with love. Where did that kind of love come from? She wondered if the answer lay in the one angel yet to be shown her.

During the next few days, a curious thing happened. Several times, Fair Angel looked down to find the kind lady standing in front of the tree, staring right up at her. There were times when she almost looked sad, or so Fair Angel thought, for she would wipe a tear from her eyes. And then, finally, a smile would light upon her gentle face and she would turn and leave the room. Once, her youngest daughter came into the room and asked her mother why she was crying. "Oh, it's just Christmas. It always makes me cry," the kind lady answered.

"Is it our new treetop angel?" the little girl asked, unconvinced by the explanation. She well remembered the night they had put up the Christmas tree.

The kind lady nodded and, with an affectionate pat on the child's face, replied, "Yes, I guess that's it." Seeing the question in her daughter's eyes, she made a promise. "I'll tell you all about it on Christmas Eve. How does that sound?"

The little girl beamed at this, and on the tree, the ornaments, including Fair Angel, stirred at the kind lady's promise. As Christmas Eve drew closer, a feeling of anticipation grew in everyone.

During this time, Fair Angel sensed a deepening degree of warmth and even forgiveness from all of the other ornaments. Occasionally, she even thought about asking Gray Mouse or the satin swan about the mysterious angel—the grandest of all, Father Christmas had said. Yet, each time she caught their eyes, she felt the need only to smile in a sincerely friendly manner. After all, she reminded herself, Father Christmas had promised her the answer. "Christmas Eve," he had said. "Wait until then." And at long last, the morning of Christmas Eve dawned.

The excitement in the house was felt by everyone. The entire day had been spent in a vast number of projects carried out by the good family. Last-minute gifts were purchased and wrapped. Plates of pastries were assembled and delivered around the neighborhood. Food was prepared for a wonderful Christmas Day dinner, and it was far into the day before things seemed to be settling down. The ornaments felt the excitement as well, and as the anticipation increased, they each rechecked their positioning on the tree. Everything must be as perfect as possible.

Twilight arrived, and the lights were lit. Fair Angel could hear voices from outside the home. Carolers had stopped and were now singing wonderful songs just beyond the window. It was a magical moment. The good family gathered around, watched, and waved a Merry Christmas as the beautiful music trailed off into the shades of evening. Soon afterward, guests began to arrive. Family and friends came in bundles of woolen scarves, capped heads, and gloved hands. Their laughter and greetings were delightful to hear, and Fair Angel felt as if she herself were about to burst with the excitement of this night. With a clattering of dishes and silverware, the humans dined and laughed and sang. Oh, this was indeed merry, thought Fair Angel—more so than she had ever imagined. So this was Christmas! This was the festive event for which she and all the other ornaments had been crafted. Or so she thought.

"Father Christmas," she whispered excitedly, "this is all so grand. I never expected it to be so—"

"Shh," he kindly said. "Remember what I said about the best being still ahead? It is nearly time." And with that, his eyes turned toward the room that was now filled with the man and his wife, their family, and their friends.

The humans seated themselves around the spacious room, and the good gentleman stood before them all. Taking a large book from the lamp stand nearby, he opened it carefully, smiling at his dear wife, who stood just at the entryway of the parlor. She looked behind her, out into the hall, and whispered something to someone there. Fair Angel tried hard to see who was in the hallway, but she could not. The kind lady then motioned to her husband, and the good gentleman began to read aloud.

"And it came to pass in those days, that there went out a decree from Caesar Augustus, that all the world should be taxed. . . . And all went to be taxed. . . . And Joseph also went up from Galilee, out of the city of Nazareth . . . unto the city of

David, which is called Bethlehem . . . to be taxed with Mary his espoused wife, being great with child." With those words, there appeared in the hallway two young children, a boy and a girl, dressed in robes of brown and beige. The boy led the little girl by her hand into the center of the parlor and stood quietly as the good gentleman continued.

He next read about the journey and the arrival into the city, and of the inns that were unable to house the two travelers. At this point three other small children, dressed as innkeepers, came into the parlor. As Joseph and Mary approached them, the first two shook their heads—no room in this inn. Finally, the third pointed toward a corner of the room, where a small child's cradle stood. The two walked toward it, and Joseph helped Mary down onto a pillow at the cradle's side. The good gentleman now read of a manger and then of a wondrous birth. The Christ child was born! With that, the little Mary took a doll bundled inside the cradle, and held it ever so gently next to her heart. The Christmas story unfolded humbly before them all, human and ornament family alike, and the words touched them deeply. But few, perhaps, were moved more than Fair Angel.

The story went next to a hillside, where shepherds were abiding in their fields by night. With that introduction, several more children entered the parlor, lifting as best they could their long robes as they walked. Some carried shepherds' staves, crooked as they were at one end, and a few of the smallest children carried toy lambs. They seated themselves in the corner opposite the manger and sat quietly as the story continued. "And, lo, the angel of the Lord came upon them, and the glory of the Lord shone round about them: and they were sore afraid." With that, a little golden-haired girl stepped into the room and took her place, standing on a bench near the shepherds. She was dressed in a delicate, flowing gown of white and gold silk, with a row of rhinestones at her throat. Atop her head sat a wreathlike crown of shimmering gold and silver tinsel, and at her back dangled a pair of gossamer wings that glistened in the gentle light of the room. In her small outstretched arms she carried a golden scroll, draped like a velvet ribbon. "Fear not," were the words of the angel of the Lord as the good gentleman read on: "For, behold, I bring you good tidings of great joy, which shall be to all people. For unto you is born this day in the city of David a Savior, which is Christ the Lord."

A strange realization stirred in the heart and mind of Fair Angel as she gazed upon this little girl, who, as the angel of the Lord, carried forth the greatest message of all. In this little girl, Fair Angel was suddenly seeing herself. The thought struck her with great force. Was this true? Her dress, her hair, the wreath, the scroll—all identical to her own! She glanced toward Father Christmas, who, to her surprise was staring back at her intently, as were Gray Mouse, the satin swan, and all of the ornaments on the tree. Could this mean what she was only now beginning to comprehend? That *she* represented the most important angel ever?

The question froze in her mind as another arose. What did it mean, to represent the angel of the Lord? Her thoughts raced; she was trying earnestly to understand.

She looked again at Father Christmas, searching for answers.

"Just watch and listen," he whispered, seeing her confusion.

The good gentleman was reading now of wise men, coming from the east, and of a star. More costumed children entered the parlor and placed jewel-encrusted containers at the feet of the little Mary, who still cradled the babe in her arms.

The magnificent story was now concluded, and the family, as they had done for so many Christmas Eves, reached out to one another. Clasping hands, they began to sing of a silent and holy night. Their voices were soft and gentle, and tears filled many eyes as the carol continued. As the song ended, a stillness rested upon all in the room, and finally, the good gentleman, taking his wife by the hand, walked across the room and stood in front of the beautiful Christmas tree. Then they turned and faced their family and friends.

He spoke first. His words of gratitude and love touched them all as he opened his heart. Then, after a long pause, he spoke ever so softly of the importance of this night and the significance of the day that would follow. His words were now of Christ, the baby born in a manger on that night long ago, and of his love for Him. Tears were now in abundance as each person in the room spoke words of a similar nature. The small children watched in perfect reverence, sensing the importance of this moment, and some, drawing in deep breaths, spoke of their love for Jesus.

Coming full circle around the room, it was now the kind lady's turn to speak. Her soft voice began much like the others, with words of gratitude for countless blessings and abiding love. It was then that she glanced to the top of the Christmas tree and, with a radiant smile to her youngest daughter, continued with something most unusual.

"I promised to tell you all a little story—one that I have never told anyone. It concerns the angel atop this tree." Eyes glanced at Fair Angel and then back again to the kind lady.

"When I was a little girl," she began, "perhaps eight or nine, I became very ill one week before Christmas. The doctors were called in, but they could not seem to get my fever down. My dear mother sat at my bedside, continually placing cool towels on my fevered head and arms. During these long hours, she would tell me stories. Many were of her childhood, but mostly they were stories from the Bible—stories of Jesus.

"One night," she continued, "after Mother had gone into great detail about the birth of Christ, including the stories of the shepherds and the wise men, I fell into a sound sleep, the best I had known in days. I dreamed of an angel. In my dream, I was a little shepherd girl, sitting on a rock on the hillside that night. And when the angel of the Lord came and told us the news of the birth, everyone left and hurried into Bethlehem. I was the only one left behind. I didn't know if I was supposed to go or stay and watch over the sheep.

"The angel asked me why I lingered on the hillside, and I told her of my confusion. At that point, the angel pulled a golden scroll from the heavens. She looked at it for a long time and then said that my name did not appear upon the scroll; therefore, I should stay here on the hillside. I was so very sad and asked her why my name was not listed. 'Perhaps,' said the angel, 'it is that you do not yet know the Lord.'

"'How do I come to know the Lord?' I asked the angel. 'By following Him,' the angel replied. And then my dream ended. I have always remembered that dream; and over these years, I have tried very hard to do just that—to follow the Lord . . . that I might come to know Him."

She looked for a brief moment at her husband. It was he who over these many years had given her all of the angels that now hung upon the tree as symbols of her goodness. Only the two of them fully understood their significance. He smiled at her, knowing the extent of her desire to follow the Savior of the world.

Her voice was now barely a whisper. "There have been times of failure, but even then I have come to feel of His love and infinite care for me—for all of us." She paused, and for a long moment stood in humble silence. At last she continued. "And so when I came to needing a new treetop angel, I had intended to buy one much like the old one if I could. Until one day, in a little shop, I spotted her. She sat alone in the corner of the store; there was not another like her. As I drew near, I could see that she was ever so much like the angel in my dream of those many years ago. Her dress was similar, but when I could see that in her hands she held a golden scroll, my heart began to pound, and I knew this would be my new angel of the Lord."

She smiled at the many dear ones who had listened to her story with their hearts, and felt she could say just one last thing. "I have longed to know if my own name could be found upon the scroll. I still don't know, but having her there at the top of this tree, I am always reminded that somewhere, perhaps, the angels are taking notes upon a golden scroll."

The room was perfectly silent as humans and ornaments alike pondered the story of the kind lady. It would become a cherished Christmas memory, one they would hold dear for the rest of their lives.

The evening had drawn to a wonderful close, and the guests parted with sweet embraces and promises to return on the morrow. The house began to settle into a gentle Christmas Eve quiet, and within a short time the family had retired for a peace-filled slumber.

In keeping with the family's tradition, the lights on the Christmas tree remained on throughout the night. The ornaments waited in silence as they watched Fair Angel reflect upon the events of the evening. More than ever, they realized the great importance of Fair Angel.

At long last, she spoke softly. "Have you always known?" she asked her question of anyone.

Father Christmas answered. "Not all of it, Fair Angel. Much of what was said here tonight, we ourselves heard for the first time as well. Your resembling the angel in the kind lady's dream, the scroll you hold in your arms—all of that is new to us. But as to who you represent—the angel of the Lord—yes, we have always known. Still, even more importantly, we have known how very vital the Lord is in the lives of these good people."

"Why couldn't you just tell me?" she asked in a whisper.

"Oh, my dear, just as knowing the Lord and following Him has forever changed the hearts of people—these people in particular—it is still a journey that must be made more or less alone. We could not tell you of the Lord, or even of the angel of the Lord, until you could see and feel all of this for yourself."

"And the angels of the lower branches?" she asked.

Father Christmas smiled. "They represent our lady's very good and kind deeds of charity and service in following Him—in coming to know the Lord. He changed her life, and she, in turn, has done all the good she can, because of Him."

Fair Angel looked at all of the charming and caring ornament faces turned toward her. How wonderful she felt! How very blessed to be a part of them in representing such goodness! The host of other angels reminded them all of loving service given in His name; her role was to remind them all that the greatest example of service on this earth came first as a babe lying in a manger.

"Thank you . . . all of you." She spoke softly, lovingly, looking at each ornament. They all looked at her, rather shyly now.

It was Gray Mouse who spoke first. "Merry Christmas, Fair Angel."

"Oh, and Merry Christmas to you, too," she eagerly replied.

"Merry Christmas!" It came from the satin swan and the cotton bears in unison.

"Thank you. And to you as well." She spoke with a growing smile.

At that moment, all of the ornaments began at once to extend to her the warmest of Christmas wishes. She returned each with a heart that was filled with joy.

Finally, she looked at Father Christmas, who had remained quiet these last few minutes. He was beaming, delighted with what had occurred this night. "What a choice tree this is—to have you as our angel of the Lord. Merry Christmas, Fair Angel."

"And to you, Father Christmas—and to us all."

After a quiet, reflective hour, Fair Angel looked down at the golden scroll she held. Were there names upon it? Yes, indeed, there were many. With a humbled heart, Fair Angel closed her eyes and smiled.

Bells in the distance chimed. Christmas Day had arrived.

Symbolism of the Angel:

Angels remind us of the heavenly messengers who proclaimed Christ's birth.

What will you and I give for CHRISTMAS this year?
Let us in our lives give to our Lord and Savior the gift of
gratitude by living His teachings
and following in His footsteps.
It was said of Him that He "went about doing good."
As we do likewise, the CHRISTMAS SPIRIT will be ours.

~ Thomas S. Monson

Angels We Have Heard on High

Angels we have heard on high
Sweetly singing o'er the plains,
And the mountains in reply
Echoing their joyous strains.

Refrain:
Gloria, in excelsis Deo!
Gloria, in excelsis Deo!

Shepherds, why this jubilee?
Why your joyous strains prolong?
What the gladsome tidings be
Which inspire your heav'nly song?

Refrain

Come to Bethlehem and see
Him Whose birth the angels sing;
Come, adore on bended knee,
Christ the Lord, the newborn King.

Refrain

See Him in a manger laid,
Whom the choirs of angels praise;
Mary, Joseph, lend your aid,
While our hearts in love we raise.

Refrain

The words to this Christmas carol are based on a traditional French carol, "*Les Anges dans nos Campagnes*"—which translates literally to "Angels in Our Countryside." French shepherds tending their flocks on Christmas Eve traditionally called out to one another, singing "Gloria in excelsis Deo, gloria in excelsis Deo"; the tune to which they sang was a late medieval Latin chorale, now the refrain for "Angels We Have Heard on High." The most common English version was translated in 1862 by Roman Catholic Bishop James Chadwick, who was born to Irish parents but spent most of his life in northeast England. While serving as a priest, he became a professor of humanities, theology, and philosophy. During the sixteen years he served as a bishop, he was first vice president and then the eighth president of Ushaw College, a Roman Catholic seminary near Durham, England, where priests are trained.

The Blessed Day

By Louisa May Alcott

What shall little children bring
On Christmas Day, on Christmas Day?
What shall little children bring
On Christmas Day in the morning?
This shall little children bring
On Christmas Day, on Christmas Day;
Love and joy to Christ their king,
On Christmas Day in the morning!
What shall little children sing
On Christmas Day, on Christmas Day?
What shall little children sing
On Christmas Day in the morning?
The grand old carols shall they sing
On Christmas Day, on Christmas Day;
With all their hearts, their offerings bring
On Christmas Day in the morning.

A MERRY
CHRISTMAS

A Christmas Bell Poem

By Eugene Field

Why do the bells of Christmas ring?

Why do little children sing?

Once a lovely shining star,

Seen by shepherds from afar,

Gently moved until its light

Made a manger's cradle bright.

There a darling baby lay,

Pillowed soft upon the hay;

And its mother sung and smiled:

"This is Christ, the holy Child!"

Therefore bells for Christmas ring,

Therefore little children sing.

SYMBOLISM OF THE CHRISTMAS BELL:
Bells have traditionally been used to indicate the beginning of a religious service, and what more joyous event than the birth of our Savior?

HOMEMADE WASSAIL

½ cup and 1 Tablespoon sugar
1 cup water
½ cinnamon stick
¼ slice fresh ginger root
1 cup orange juice
½ cup lemon juice
2 cups apple juice
2 whole allspice berries
¾ teaspoon whole cloves

1. In a large saucepan, combine sugar and water. Boil for 5 minutes. Remove from heat, and add cinnamon sticks, allspice berries, cloves, and ginger. Cover and let stand in warm place for 1 hour.
2. Strain liquid into a large pot. Just before serving, add juices and cider and quickly bring to boil. Remove from heat and serve.

YUMMY CREAMY HOT COCOA

⅓ cup unsweetened cocoa powder
¾ cup white sugar
1 pinch salt
⅓ cup boiling water
3½ cups milk
¾ teaspoon vanilla extract
½ cup half-and-half cream
Optional: marshmallows, crushed peppermint candy, and sprinkles.

1. Combine the cocoa, sugar, and pinch of salt in a saucepan. Blend in the boiling water. Bring this mixture to a soft boil while you stir. Simmer and stir for about 2–3 minutes. Becareful that it doesn't scorch.
2. Stir in the milk and heat until very hot, but do not let it come to a boil. Remove from heat and add vanilla.
3. Divide between 4 mugs. Add the cream to the mugs of cocoa to cool it to drinking temperature.

Optional: top with marshmallows, crushed peppermint candy and sprinkles.

Did You Know?

Wassail, a popular Christmas drink made with apple cider, is from the Old Norse ves heill, which means "good health."

In November 2010, Nestlé made The World's Largest Cup of Hot Chocolate (634.01 US gallons) in Mexico.

The Animals' Christmas Tree

By John P. Peters

Once upon a time the animals decided to have a Christmas tree, and this was how it came about: The swifts and the swallows in the chimneys in the country houses, awakened from their sleep by joy and laughter, had stolen down and peeped in upon scenes of happiness, the center of which was always an evergreen tree covered with wonderful fruit, bright balls of many colors, and sparkling threads of gold and silver, lying like beautiful frost-work among the green fir needles. A sweet, fairy-like figure of a Christ Child or an angel rested high among the branches, and underneath the tree were dolls and sleds and skates and drums and toys of every sort, and furs and gloves and tippets, ribbons and handkerchiefs, and all the things that boys and girls need and like; and all about this tree were gathered always little children with faces oh so full of wonderment and expectation, changing to radiant, sparkling merriment as toys and candies were taken off the tree or from underneath its boughs and distributed.

The swifts and swallows told their feathered friends all about it, and they told others, both birds and animals, until at last it began to be rumored through all the animal world that on one day in the year the children of men were made wonderfully happy by means of some sort of festival which they held about a fir tree from the forest. Now, of course, the tame animals and the house animals, the dogs and the cats and the mice, knew something more about this festival. . . . And when they were asked about the Christmas tree, they told still more wonderful stories than the swifts and the swallows from the chimneys had told, for some of them had taken part in these festivals, and some had even received presents from the tree, just like the children.

They said that the tree was called a Christmas tree, because that strange fruit and that wonderful frosting came on it only in the Christmastime and that the Christmastime was the time when men and women and little children, too, were always kind and good and loving and gave things to one another; and they said, moreover, that on the Christmas tree grew the things which everyone wanted and which would make them happy, and that it was so because in the Christmastime everyone was trying to make everyone else happy and to think of what other people would like. This, they said, was what they had seen and heard told about Christmas trees. They did not quite understand why it was so, but they knew that the Christmas tree, when rightly made, brought the Christmas spirit, and they had heard men say that the Christmas spirit was the great thing and that it was what made everyone happy.

Well, the long and the short of it was that the animals talked of it in their dens and on their roosts, in the fields, and in the forests, wild beasts and tame alike—the cows and the horses in their stalls, the sheep in their fold, the doves in their cotes, and the poultry in the poultry yard, until all agreed that a Christmas tree would be a grand thing for the wild and tame alike. Like the men, they, too, would have a tree of their very own. But how to do it?

Then the lion called a meeting of all the creatures, wild and tame; for you know the lion is king of beasts, and when he calls they all must come. You know, too, that before and during and after these animal congresses there is a royal peace. The lamb can come to the meeting and sit down by the wolf, and the wolf dare not touch him; the dove may perch on the bough between the hawk and the owl and neither will harm him when the great king of beasts has summoned them all together to take counsel. But you know all about the rules of the animals, for you have read them in books, and you have seen the pictures: how the lion sits on his throne with a crown on one side of his head, and all the other creatures gather about—the elephant, and giraffe, the hippopotamus, the buffalo, wolves and tigers and leopards, foxes and deer, goats and sheep, monkeys and orangutans, parrots and robins and turkeys and swans and storks and eagles, frogs and lizards and alligators, and all the rest besides.

Then, when the lion had called the meeting to order, the swifts and the swallows told what they had seen, and a fat little pug-dog, with a ribbon and a silver bell about his neck, wheezed out a story of a Christmas tree that he had seen and how a silver bell had grown on that tree for him and a whole box of the best sweets he had ever dreamed of while he lay comfortably snoozing on his cushion before the fire. And a Persian cat, with her hair turned the wrong way, mewed out her story of a Christmas tree that she had attended and told how there was a white mouse made of cream cheese for her creeping about beneath the branches.

Then the monkeys chattered and the elephants trumpeted, the horses neighed, the hyenas laughed, and each in his own way argued for a Christmas tree and told what he would do to help make it.

The elephant would go into the forest and choose the tree and pull it up. The buffaloes would drag it in. The giraffe would fix the ornaments on the higher limbs because its neck was long. The monkeys would scramble up where the giraffe could not reach. The squirrels could run out on the slender twigs and help the monkeys. The birds would fly about and get the golden threads and put them on the tree with their beaks. The fireflies would hide themselves among the branches and sparkle like diamonds, and the glowworms promised to help the fireflies by playing candles, if someone would lift them up and put them on the branches. The parrots and paroquets and other birds of gay plumage would give feathers to hang among the branches, and the hummingbirds promised to flutter in and out among the twigs, and the sheep to give white wool to lie like snow among the boughs.

Then the parrots screeched and the peacocks screamed with delight, and you and I never could have told whether anybody voted aye or nay. But the lion knew, and the owl, for he was clerk, set it down in the minutes, as the lion bade him, that all the birds and beasts would do their part. So each planned what he could do. Even the little beetle, who makes great balls of earth, thought that if he could only once see one of those gay balls that grow on the children's Christmas tree, he might make some for the animals' tree. Different birds and beasts told of the oranges and apples and holly-berries and who knows what they could get and hang upon the tree. You see the animals came from many places, and then, too, they could send the carrier pigeons to go and bring fruit and berries from, oh, so far away.

And so they arranged how they would ornament the tree, and the next thing was to decide what presents should be hung on the tree or put beneath its boughs, for each one must have his present. Well, after much discussion in roars, and bellows, crows and croaks, lows and screams and bleats, and baas and grunts, and all the other sounds of birds and beast language, it was voted that each might choose the present he wished hung on the tree. The clerkly owl should call their names one by one, and each might declare his choice. So they began. The parrots and the macaws thought that they would like oranges and bananas and such things, which would look so pretty on the tree, too; and so they were arranged for. The robins and the cedar birds chose cherries; the partridges, partridge berries' the squirrels, the red and grey and black nuts and apples and pears. The monkeys said the popcorn strings would do for them, and the cats and dogs, remembering the Christmas gift which the pug-dog and Persian cat had told about, asked for tiny mice made of cream cheese or chocolate.

By and by it came the pig's turn to tell his choice. "Grunt, grunt!" said the pig. "I want a nice pail of swill hung on the very lowest bough of all."

"Ugh!" said the black leopard, so sleek and so clean.

"Faugh!" said the gazelle, with his dainty sense of smell.

"Neigh!" said the horse, so daintily groomed.

"What?!" roared the lion. "What's that you want?"

"A pail of swill," grunted the pig. "Each one has chosen what he wants, and I have a right to choose what I want."

"But," roared the lion, "each one has chosen something beautiful to make the tree a joy to all."

"Grunt, grunt," said the pig. "The parrots and macaws are going to have oranges and bananas; and the robins and the cedar birds, red cherries; the partridges, their berries; the squirrels, nuts and apples and pears; the dog and the cat, their cream and chocolate mice. They all have what they want to eat. Grunt, grunt," said he. "I will have what I want to eat, too, and what I want is a pail of swill."

Now, you see it had been voted, as I told you, that each should have what he wanted hung on the tree for him, and so the lion could not help himself. Angrily the lion had to roar: "If the pig wants swill, a pail of swill he must have, hung on the lowest bough of the tree!"

Then the wolf's wicked eyes gleamed, for his turn was next, and he said: "If the pig has swill because he wants swill to eat, I must have what I want to eat, and I want a tender lamb, six months old." And at that all the lambs and the sheep bleated and baaed.

"Ha, ha!" barked the fox. "Then I want a turkey!" And the turkeys gobbled in fear.

"And I," said the tiger, "want a yearling calf." And the cows and the calves lowed in horror.

"And I," said the owl, the clerk, "I want a plump dove."

"And I," said the hawk, "will take a rabbit."

"And I," said the leopard, "want a deer or a gazelle."

Then all was fear and uproar. The hares and rabbits scuttled into the grass; the gazelles and the deer bounded away; the sheep and the cattle crowded close together; the small birds rose in the air in flocks; and the Christmas tree was like to have come to grief and ended, not in Christmas joy, but in fear and hatred and terror.

Then a little lamb stepped out and bleated: "Ah! King Lion, it would be very sad if all the animals should lose their Christmas tree, for the very thought of that tree has brought us closer together, and here we were, wild and tame, fierce and timid, met together as friends; oh, King Lion, rather than there should not be a tree, they may take me and hang me on it. Let them not take the turkeys and gazelles and the calves and the rabbits and all the rest that they have chosen. Let the tigers and leopards and wolves and foxes and eagles and hawks and owls and all their kind be content that their Christmas present shall be a lamb; and so we may come together again and have our happy Christmas tree, and each have what he wishes."

"But," said the lion, "what will you have? If you give yourself, then you will have no Christmas present."

"Yes," said the lamb, "I, too, shall have what I want, for I shall have brought them all together again and made each one happy."

Then a dove fluttered down from a tree and landed on the ground beside the lamb, and very timidly and softly she cooed: "Take me, too, King Lion, as the present for the owls and the hawks and the weasels and minks, because for them a lamb is too big. I am the best present for them. Take me, King Lion!"

Then the lion roared: "See what the lamb and the dove have done! My food, oh, tigers and leopards and wolves and eagles and all your kind, is like your food; but I would rather eat nothing from our Christmas tree than take this lamb or dove for my present."

Then all the beasts kept still, because the lion roared so loud and angrily, and the birds that were flying away settled on the branches of the trees, and the gazelles stopped their running and turned their heads to listen, and the rabbits peeped out through the grass and brush where they had hid.

Then the lion turned to the pig and roared: "See this lamb and this dove! Are you not ashamed for what you have done? You have spoiled all our happiness. Will you take back your choice, you pig, or do you wish to ruin our Christmas tree?"

"Grunt, grunt," said the pig. "It is my right. I want something good. I don't care for your lambs and your doves. I want my swill!"

Then the lion roared again: "Have all chosen?" and all answered, "Yes."

"Then," said the lion, "it is my choice."

And all said: "It is."

"I love fat and tender pigs. I choose a pig for my Christmas gift," roared the lion.

Did you ever hear a pig squeal? Oh, how that pig squealed then! And he got up on his fat little legs and tried to run away, but all the animals gathered around in a ring, and the hyenas laughed, and the jackals cried, and the dogs and the wolves and the foxes headed him off and hunted the poor pig back again. Then, when the pig found that he could not run away, he lay down on his back with his feet in the air and squealed with all his might: "Oh, I don't want the swill; oh, I don't want the swill! I take it all back! I don't want anything!"

But at first no one heard him because all were talking at once in their own way—barking and growling and roaring and chattering; but by and by the lion saw that the pig was squealing something, so he roared for silence, and then they all heard the pig squeal out that he did not want any swill. And the lion roared aloud: "You have heard. Has the owl recorded that the pig will have no swill?"

"Yes," said the owl.

"Then," said the lion, "record that the lion wants no pig."

Then the tiger growled: "And I want no calf," and one by one the leopard and the eagle, the wolf and the fox, the hawk and owl, and all their kind, took back their votes.

And so it came about that the animals did have a Christmas tree after all; but instead of hanging lambs and doves upon the tree, they agreed that they could hang little images of lambs and doves, and other birds and animals, too, perhaps. And by and by the custom spread until the humans came to hang the same little images on their trees, too, and when you see a little figure of a lamb or a dove on the Christmas tree, you may know that it is all because the lamb and the dove, by their unselfishness, saved the animals from strife; for neither thought what he wanted from the tree, but each was ready to give himself for the others, so that they might not fight at Christmastime.

How can we give to the Lord? What shall we give to him? EVERY kind word to our own, EVERY help given them, is as a *gift* to God, whose chief concern is the welfare of his children. Every gentle deed to our neighbor, every kindness to the poor and suffering, is a gift to the Lord, before whom all mankind are equal. Every conformity to the Lord's plan of salvation—and this is of first importance—is a direct *gift* TO GOD, for thereby we fit ourselves more nearly for our divinely planned destiny.

-John A. Widtsoe

Symbolism of the Dove:

Doves signify peace on earth and the peace bestowed by the Holy Ghost.

MOST POPULAR Christmas Toys THROUGH THE YEARS

- 1910s—teddy bear, erector set, electric train
- 1920s—Crayola crayons, Raggedy Ann doll, Tinker Toys (Did you know that until the 1930s Crayola crayon boxes included only eight crayons?)
- 1930s—Monopoly, Viewmaster Slide Viewer (Did you know more than 200 million Molopoly board games have been sold worldwide?)
- 1940s—Scrabble, Slinky, Silly Putty (Did you know more than 300 million Slinkys have been sold worldwide?)
- 1950s—Yahtzee, Barbie, Hula hoop, Play-Doh (Did you know the first Barbie doll wore a black and white swimming suit and was available in blonde and brunette? Did you know Play-Doh was originally invented to be a wallpaper cleaner?)
- 1960s—Easy Bake Oven, G.I. Joe, Etch-a-Sketch, Action Man, Rock 'Em Sock 'Em Robots (Did you know G.I. stands for "Government Issued" and the Joes were marketed as action figures not dolls?)
- 1970s—Uno, Dungeons & Dragons, Pong, Connect Four, Star Wars, Speak and Spell (Did you know that the Uno world championship is held every year in Moscow, Russia, and more than seventy-one countries compete?)

- 1980s—Rubik's Cube, Koosh Ball, Transformers: Optimus Prime, My Little Pony, Teddy Ruxpin, Teenage Mutant Ninja Turtles, Lego (Did you know a Koosh ball is made from about 2,000 rubber strings? Did you know the name *Lego* comes from the abbreviation of the Danish words "leg godt," which means "play well"?)

- 1990s—Game Boy, Furby, Tickle-Me-Elmo, POG, Power Rangers, Buzz Lightyear, Beanie Babies (Did you know the most popular game for Game Boy was Tetris? Did you know Buzz Lightyear's name was inspired by Apollo 11 astronaut Buzz Aldrin?)

- 2000s—Razor Scooters, Playstation 2, Bratz dolls, RoboSapiens, Tamagotchi Connexions, Playstation 3, Nintendo Wii, Nintendo DS, Xbox 360, The High School Musical Dance, Ben 10: Alien Creation Chamber (Did you know the Playstation 2 is the best-selling game console ever, with more than 150 million sold, and the Nintendo DS is the best-selling handheld game console, with more than 149 million sold?)

Did You Know?

Toys for Tots, a well-known charity that collects toys for disadvantaged children at Christmas, held its first toy drive in 1947. That first year, the program collected 5,000 toys to distribute. In 1991, the Secretary of Defense officially authorized the U.S. Marine Corps to work with the Marine Toys for Tots Foundation. The following year, Marine Reserve Units collected and distributed more than 7.4 million toys. The Marine Toys for Tots Foundation provided more than 250,000 toys for children who were victims of Hurricane Andrew. Over its life span, Toys for Tots has distributed more than 469 million toys to more than 216 million children.

Anniversary

By Margaret E. Sangster

The little boy sat quite alone on the hilltop, his shepherd's crook across his knees, his small square lunch basket beside him. He made an odd distorted shadow in the white light of the moon, for even the shawl that his mother had woven of lamb's wool could not hide the ugly hump that lay between his shoulders.

Far below him, dotting the hillside with irregular shadows, were the sheep. The majority of them slept, but a few wandered aimlessly up and down the slope. The little boy, however, was not watching the flock. His head was thrown back, and his wide eyes were fixed on the sky. There was an intensity in his gaze and a strange wistful smile on his lips.

The boy was thinking, "Perhaps it will happen again. Perhaps, though a third of a century has gone by, I shall be privileged to see the great star and hear the angel voices as my father did."

The moon, riding high in the heavens, went under a black cloud. For a moment the world was dark. The little boy sighed and lowered his eyes. "Though it is the time of anniversary," he breathed, "there will be no star this night. Neither will the angels sing . . ."

The time of anniversary. How often he had listened to the story of the miracle that had taken place so long ago! The little boy's father had been a little boy then—he had been the youngest of the shepherds on that glorious occasion when an angel anthem sounded across the world and a star shone over the tranquil town of Bethlehem. His father had followed that star; with other shepherds he had come to the stable of the inn. Crowding through the narrow doorway, he had seen a woman with a baby in her arms.

"But," his father would say, "she was no ordinary woman! There was something in her face that made one think of a . . . lighted candle. And there was a tenderness in her smile that the very cattle felt, for they drew near to her, and seemed to even kneel. It was not completely her beauty—although beauty she did possess! It was a shine from within."

"And the baby . . . what of the baby?" the little boy would ask.

The father's hand habitually touched his small son's shoulder at this point—touched it and drew away as if the brief contact caused him anguish; the hump, high and distorted, was so obvious.

"The baby," he said, and his voice grew hushed, "was as unlike other infants as his mother was different from other women. Scarce an hour old when first I glimpsed him, yet there was a sense of wisdom on his brow, and his tiny, upcurled hands seemed so tender, yet even then to hold power. I found myself kneeling as the cattle knelt, and there was moisture upon my face; and though I was a lad tall for my age—I was not ashamed."

Alone on the hillside, the little boy could almost hear the sound of his father's voice in the stillness; his father's voice telling the story of the marvelous infant and of the Wise Men who had come to visit, following the path of the star. They had come bearing gifts, the fame of which traveled through all the land. Often he had heard of the gold and frankincense and myrrh, and he had shivered at the tale of the great but cruel king who had ordered death to all the infants. Often he had thrilled to the danger and excitement of a worried young mother and her sober husband who had stolen away into the land of Egypt with their child.

"Many of us thought that the child had been captured and slain by Herod," the little boy's father invariably finished, "until a decade passed and we heard rumors of a youth who bore his name, who lectured in a temple at Jerusalem to a group of learned doctors. A few years ago we heard that this same youth, now grown older, had organized a group of men, that with them he was journeying from place to place preaching, teaching, and aiding the needy. "And," (here the little boy's father had a habit of lowering his voice and glancing seriously around the room), "there are some who say he has become a Messiah, and that he does more than just help the cause of the common people. There are some who say that he performs wonderful deeds—healing the sick, and the blind, and the lepers—even raising the dead."

Once at this point the little boy interrupted, "Oh, I would that I might meet him. I would that he might take the hump from my back and make me strong and straight like other children."

With a loving finger laid against her son's lips, the little boy's mother warned silence. "What must be must be," she told him. "You were born that way, my son. It is better," looking at her husband, "that we change the subject! There might be listening ears."

It was growing cold on the hillside. The child drew the shawl closer about his tired body and wished that he were not a shepherd. Shepherds led a lonely life—they did not fit into the bright places of the world. Rooms that were gaily lighted at eventide were for men and boys who worked hard by day and earned their moments of ease; they were not for shepherds. But what else could a crippled boy do besides tend sheep?

Yawning wearily, the little boy looked up at the sky. From the position of the moon, he judged it to be about middle night. It was still a long while before sunrise, still hours before someone would come to take his place and he could limp home. Yet middle night had its good, too! For at that time he could break his fast and partake of the lunch his mother had packed so neatly into a basket.

As he reached for the basket and opened it slowly, the little boy was wondering what had been prepared for him tonight by his mother. He found a flask of goat's milk, and nearly a loaf of crusty, dark bread, and some yellow cheese. He also found dried figs, sugary with their own sweetness. Wrapped separately, he came upon a real treat—a cake made of eggs and sifted flour with lemon in it—and raisins!

He had expected the bread and the cheese and the milk. Even the figs he had expected. But the cake was a surprise—the sort of surprise that happened seldom to break the monotony of watching his father's sheep. His eyes gleamed as he surveyed it, and some of the sadness went out of him. Carefully he set the basket down and spread on the ground beside him the square of linen in which his mother had folded the lunch. Carefully he laid out the flask of milk, the bread, the cheese, but not the cake, which he left tucked away in the depths of the basket. He left it there so he might not be tempted to eat it first!

"It is so good to be hungry," he said aloud. "Yes, and to have food."

Suddenly, from somewhere just behind him, a voice spoke. It was not a loud voice, and yet it seemed to carry beyond the hillside.

"Indeed, yes," said the voice. "It is good to be hungry and to have food and to . . ."

Startled, for he thought he was quite alone with his thoughts and the drowsing sheep, the little boy glanced back across his crooked shoulder. He saw a man standing upon the brow of the hill, silhouetted against the moonlit sky. Ordinarily he would have been afraid, for there were sometimes cruel robbers in the middle of the night. But somehow the sight of this man, who was tall and muscular, failed to frighten him. He did not know why he instinctively completed the man's unfinished sentence.

"And to share it," he murmured. "You are a stranger, sir?"

The man came closer to the child and stood looking down on him. "No, not a stranger," he said slowly, "never a stranger. As it happens, my journey started not far from this very place, started years before you saw the light, my lad. I am on my way to complete the circle."

Although he couldn't imagine what the man meant, the boy made swift response.

"I was about to eat my lunch," he said, pointing at the square of linen on which he had arranged the food from his basket. "One grows hungry on the hillside. I am a shepherd, sir. I tend my father's flock, and each night my mother packs for me a simple meal. Will you be seated—and break bread with me?"

The boy hesitated shyly, "Perhaps you will talk with me as we eat? It grows lonely on the dark hillside. I long at times for companionship."

The man continued to peer down from his impressive height. His eyes held a warm glow. It was as if a candle burned somewhere behind them, the little boy thought. He recalled words that his father had spoken when he described a woman in a stable. He felt so comforted by the man's glance that he smiled up into the kindly face, and the man spoke again.

"It is a strange coincidence," he said, "the fact that you are a shepherd, for I also tend my father's flock! And I also . . ." his face shone with a luminous smile, "have often grown lonely waiting for the gates of dawn to open. Are you sure," the man began to gracefully seat himself upon the ground, "that you have sufficient nourishment for two? I should not like to deprive you of anything."

Gazing, fascinated, into the man's face, the little boy replied, "But yes! I have a large flask of goat's milk, and some yellow cheese, nearly a loaf of bread and ten figs. And"—for a second he hesitated—"that's a great plenty," he finished. He did not mention the cake, still wrapped in the basket. For a cake—a cake made of sifted flour and eggs and lemon and raisins—was indeed a rare delicacy. And it was not a very big cake.

The man bent forward to re-tie the thong of his sandal. The little boy saw that the sandal was covered with dust. He tried to keep his eyes from glancing toward his lunch basket as he tore the crusty brown bread into fragments.

"Perhaps your feet are aching," he said as he placed the fragments in the center of the linen cloth. "This hill is hard to climb. I am close to being spent when I reach the summit of it, but I must needs sit high so I can watch all the sheep."

The man said slowly, "I have climbed steeper hills than this, my lad, and know there are steeper hills to come. My feet do not ache. How long"—abruptly changing the subject—"have you been crippled?"

The little boy would have resented such a display of curiosity if the inquiry had come from an ordinary person. But for this man, the question seemed a natural one, to be answered naturally.

"Why," he said, "I have never been without a hump between my shoulders. I hate it, but"—and he began to quote his mother—"what must be, must be!" Then his childish face became a trifle unchildish. "Still, it is hard to go through life looking like one of the camels that the Wise Men rode when they came from the East with their caravans—"

The man interrupted, "What, lad? You know of the Wise Men from the East? How does it happen that you should mention them to me on this night? It is very curious!" The man began to partake of a piece of the crusty dark bread.

Laughing softly, the little boy answered, "I suppose the Wise Men are in my mind because this is the time of anniversary, and I have been thinking of the baby that was born in a stable. I was hoping—before you arrived—that once again the great star might shine and the angels might sing. I have, in fact, been watching the sky rather than the sheep."

The man asked another swift question. "What do you know about these holy things—about the star and the song? You are so very young!"

The little boy exclaimed, "All Bethlehem heard about the star, and the infant who lay in the manger because there was no room at the inn. I know, perhaps more than the others, for my father, a child then, was one of the shepherds who saw the light from the heavens and heard the angel music. Will you . . ." The little boy had taken the flask of goat's milk in his hands. "Will you share with me this cup, sir? For, perhaps you thirst."

The man took the flask from the lad's small hands. His fingers were powerful, and yet as gentle as a woman's. He said, "I will share this cup with you lad, for I do thirst."

Then he watched the man drink deeply. The little boy thought it must be tiring to tramp from place to place.

He said, on impulse, as the stranger set down the flask, "Will you tell me, sir, of some of the towns in which you have stayed?"

The man answered, "Ah, yes, my lad, I have seen many towns—Capernaum, Nazareth, Jerusalem, and many, many others. Each has some good and some bad. Each has some poverty and pain rubbing shoulders with wealth and ease. In every city I have found health on one hand and illness on the other—and in each city more deeds to be done than one short lifetime can accommodate."

"Why, sir, you are still young and strong. You have many years left. How old are you, sir? I turned ten in the spring," the boy added.

The man's voice was muted as he replied, "I am more than three times your age, lad."

"When is your time of birth, sir? The boy asked suddenly.

The man smiled his beautiful, luminous smile. "It's odd that you should ask, dear lad, for this is my day of birth. You, quite unknowingly, are giving me an anniversary feast—and never has a feast been more welcomed. I was weary and forlorn when I came upon you."

"Weary and forlorn!" the little boy queried. "Haven't you any people of your own? People with whom you can be happy on the day of your birth? When my birthday arrives, mother prepares a real feast for me and gives me gifts. This shawl I wear, have you noted it? She wove it for my last birthday."

The man reached over and rested his hand on the little boy's knee. "I fear," he said, "my loved ones are not near enough just now to celebrate with me. But maybe there will be a gift for me at my journey's end."

The little boy's knee felt a tingle under the pressure of the friendly hand. He asked, "When, sir, shall you come to your journey's end?"

The man did not meet the child's gaze but solemnly replied, "Perhaps very soon!"

The little boy looked worried. He said, "You don't look happy about it. Don't you want to come to the end of your travels? Don't you want to reach home and see what gift they have for you?"

The man hesitated ever so slightly. "Yes," he said at last, "I want to reach home. But the gift, it may be too beautiful to bear or too heavy for me to carry. I suppose," his face looked pensive in the white moonlight, "I should be getting on, but you have made this birthday very wonderful, my lad."

Peeping down at the white cloth with its remnants of bread and cheese, thc little boy thought, "There seems to be as much as ever. He couldn't have liked it." Slantwise he contemplated the man's face, and suddenly he was swept with a burning sense of shame. The boy cried out, one word tumbling over the other, "You did not enjoy your food, sir! You have not had a true birthday feast. That is because I have been selfish and mean!" In a confessing tone, the boy continued, "I have a cake in my basket, a cake I was saving to eat alone, after you left. It is a cake of sifted flour and eggs and lemon and raisins, and I love cake! But now," the little boy's voice quivered, "I would not enjoy it if I ate it all alone, sir. I have desire to give the cake to you—as my birthday gift to you. Perhaps you will eat it later, when the chill of early morning has set in and you are on the road."

The man did not speak. His eyes were like stars now, instead of candles, as he watched his small host lift the cake from the basket and display its rich goodness. It was only when the lad extended it toward him that he broke into speech.

"Ah, my lad," he said, "you have sustained me with your bread, and we have drunk deep of the same cup. And now, we will share this cake, which shall be, through your bounty, my birthday cake. We will apportion it equally, and we will eat of it together, you and I. And, as I walk alone along the road, I shall remember a little lad's generosity."

Gravely, as if he were handling something infinitely precious, the man took the rich cake into his fingers. Carefully he divided it so the two sections were equal, and said, "Bless unto us this food, my Father." The little boy was startled, for there was no one else upon the hillside. Then the man continued, "This is the cake of life, lad. Enjoy it to the last crumb." So he and the little boy ate the cake together, and the little boy thought he had never tasted such good food. It was as if the cake's richness were, verily, the richness of life! As he licked the last crumbs from his fingers, he felt as if he were gathering force and vigor and purpose. In his mind, for no reason at all, he saw a picture of himself, big and handsome and brave, striding down the road with his weakness, the ugly hump, cast from him.

"It's like a vision," he said aloud. But when the man asked, "What do you mean, lad?" the boy hung his head and was unable to answer.

Indeed, he was silent so long that the man's hand came to rest lightly upon his shoulder—lightly, but oh so firmly! There was something in the touch that made tears hang on the little boy's eyelashes.

"Oh," he cried, "do not leave me, sir! We could be such friends, you and me. Come with me to my home and dwell with my family. My mother will bake many cakes for you, and my father will share with you of his plenty. And I, you can have my bed, and even this fringed shawl that I wear. Oh, do not journey on, sir! Stay with me, here in Bethlehem."

The man spoke, his voice like a great bell tolling over hill and valley. "I must go on. I must be about my Father's business. But I shall never leave you, my lad. Lo, I am with you always, even unto the end of the world!"

Bowing his head in his hands, covering his misted eyes, the little boy was aware of the man's firm fingers traveling up from his shoulder until they touched his hair. But now he couldn't speak, for a pulse drummed in his throat. When he raised his head, the man was gone, and the hillside empty, save for the shadows of the sheep, which were asleep.

The little boy sobbed once, sharply, with a sense of loss and then struggled to his feet. Only, he didn't have to struggle really, for there was a curious lightness about his body and a feeling of freshness and peace—a peace that transcended the pain of parting. But it was not until he pulled his fringed lamb's wool shawl tighter across his back, that he realized how straight he was standing and how straight he would now always stand.

Symbolism of Christmas Carols:

Carols represent the songs sung by the angels when they proclaimed the birth of the Savior.

Carol of the Christmas Morn

By Eugene Field

Carol of the Christmas morn—
Carol of the Christ-child born—
Carol to the list'ning sky
Till it echoes back again
"Glory be to God on high,
Peace on earth, good will tow'rd men!

Did You Know?

The largest group of carol singers was 25,272 people. The choir, Godswill Akpabio Unity Choir (Nigeria), sang a medley of "The First Noel," Joy to the World," "O Christmas Tree," "Hark! The Herald Angels Sing," "Once in Royal David's City," and "O Come All Ye Faithful" on 13 December 2014.

A Bright
and Happy
Christmas

On a Cold Christmas Night

By Lyman Hafen

Christmas Day was drawing heavily to a close. The bright light of morning had crossed over to the gray shadows of evening. Where there had been joy and laughter there was now complacency and silence. Where there had been energy and goodwill, now there was weariness and indifference. The day was ending like any other built up to be more than it can ever be.

Yet it had been a perfect Christmas morning. My seven-year-old daughter had awakened my wife and me well before daylight. Our Sara, a radiant, blue-eyed girl with curly brown hair, had been looking forward to Christmas with the full intensity of her heart for weeks. I felt that precious little heart beating like the breast of a captured bird as she snuggled in bed between us and began to make her case that it was time to get up.

"It's too early," I whispered. "Santa probably hasn't even been here yet."

"Oh yes! He's been here, Daddy," Sara said. "I already looked."

"That's against the rules," I said.

"I know," Sara said. "But I couldn't help it. It's taken so long for Christmas to come. We've got to get up and open the presents."

And so we did. Sara awoke her little brother Jake, and my wife and I followed them down the hallway and into the living room that was awash with the red, blue, and green lights of the Christmas tree. For two hours there was magic in that room. There was exultant laughter and blissful smiles; there was so much pent-up joy in the house I thought it might at any moment explode.

Now it was all a hollow echo. Our stomachs were full of turkey and rich pie, and the living room was strewn with piles of expensive gifts, but the day's early promise had vanished as completely as the brightly wrapped packages that had sat for weeks beneath the tree. Through the long holiday season it had all built to a high Christmas-morning crescendo, but now whatever it was we had been anticipating had come and gone, and we were left in its wake with wanting hearts and sagging spirits. Something very important was missing.

I lay fully extended in my recliner, looking up through the celestial window in our living room. Out in the gray twilight of dusk, I saw the first star of evening appear. As I struggled for an answer to what it was that was missing, I felt a gentle tap on my shoulder. It was Sara.

"Daddy?" she said.

I snapped out of my trance and turned my head toward her. She was so close that the tip of my nose nearly brushed the tip of hers. The brilliant light of the morning had gone out of her eyes, but they still managed to hold all the hope of the world. And in those longing eyes, in that revealing moment, I saw all eternity.

"I wish Christmas wouldn't be over," she said.

I sat up in the chair and lifted my forlorn little daughter onto my lap. She curled into a ball in my arms and snuggled her head beneath my chin. I held her tight and felt as if I could hold her safely away from the cold world out there, away from the distress, the disappointment, the disillusionment of this life. In that quiet

moment I realized that I could also be shielded from those very things. My Father could protect my heart from that emptiness even better than my arms could keep it from touching Sara. The quiet whisper of the Spirit overwhelmed me. My heart had never burned so bright with love, nor had it ever been so charged with a desire for that love to fill the heart of another. I looked out the window again at the single shining star in the heavens. I wanted to believe that what Sara was asking was possible, that Christmas didn't have to be over.

"I can't wait for Christmas to come again," she said. "I wish it were tomorrow."

"I wish it were too," I said. "But it's three hundred and sixty-four days until Christmas comes again."

"Too many days," Sara whimpered. "I can't wait that long."

My eyes were still fixed on the bright evening star when a distinct understanding came into my heart. Christmas did not have to be over. It never has to be over. The answer was obvious to me now, and a way to share that answer with my daughter came clearly to my mind.

"Let me tell you a story," I said. "It's a story about a Christmas Day long ago when Grandpa Great was a little boy."

"Grandpa Great who is almost ready to die?" Sara asked.

"Yes. Grandpa Great who lives in the care center and can't get out of bed."

Sara tilted her head back and looked up at me in wonderment. "Grandpa Great was a little boy?" she asked.

"Of course he was," I said. "And he looked forward to Christmas just as much as you do. And he didn't want Christmas to end any more than you do either. And one Christmas he learned how to be as happy on every day of the year as he was on Christmas morning."

"Tell me the story, Daddy," Sara said.

And I did . . .

Jesse lived on a farm a mile from town in a high mountain valley. It was many years ago, before there were buses to carry little boys and girls to school or tractors to plow the fields. In the spring and summertime Jesse helped his father with farm chores. He would heft the heavy harnesses off their hooks in the tack shed and carry them out to the barnyard, where his father would drape them over the shoulders and backs of old Buck and Dan, the workhorse team that pulled the plow in spring and the mower and hay wagon in summer. During those long, sun-drenched days that started before daylight and ended well after dusk, Jesse drove the team and wagon through the fields as his father and two hired men pitched hay onto the wagon bed. Then they would ride the wagon to the barn, and Jesse would help pitch hay into the loft until his arms were so tired he thought they might fall off. Day after day, week after week, they would store up the hay for winter.

"We've got to make hay while the sun shines," Jesse's father would say if Jesse looked the least bit like he might complain. "Fall will be here before we know it, and then the snow will fly."

Jesse both dreaded and anticipated the arrival of fall. He dreaded it because it meant he had to go back to school, which meant—rain, snow, or shine—he had to walk the long mile to the little gray schoolhouse in town and then back again each day. Yet in another part of his heart he joyously anticipated fall's arrival because he knew that once the potatoes were in and the harvest was finished, his father would take the old .30-30 rifle down from its rack above the fireplace and they would pull their chairs up to the kitchen table on a golden autumn evening and clean the gun and start to talk about where the big bucks would be running this year.

For Jesse there were two mornings in the year that stood out gloriously from all the rest. One was the morning when he and his father would roll out of their warm beds and set off into the cold darkness in search of their winter supply of venison. The other was Christmas, when Jesse hoped, year after year, to get a rifle of his own.

Jesse often dreamed of the hunt, imagining how it would be that year. Then, when it would finally come, on a magical October morning long before daylight, he would follow his father out through the moon-glazed snow. He would be bundled in his sheepskin-and-denim coat and his cap with the flaps that pulled down over his ears. The icy snow would crunch beneath his boots, and every few steps a boot would break through the crisp top layer of snow as if through a pane of glass. Jesse's leg would sink to the knee, and he would lurch forward against the painfully sharp edge of the snow. Then he would awkwardly pull himself free again and eagerly press forward, undaunted.

By daylight Jesse and his father would be perched on a granite pinnacle above a deep draw in the mountains east of the farm. There they would sit in the silence of the bone-cold morning, looking down into the draw and gazing out across the beautiful valley where the farm lay under a rolling blanket of snow. Before long the deer would begin to move. And finally, after what seemed an eternity, a majestic buck—one that looked suitable to feed the family all winter—would appear out of an oak thicket. Jesse would watch in awe as his father raised the rifle to his shoulder and, with one perfect shot, secured his family's meat supply for the long, hard winter to come.

Jesse admired his father with all his heart. More than anything, he wanted to be just like him. And that is why, more than anything, Jesse wanted a .30-30 rifle of his own that Christmas. He had begun asking for a rifle when he was seven years old. Every fall between the morning of the deer hunt and the morning of Christmas, Jesse would ask the same question each day. First he would ask his mother. Then he would ask his father. "Can I have a rifle for Christmas this year?"

Each time he asked the question, he got one of two answers. "I don't think you're quite old enough yet," or, "We'll see."

Then Christmas morning would come, and Jesse would jump out of his comfortable covers and bundle into his stiff clothes. With the milk bucket in one hand and the coal-oil lantern in the other, he'd make his way out through the icy darkness to the barn where it was his responsibility to milk the cow and feed old Buck and Dan and the broodmares before coming back in to Christmas. In the meantime his father would be down at the stock pens feeding the other cows.

When the chores were all done, the family would meet at the foot of the Christmas tree in the parlor, and Jesse would begin to rustle through the presents Santa had miraculously left the night before. Each year he would pull all the beautifully wrapped packages out from under the tree, praying that somewhere in the pile he would come upon a long, narrow package. And each year his high hopes would eventually dwindle to sharp disappointment as he opened the last of the presents.

Then came the summer when Jesse turned twelve. He was getting bigger every day, and every day he was able to do more to help his father. He took pride in not only driving the team and wagon during hay loading, but in jumping off and helping load the wagon as they made their way down through the forever fields. Jesse's father seemed pleased with his son, and at least once a day he would praise the boy for his good work.

Jesse knew things were truly beginning to change the morning his father put his hand on Jesse's shoulder and told him he had something very important to talk to him about. As they lay in the shade under the hay wagon after eating their lunch that day, his father propped himself up on his elbow and looked at Jesse thoughtfully, the way he looked at a man when he was talking business with him.

"I'm very pleased with the way you help me," his father said. "You're working hard enough now that I should be paying you. I wish I could pay you with money, but we don't have much cash, and what we do have must be saved for necessities. So I want to offer you something else. The new broodmare is going to have a colt this winter. When the colt is born, it will be yours."

Jesse's heart swelled like a balloon, and he sat up with such excitement that his head bumped the bottom of the hay wagon. He rubbed his head and started laughing, and his father began to laugh as well. "You mean the colt will be my own?" Jesse asked when he finally stopped laughing. "My very own?"

"Your very own," his father assured him.

"Could I break him myself and ride him to school?" He had never felt quite so excited, so absolutely grateful.

"Yes," his father said. "He will be yours to do with as you wish, as long as you take care of him properly."

"I'll take care of him better than any horse has ever been cared for," Jesse promised. "You'll see, Dad. I'll break him right and I'll comb his mane and tail every day and I'll see that his feet are kept trim and I'll feed him every morning and night and I'll never run him back to the barn—" Jesse paused to take a breath. "You'll see, Dad. You'll see."

"I know you will, son. And the broodmare will need special care this fall and winter," his father replied. "I didn't know she was with foal when I made the deal with the old horse trader from the desert last spring. The good news is that she's going to have a colt. The bad news is that the colt will be born in the dead of winter, which is a difficult thing up here in the cold mountain country."

"I'll take care of the mare, Dad," Jesse said. "I'll take the best care of her, and everything will be fine no matter how cold it gets this winter."

The rest of the summer passed in a blaze of glory. Every night Jesse lay in bed looking at the dark ceiling of his room, lost in a jumble of thought. He imagined a beautiful blaze-faced colt jumping and prancing out across the meadow. He could see himself next summer, breaking the colt to halter, and the summer after that saddling it for the first time, and then in the fall, climbing up into the saddle and riding his own horse to school. Imagine that—no more walking the long mile to town, but every day riding proudly into the school yard on a long-legged, wonderful horse.

Before he knew it, the soft summer days had stiffened into the crisp days of autumn. Every morning before school Jesse hustled out to the barn to milk the cow and feed old Buck and Dan and the broodmare. The mare was getting larger and larger, and every morning Jesse would drop down onto his chest and roll under the bottom board of the stall. Then he'd stand next to the mare and rub her sleek neck and talk to her at length about the colt inside her and how much he was looking forward to it being born. The mare would turn her head and look at him through her satiny black eyes and nuzzle her face into the warmth of his jacket. Then Jesse would hurry back to the house for breakfast.

On a golden autumn evening that October, Jesse's father hefted the .30-30 rifle down from above the fireplace and laid it on the kitchen table. The two of them sat down, and Jesse watched as his father cleaned the gun in preparation for the deer hunt the next morning. His father whistled, and his eyes were bright. Jesse thought he had never seen his father this happy before. It had been a good season; the hay loft was full and the potato yield had been better than ever and prices were strong. The excitement of the moment lasted clear through the evening, and Jesse couldn't wait to greet the dawn.

The next morning before daylight, Jesse and his father climbed to the top of a rocky ledge that overlooked a promising draw where deer might well appear as soon as day broke. As they waited in the cold morning quiet, Jesse asked his father if he could look through the rifle's sights, and his father willingly handed him the gun. Jesse brought the butt of the rifle to his shoulder and hoisted the heavy barrel into position. He was pleased at how comfortably the rifle fit him. He was no longer too small for the gun, and his father seemed to notice.

"Won't be long and you'll be the one who bags our winter meat," his father said. Jesse took this as the perfect opportunity to ask the question that hung on the edge of his tongue.

"Do you think I could get a rifle for Christmas this year?" Jesse asked with even more expectation than usual.

"Maybe so," his father said.

Jesse could not believe what he'd heard. It was not, "We'll see," or, "You're not quite big enough yet." It was, "Maybe so." The words filled Jesse's heart with wonder and hope, and he looked at his father excitedly, his eyes wide.

"Maybe so," his father repeated with a smile as he clapped Jesse on the back.

Now it was almost impossible to wait for Christmas. Jesse considered himself the luckiest boy in all the world. On feet light as clouds he floated the mile to school each day. After school, he floated all the way home. The thought of having his very own rifle began to upstage every other thought in his mind. Though he continued to check the broodmare and place fresh straw in her stall each morning, and though the last thing he did before going to bed at night was to check her again, he grew less and less concerned for the mare and more and more enthralled with the idea of getting his own rifle. Almost every night he dreamed of beautiful blue-barreled rifles, and he constantly prayed for the days to pass more quickly.

Finally it was Christmas Eve. The day passed as slowly as a melting icicle, and Jesse spent most of it tromping through the low hills east of the farm, imagining himself with his own gun. He paid little mind to the mare that day. He had grown weary of waiting for the colt to come, and his thoughts glowed with the vision of a brand-new rifle. As the day drew to a close, Jesse knelt in prayer with his mother and father, but his heart pounded so hard and his head was so full of anticipation that he did not hear the words his father prayed.

"Help us remember Him before whom a few gifts were laid in that lowly manger," Jesse's father prayed. "Help us to remember the many gifts He has spread before us, thereby providing an unending Christmas."

As Jesse was caught up in visions of stalking regal bucks with his handsome new rifle, his father continued to pray for the true spirit of Christmas—for the gift of being able to think of others more than self, for the blessing of being able to find joy in giving, and for the ability to understand and appreciate the most important gift of Christmas.

The sound of the words entered Jesse's ears, but their meaning did not register in his heart. He was too full of exhilaration and too swollen with expectation to allow the words of his father's prayer to settle into his soul.

He went to bed that night with his heart galloping in his chest and his mind racing with thoughts of hunting. Not long after Jesse had gone to bed, his father came into the room and sat down on the bed beside him. Jesse saw his father's form as a dark silhouette against the pallid moonlight sifting in from the window.

"Jesse?" his father said as he laid his heavy hand on Jesse's shoulder. "The mare looks awfully close to foaling. Be sure to check her and change her straw first thing in the morning before you come in for Christmas."

"I will," Jesse said.

His father patted him on the shoulder then walked out of the room while Jesse lay there thinking. The mare had seemed ready to foal for days, and every morning for the past week he had plodded out to the barn to check her. Every morning it was the same—the mare standing in the corner of the stall and no colt. Jesse had grown impatient with the morning routine that began with excitement and hope but ended with disappointment. He was pleased that on this night, at least, he could look forward to something else in the morning—and with all his heart he hoped it would be a brand-new .30-30 rifle.

On Christmas morning Jesse awoke as he always did in the cold, early darkness. As he rolled out of the warm covers, he heard the back door softly shut, and he knew his father was already on his way down to the stock pens to feed. Jesse hurried now, realizing he would have to work quickly to finish his chores and get back to the house by the time his father did. He wanted to start opening presents as soon as possible, and the only thing standing between him and the presents were the chores to be done in the barn.

He pulled on his frigid pants, shirt, socks, and boots, then bundled into his coat and put on his cap, pulling the flaps down over his ears. In the kitchen he grabbed his deerskin gloves and lit the coal-oil lamp. With the lamp in his right hand and the milk bucket in his left, out the door into the frosty morning he went. He trotted down the icy path to the barn, catching his balance now and then as his feet slid this way and that. He unlatched the big barn door and slowly pulled it open. The door moaned and groaned in protest of its frozen hinges.

Just inside the door stood the milk cow in her milking stanchion, waiting to be fed her hay and offer up her milk. Jesse hung the lantern on a hook by the door and scurried down to the far end of the barn to the horse stalls. Old Buck's stall was first, then Dan's, then the broodmare's. With the lantern at the other end of the barn, the light was gray and dim.

Jesse went straight to the broodmare's stall and peered skeptically through the boards. He could see the dark shape of the mare; she was standing in the corner like she always did in the morning, and he immediately noted, as he had already mostly expected, that she was standing alone. He didn't give it another thought. There were other things on his mind this morning. His heart leapt as he imagined the rifle in his hands, the heft of its ample weight, the crack of its shot, and the feel of its kick against his shoulder. The mare would have her colt when she would have it. Today was the day for the rifle.

Quickly and with an air of impatience, Jesse tossed a pitchfork full of hay beneath the bottom board of the mare's stall. He was in too big a hurry to change the straw; it was something he could do later. He fed Old Buck and Dan, then hustled back to the other end of the barn and began to milk the cow. His palms and fingers worked in perfect rhythm, and the musty, cold barn filled with the rapid *spish-spish-spish* of his milking. Never had he filled the bucket so swiftly. He set the lantern and the full, steaming bucket of milk in the snow just outside the barn door. Then he began to push the groaning door closed. As he did so, he thought he heard a sound from the far end of the barn. It was a strange sound, and he stopped silent for a moment and listened carefully in the crisp, still air. There was no more sound until he started to close the door again, and in his haste to get up to the house and open his presents he convinced himself that all he had heard was the moaning of the heavy barn door.

A ribbon of steam trailed from Jesse's mouth as he huffed up the icy path to the house. The promise of Christmas Day was beginning to present itself with a faint hint of light over the mountains to the east. At the house his mother had a cup of steaming cocoa waiting. He sipped it carefully, warming inside as his heart boomed harder and harder in anticipation of discovering what lay beneath the tree in the parlor. His father returned from the stock pens and asked Jesse how the mare was. "Same as every morning," Jesse answered.

Without further delay they went in and started opening presents. Jesse opened a large package and pulled out a splendid, blue denim coat. The coat, lined with sheepskin, was just like his old one, but bigger and new. From another package he pulled a pair of glorious-smelling leather boots, and from another, a bright new pocketknife.

One by one the presents disappeared from beneath the tree until the hard truth finally settled on Jesse. There was not a package remaining under the tree—

even with the greatest leap of faith or imagination—that could possibly contain a rifle inside.

Jesse stood up and walked slump-shouldered across the room and sat down heavily on a pinewood chair. He buried his face in his arms, and his mother and father came over and knelt at either side of him.

"You're not quite old enough for a rifle yet," his mother said in a consoling voice.

"The day will come when you will have your rifle," his father promised.

There was a long pause before Jesse finally raised his head. His eyes were moist, and his face was creased with sadness. "I wanted a rifle more than anything," he said sorrowfully.

"I know you did, son," his father said regretfully. "But this was not the year for you to get a rifle. Someday you'll understand."

"It's not fair," Jesse said. "Why couldn't I get it this Christmas? You said I might be able to get it this year. It's too long to wait another year."

"You've received such wonderful gifts this Christmas," Jesse's mother said. "Just look at what you've been given."

Jesse raised his glistening eyes and took stock of all the gifts and bright wrapping strung about the room. But he could not see what his mother saw. He could only see what wasn't there, and he buried his face in his shirtsleeve and sobbed uncontrollably.

The rest of the day Jesse thought of nothing but his misfortune. He bundled up in his new clothes, tucked his new pocketknife into his pocket, and with his shoulders hunched against the bitter wind, he set out toward the mountains to the east.

For hours he slogged through the heavy snow, weaving in and out of the tall pines. By midday he found himself sitting on a tower of rock overlooking a magnificent ravine where he imagined the sight of a grand buck prancing down through the glittering trees. But there were no deer in the draws now. They had all moved to lower country. Jesse sat there in the brittle air feeling sorry for himself, thinking of nothing except how unfair it was that he hadn't gotten a rifle for Christmas. His heart was so full of disappointment there was no room for anything else but gloom.

It was late afternoon before he got back to the house. He stomped the snow off his boots on the back porch and stepped through the door into the warm kitchen. The house was full of the smell of turkey and pies, and his mother immediately encircled him in her arms, wondering where he had been and if he was all right. She scolded him for not telling her where he was going or how long he would be gone.

"Where's Dad?" Jesse asked after apologizing.

"He went down to the barn just now," his mother answered.

A dark feeling seized Jesse's heart. Since he had shut the barn door that morning, he had not once thought of the mare. He had been so swallowed up in self-pity he had completely forgotten his responsibility.

Out the door he flew, and down the path he scampered to the barn. He unlatched the heavy door, and with all his might he tugged it open. Soft evening light washed into the barn. Jesse stood in the doorway and peered all the way down to the horse stalls. What he saw in that moment was something he would never forget—not in this life or through all eternity. He saw it with his eyes and at the same time saw it with his heart, and it left him frozen, confounded, and afraid in the bitter-cold doorway of the barn.

Just outside the mare's stall, in a pitiful little heap, lay a motionless newborn colt. Next to the colt knelt Jesse's father.

Jesse started to move but his legs were numb with shock, and he fell in a lump on the icy ground. He gathered himself up, hurried down to the stall, and fell to his knees at the side of a delicate red colt with a beautiful white star on its forehead. Its eyes were closed, and it lay perfectly still in the gray light of the barn. Jesse's heart fell like a rock to the bottom of his stomach. He ran his fingers through the colt's soft coat, and he started to cry. He bent over the colt and cried harder and harder and stroked it more and more until, in a moment of simple promise, he felt a hint of warmth pass into his fingers, and he saw the colt's little belly slowly lift and fall in the faintest motion of breathing.

"Is he alive?" Jesse asked.

"Barely," his father said.

"Why is he outside the stall?"

Jesse's father pointed to the space between the bottom board of the stall and the straw-covered ground. It was the space Jesse liked to roll through, rather than open the gate, when entering the stall. It was also the space he tossed the mare's hay through when he fed her every morning and evening. Looking through the gap now, Jesse could see the mare's front knees and hooves prancing nervously on the other side of the fence. He looked up and saw the mare's face hovering over the top board of the stall, her terror-filled eyes glaring down on him. Then he suddenly realized what had happened.

When the mare had lain down to give birth to the colt, she must have settled next to the edge of the stall, and the colt had come into this world beneath the bottom board of the fence—coldly and cruelly separated from its mother. In the same instant he realized what had happened, he comprehended his guilt. The mare in the stall, the colt outside the stall, and both incapable of doing anything about it. Jesse was overcome with shame and remorse. There lay a helpless colt, his colt, separated from its mother and in need of warmth and milk, and it was Jesse's fault for not being there when he should have been.

"How long has he been here?" Jesse asked.

"I don't know," his father said. "Judging by how weak he is, and how dry his coat is, and how much tromping the mare has done in her stall, I would say he was probably born about the time we were opening our presents this morning."

Jesse ran his fingers down the colt's neck and admitted to himself how dry its coat was. His father was right. The colt had been in the world long enough for the moistness of its birth to have thoroughly dried. Jesse's heart sank further as he was forced to admit that the colt had probably been born early that morning while he was opening his presents in the house and that it had lain there through all of Christmas Day, through all the hours that Jesse had sulked about in the mountains. The handsome little red colt had lain there in the frigid air all day. It was a miracle the colt was still alive and hadn't starved.

Still alive! Jesse's thoughts began churning. "What can we do?" he cried. "We can save him, can't we?"

"I'm afraid it might be too late," his father said. "He's too weak to stand and nurse, and I don't know if the mare will even accept him now."

Jesse instinctively jumped to his feet. Without another thought he ran to the house, a white billow of steam trailing him. From the pantry shelf he grabbed the clear glass bottle and rubber nipple he had used to feed an orphaned calf the previous spring. As he trotted back down the frozen path to the barn, Jesse's eyes rose to the horizon above the mountains, and he saw the first star of the evening. It was a fleeting glance, but the image of the star burned a deep imprint on his heart. When he got back to the barn his father had already haltered the mare and led her out of the stall. The mare stammered around her newborn colt, sniffing and nuzzling it. Strangely enough, she now seemed only mildly interested in the colt, as if it didn't belong to her.

Without even asking his father for advice, Jesse began to stroke the mare and talk to her softly. He worked his way slowly and carefully to her milk sack and prayed that she would allow him to fill the bottle with her warm, life-giving milk. It took several tries and more patience than Jesse had ever mustered, but finally the mare relented and stood still long enough for him to squirt the bottle full of her milk.

He then sat down in the straw and lifted the colt's dainty head onto his lap. He teased the colt's mouth with the nipple for a long, long time before it finally opened its eyes and began to lick at the bead of milk with its dry tongue. Eventually, with some coaching from his father, Jesse finally coaxed the colt to take the nipple into its mouth, and once the starving baby horse began to suck, the bottle quickly emptied.

Jesse repeated the process two more times, milking the mare and nursing the colt. Then his father told him it was enough. The two of them lifted the colt and carried it through the gate into the stall and laid it down on the soiled and grungy straw that Jesse hadn't bothered to change that morning. They led the mare back into the stall and shut the gate. Then Jesse's father said, "We need to leave them alone now."

Later that night they came back and found the colt still lying in the same place and in the same position where they had placed him earlier. "We'll have to stay with him," Jesse's father said. "We'll have to hand-feed him every half hour or so until he's strong enough to get up and feed himself."

"I'll stay with him," Jesse said. "I'll bring my bedroll out and take care of him until morning."

And that is what Jesse did.

While the rest of the world went to bed, languidly leaving one Christmas Day behind and longingly dreaming of another three hundred sixty-four days away, Jesse stayed up all night with his newborn colt and did everything in his power to keep the slight and frail animal alive until morning. Every thirty minutes he milked the mare and nursed the colt. Between feedings he fell onto his bedroll next to the colt and rested and prayed. He prayed that the colt would live, and he pleaded for forgiveness for neglecting his duties and promised his Heavenly Father he would never be selfish again. As the night passed into early morning, Jesse curled up close to the colt and rubbed its neck and back. He talked to the colt in a soft whisper and told it he was sorry for the way he had acted. "You're the best

Christmas gift I could have ever asked for," Jesse said. "Please don't die."

By the light of the coal-oil lamp, Jesse looked into the colt's wondrously dark eyes, and his heart burned with love. He noticed again the beautiful white star on the colt's forehead, and he remembered the lone star over the mountains he had seen the evening before. "If you live," Jesse whispered to the colt, "I will call you Star. And I promise I will take care of you better than any colt has ever been taken care of. I will never forget you again."

As the light of a new day began to filter into the barn, the gangly little horse started fumbling to his feet. Before long he was standing crooked and wobbly on delicate legs, and soon thereafter was feeding himself at his mother's side.

Jesse watched it all with a grateful heart and thanked his Heavenly Father for what he had learned that night. During the long night there had been plenty of time for Jesse to contemplate the gifts that made Christmas so exciting, the fleeting gifts that came and went just as Christmas Day itself did. He thought of gifts anxiously anticipated that only ended up hanging on a wall or sitting on a shelf. But he thought even more about the gifts that were his every day—of parents who loved him, legs to walk on and food to eat, the beautiful mountain valley where he lived, and the warm and comfortable home where he was sheltered every day. And he thought about the gift that started Christmas two thousand years ago—the gift that was signaled by the bright star over Bethlehem. The gift of God's son. These gifts, he came to understand that night, were the most precious of all, and they were gifts that were his every day.

Never again did Jesse allow Christmas to swallow him up in selfish concerns. On that long-ago night after Christmas, he came to understand that the most important gifts were the ones given from the heart, the ones given without thought of self.

And as he grew older, Jesse taught his own family that if they would forget about receiving and concern themselves only with giving, Christmas would never be a disappointment; Christmas would never be over . . .

Sara lay motionless in my lap. There was silence for a very long time. Finally she looked up at me, and my heart warmed as I noticed the light that had returned to her eyes.

"When Star got big, did Grandpa Great ride him to school every day?" Sara asked.

"He certainly did," I said. "And when Grandpa Great turned fourteen, he finally got a beautiful new rifle for Christmas. But that rifle was never so precious to him as his horse named Star. Jesse rode the horse everywhere he went, and every time he looked at that big bright star on his horse's forehead, he thought of what he learned on the night after Christmas when he was twelve years old. And at night when he looked up at the stars in the heavens, he thought of them all as Christmas stars, and he remembered that as long as he cared more about others than about himself, every day of the year could be Christmas."

Sara smiled at me and wrapped her arms around my neck. I looked again out the upper window of the living room and saw that the first star of evening had been joined by myriad others. I held Sara tight and whispered in her ear, "Do you still wish Christmas Day wouldn't end?"

She released her hold on me, tilted her head back, and looked at me with all the sincerity of her heart. "No," she said.

"Then what do you wish?" I asked.

"I wish we could go visit Grandpa Great."

And we did.

Once within a Lowly Stable

Once within a lowly stable,
Where the sheep and oxen lay,
A loving mother laid her baby
In a manger filled with hay.
Mary was the mother there,
And the Christ that baby fair.

God sent us this loving baby
From his home in heav'n above,
And he came down to show all people
How to help and how to love.
This is why the angels bright
Sang for joy that Christmas night.

Best known for co-writing with her sister, Mildred J. Hill, Patty Smith Hill helped craft the tune to "Good Morning to All," which became an equally popular song, "Happy Birthday to You." She later wrote this song for the Christmas season. Patty had a creative approach to many of her passions. Besides writing songs, she also used her imaginative curriculum to lay the foundation for the standards of kindergarten education, which would later be adopted into the United States public school system.

It Came upon the Midnight Clear

It came upon the midnight clear,
That glorious song of old,
From angels bending near the earth
To touch their harps of gold:
"Peace on the earth, good will to men
From heav'n's all-gracious King."
The world in solemn stillness lay
To hear the angels sing.

Still thru the cloven skies they come
With peaceful wings unfurled,
And still their heav'nly music floats
O'er all the weary world.
Above its sad and lowly plains
They bend on hov'ring wing,
And ever o'er its babel sounds
The blessed angels sing.

For lo! the days are hast'ning on,
By prophets seen of old,
When with the ever-circling years
Shall come the time foretold,
When the new heav'n and earth shall own
The Prince of Peace their King,
And the whole world send back the song
Which now the angels sing.

The lyrics of "It Came upon the Midnight Clear" were originally written as a poem in 1849 by Edmund Sears, who was reflecting on some of his melancholy experiences as a Unitarian minister in Wayland, Massachusetts. Sears had graduated from the Harvard Divinity School and had preached as a missionary in Toledo, Ohio, before becoming a minister in Massachusetts, where he served congregations in three different areas. Oliver Wendell Holmes once said that the hymn was "one of the finest and most beautiful ever written." Inspired by the poem, musician Richard Storrs Willis—an editor and critic for the *New York Tribune* who had studied music in Europe with Felix Mendelssohn—composed the music to the carol in 1859. Prior to Willis's composition, the poem was sung to a tune adapted from a traditional English melody.

Here comes a big hearty wish for a Merry Christmas.

Fence Mending

By Fred Crowley

It was a cold December morning only three days before Christmas, and Carl was puzzled. He had just returned from an overnight trip to the cattle auction in Dalhart and was standing at his pasture fence. The tracks in the snow told a story that he couldn't believe. It was obvious that while he was away, his cattle had broken through the fence and someone had herded them back in and neatly spliced the damaged wires. He could see who that someone was by the footprints tracked through the snow. Only one man in this whole valley had a size seventeen boot: Alan Sanders.

And that's why Carl was puzzled. Why would Alan Sanders, of all people, fix his fence? He hadn't spoken to Alan for eight years, and it was all because of those four blasted tires and ninety bales of hay.

Four tires! After eight years, four tires didn't seem like much, and he shook his head in wonderment at his foolish pride. He had been partners with Alan back then. In those days, they'd shared farm equipment and worked as a team to provide for their families. Together they'd produced the finest alfalfa hay in the county.

When the farmwork was slow during the Christmas season, they would all get together and enjoy good food and good company—but not anymore. That was before the day of the bales and the tires. He could remember every detail of that day perfectly, because he had relived it over and over again in his mind every day since then.

Alan had bought tires for his own truck out of the partnership's hay profits. Carl had objected, saying that the money for the tires should have come from Alan's personal account. "No," Alan had argued, "it's an equipment expense." The argument was a silly thing, and it should never have gone as far as it did, but by the time it was over, it was too late. Pride had driven a deadly wedge into the friendship.

That very afternoon, Carl had backed his trailer up to Alan's barn and taken ninety bales of hay as repayment for the tires. Carl and Alan had not spoken to each other since. Each man withdrew his equipment from the alliance, and a lifelong friendship withered and died like a drought-stricken crop.

Although their wives, Jennie and June, tried to mend the breach, pride had kept both men from giving in. Carl had missed Alan's friendship many times through the years, but every time that thought came into his mind, he brushed it away by reminding himself that it was Alan who had wronged him first.

But on this day, during the Christmas season, as he looked at those tracks in the snow, the words of the Lord came back to his mind for the hundredth time since he'd read them last Thursday from the eleventh chapter of St. Mark: "Forgive, if ye have ought against any: that your Father also which is in heaven may forgive you your trespasses. But if ye do not forgive, neither will your Father which is in heaven forgive your trespasses."

Those words seemed like a warm breath blowing across his cold and hardened heart, softening it and restoring it to life. In an instant Carl knew what he

had to do. He turned from the pasture, walked quickly to his pickup, and drove directly to his barn.

Late that afternoon, Alan Sanders heard a light knock at his door. When he answered, he saw Carl Pearson waiting silently on the front porch looking down at the welcome mat.

"What do you want?" Alan asked quietly.

"Can you spare a few minutes? I've got something I need to say," Carl replied.

Alan stood silent for a few beats of his heart. "I suppose so," he said finally as he stepped away from the door and motioned to the couch. Carl slowly removed his hat, wiped his boots, and stepped into the room that was filled with so many happy memories of the past. He sat uneasily on the edge of the couch. He noticed that Alan was wearing large slippers and saw that he limped as he moved to a chair. Carl held the brim of his hat with both hands and worked it around and around as he spoke. "Alan." He cleared his throat. "I wanted to thank you for fixing my fence yesterday. I appreciate it."

Alan frowned in surprise. "What fence? I haven't left this house for five days. I dropped a piece of pipe on my foot last week, and today's the first time I've been able to walk on it at all."

"But I thought . . ." Carl sat confused for a moment and almost backed out of his plan, but at the last second he decided to plow on.

"Alan, I'm here about something else too. It's about the hay. I was wrong. I've returned the ninety bales. They're outside on my trailer. I'm sorry I've been so foolish."

Alan lowered his gaze and stared at the floor for a few moments while he worked his jaw muscles.

Four tires and ninety bales of hay. What had it cost their friendship? Six graduations, four weddings, three funerals, two grandkids born, and eight years. Eight wasted years! Eight Christmas seasons, come and gone.

"I can't take those bales, Carl. It wouldn't be right . . . 'cuz I've been a fool too. I'm sorry myself."

"But, Alan, it's not my hay! I can't keep it. That would be wrong. It's out there loaded on the trailer right now. I've got to do something with it . . ."

Christmas morning found old farmer Tom Crawford standing in his dilapidated barn staring at ninety bales of new hay of a quality he'd never been able to afford. There were two sets of tracks leading from the stack out of the barn, side by side in the dust—a pair of boots, and a pair of what must have been very large slippers. Propped against the bales was an empty feed sack with a message printed in bold block letters:

Merry Christmas, Tom!
From two old fools

Tom Crawford crumpled to his knees and offered his quavering thanks to God for this wondrous gift that would get his struggling calves through the winter.

And somewhere in the rising Christmas dawn, unheard by Tom as he prayed, there was a whisper of white satin robes as angels hastened to tell the story of two good men and their glorious Christmas deed . . . and of two good women, Jennie and June—their wives—who had mastered the art of fence repair in the pasture while wearing the size seventeen boots they'd sneaked from Alan's closet.

"It is possible for Christ to be born in men's lives, and when such an experience actually happens, a man is 'in Christ'—Christ is 'formed' in him. This presupposes that we take Christ into our hearts and make Him the living contemporary of our lives. He is not just a general truth or a fact in history, but the Savior of men everywhere and at all times. When we strive to be Christlike, He is 'formed' in us; if we open the door, He will enter; if we seek His counsel, He will counsel us. For Christ to be 'formed' in us, we must have a belief in Him and in His Atonement. Such a belief in Christ and the keeping of His commandments are not restraints upon us. By these, men are set free. This Prince of Peace waits to give peace of mind, which may make each of us a channel of that peace."

~ Howard W. Hunter

Let It Snow

- The Guinness Book of World Records states that the largest reported snowflake was fifteen inches across and eight inches thick!

- The largest snowball fight was held between 5,834 people in Seattle, Washington, on January 12, 2013.

- The tallest snowman was built by residents of Bethel, Maine. It took a period of one month to achieve the height of 122 feet 1 inch.

- The record for the most people making snow angels at the same time and place is 8,962 people. The event was organized by the State Historical Society of North Dakota in 2007.

- About 80 percent of all the freshwater on earth is frozen, accounting for about 12 percent of the planet's surface.

- Not every heavy snowstorm is a blizzard. A storm is classified as a blizzard only if it meets three specific criteria: winds must blow at least 35 miles an hour, visibility must be less than a quarter of a mile, and the storm must last at least three hours. Other specific classifications of snowstorms include a snowsquall (heavy snowfall, strong winds, but only last a short time) and a snowburst (intense snowfall that results in a rapid accumulation of snow).

- A typical snowflake falls at an average speed of 1.5 mph, but some "rimed crystals," or particles of supercooled water, can travel as fast as 9 mph!

- In March of 1992, after a record-breaking winter of snowfall—more than 162.5 inches—the Syracuse Common Council in New York unanimously declared: "Be it resolved, on behalf of the snow-weary citizens of the city of Syracuse, any further snowfall is expressly outlawed in the city of Syracuse until December 24, 1992." Unfortunately for them, the new law didn't work; it snowed two more inches only two days later.

- Every year the World Ice Championships are held in Fairbanks, Alaska. It began in 1990 as a week-long competition between eight teams. Now it

has grown to a month-long challenge featuring seventy teams. One unique aspect that makes this festival family friendly is the Frozen Kids Park, which is just like any other playground except carved completely from ice. It includes rides, slides, and mazes for everyone to enjoy.

- "White Christmas" is an Irving Berlin song written around 1940. There have been more than five hundred versions of it recorded, including some in several different languages, but the most popular version is the 1942 version from Bing Crosby. It has sold more than 100 million copies worldwide. In 1999, National Public Radio compiled a list of the hundred most important American musical works of the twentieth century, Crosby's "White Christmas" made the list at number two (behind only Judy Garland's "Over the Rainbow").

HOMEMADE SNOWDROPS

1 cup butter
½ cup confectioners' sugar plus
1 cup for dusting
½ teaspoon salt
1 cup finely chopped almonds
1 Tablespoon vanilla extract
2 cups sifted all–purpose flour

1. Cream butter in a mixing bowl. Gradually add sugar (½ cup) and salt. Continue creaming until light and fluffy.
2. Add nuts and vanilla extract. Blend in flour gradually. Mix thoroughly.
3. Shape into teaspoonful balls. Place on ungreased cookie sheet. Bake at 325 degrees F. for 15–20 minutes.
4. Sprinkle some of the confectioners' sugar over cookies while still on the sheet. Cool before removing from cookie sheet.
5. Place some confectioner's sugar in a plastic bag and place some of the cookies inside. Gently shake well so the sugar completely coats the cookies.

CHRISTMAS MACARONS

1 cup slivered almonds
2 cup confectioners' sugar
3 large egg whites
¼ teaspoon salt
8 drops green liquid food coloring
¼ teaspoon almond extract
4 ounces bittersweet chocolate

1. Preheat oven to 300 degrees F. Line 2 large cookie sheets with parchment paper.
2. In food processor with knife blade attached, process almonds and 1 cup sugar until powdery, occasionally scraping bowl with rubber spatula. Add remaining sugar; pulse until combined. Transfer to large bowl.
3. In mixer bowl, beat egg whites and salt on medium speed until soft peaks form. Beat in food coloring and almond extract. Increase speed to high and beat just until stiff peaks form when beaters are lifted. With rubber spatula, fold egg whites into almond mixture until blended. Batter will be just pourable and sticky.
4. Transfer batter to pastry bag fitted with ½-inch round tip. Holding bag about ½ inch above parchment, pipe 1-inch rounds spaced 1½ inches apart (batter will spread). Let stand 20 minutes.
5. Bake one cookie sheet at a time, 18–19 minutes or until bubbles around bases of macarons are firm to the touch but tops are not browned. Cool on wire rack. Repeat with second cookie sheet.
6. When cookies are cool, spread chocolate on the bottoms of half the macarons, using about ½ teaspoon for each. Top each with another macaron, bottom side down. Let stand until chocolate hardens, about 45 minutes.

LEOPARD

One Christmas Eve

By Jerry Borrowman

Kyle Byland looked out the train window for perhaps the 500th time that morning into the dazzling "white out" caused by the worst blizzard since the turn of the century. As a low moan escaped from the back of his throat, he had to force himself to relax his tightly clenched hands.

"You'll go snow blind if you keep staring out the window."

Kyle jumped at the sound of the woman's voice. "Pardon me?" He glanced at her moodily before dropping his eyes.

"I said you're likely to go temporarily blind if you keep staring into the storm."

Now he looked directly into the woman's eyes for the first time since the porter had seated them and saw that she was quite attractive with rich auburn hair and remarkable green eyes. A light blush on her cheeks provided color and warmth to her features. Still, she was being meddlesome at a time he didn't want to be meddled with.

"Thank you . . ." long pause ". . . for your concern." He looked down at the menu, which he'd ignored up until this point.

"I'm a nurse, you see, and I spend each winter in Park City, where a great many skiers are brought in with that very condition. It's quite frightening and very painful until it subsides."

Kyle glanced up sharply. "I hardly think that an occasional glance out a window is enough to give me snow blindness." He was irritated for even responding to her absurd warning.

"You're probably right. I suppose I was curious as to why you're so concerned about the storm and simply hoped to strike up a conversation. We seem to be making good progress in spite of the snow."

Kyle let out an involuntary sigh because he knew he'd have to explain himself.

"It's just that I'm concerned that the storm will cause me to miss my connection to Salt Lake City when we arrive in Ogden. I have an important event tonight that I simply can't miss."

"Ah . . . I see."

How could she see? This was the one thing he'd wanted to do since he first attended an organ concert at the Tabernacle years ago. Now, after going to extraordinary lengths to prepare, he was finally to give the first major concert of his life before a distinguished audience of the most prominent citizens of Salt Lake City. Except for the storm which will end it all. Even the voice in his head sounded bitter. He expected her to inquire more about the event, but this time it was she who remained silent. He thought that rude, so, clearing his throat, he added, "I'm supposed to perform at a concert on Temple Square tonight."

"Really! What a delightful a way to spend Christmas Eve."

"Well, it's actually scheduled for very early in the evening so everyone can go home and be with their families. That's why it's crucial that I catch the 2:15 p.m. from Ogden. The 3:30 is absolutely the last train I can catch and still hope to make it for the concert at 6:30 p.m."

"I can see why it's so urgent."

"What can I get you folks?" Kyle was startled as a waiter appeared from behind his elbow.

"I'll have the . . ." and then he caught himself as the waiter raised an eyebrow. She should order first, you idiot! "Excuse me," he said weakly. "After you . . ."

She smiled. "I'll have the roast beef and red potatoes . . . and some milk, if you have it."

"Certainly, ma'am. And you, sir?"

Having grown up in a typically lower-middle class family, Kyle was still a bit awed each time someone waited on him. While his father had been fortunate enough to keep a job, even in the darkest days of the Depression that had started six years earlier in 1929, they'd never been able to afford the luxury of eating out at restaurants. So, Kyle felt a bit awkward ordering food in the luxury of a well-appointed Union Pacific dining car.

"Uh, I'll have the same, if you don't mind, except that I'd like water instead of milk."

"Yes, sir." The waiter turned to the lady and smiled. "It will be just a few minutes." While this was going on Kyle found himself staring at the single fresh rose in a crystal vase set next to the curtain by the window. It was a deep crimson red, which stood out in beautiful contrast to the whiteness of the window.

He started to say, "I wonder how they get fresh flowers in the middle of the winter?" at exactly the same time she started to say "So, you're a singer?" They both stumbled a second time while trying to allow the other to go first. Finally, she insisted.

"I was just wondering how the railroad can place a fresh flower in the middle of a table in the middle of winter. Everything about trains and their passenger service is amazing to me."

"As it turns out my father works for the railroad. They buy them from hot-house nurseries at strategic points along the line. This flower probably comes from St. Louis."

"Oh—I didn't even know there were such things as hot-house nurseries and here I am enjoying their output."

She laughed. "You really are a curious person. I doubt many on this car ever thought about the flowers. Perhaps it's your artistic temperament?"

"I suppose so. My mother is always chiding me for being totally unaware of people, yet keenly aware of colors and music. It's embarrassing when a friend passes by and I ignore them because I'm gazing off at a painting or a unique building."

"Yes, I can see how they'd be upset. But, perhaps you need such thoughts to give proper expression to your feelings."

Kyle fumbled with his glass. No one had ever spoken to him this way. She really is beautiful. "Well, no matter how hard I try I can't seem to act differently, so I find myself apologizing to others when they force me out of some reverie."

The waiter returned with two plates of steaming hot potatoes and a modest portion of sliced roast beef covered in a rich brown gravy. After waiting for her to take the first bite, Kyle lifted his fork and quickly found himself savoring the taste in his mouth. He had to consciously slow himself down, or he'd eat the whole plate in just a few mouthfuls, probably the result of his anxiety about the concert.

"So, you're a singer in the Choir, then?"

"What? Oh, no, I play the organ. I get to play a medley of Christmas hymns on the great Tabernacle Organ. It's something I've wanted to do, and now I finally get the chance." Then, looking out the window for the 600th time, "But the blizzard may take it all away from me. Even if we make it, by some miracle, who would want to come out on a night like this?" He recognized the bitter edge to his voice but was powerless to conceal it.

"We're just an hour from Ogden, and it's barely approaching noon, so it seems very likely that we'll make it. Surely you shouldn't give up so soon."

Kyle was about to reply when there was a grinding noise in the carriage underneath their feet. Some of the water in his glass spilled onto his lap from the sudden movement.

"What the?" he started to say just as the train came to an abrupt halt. The chatter in the room increased dramatically as people speculated about what was going on. Kyle's demeanor immediately darkened, and the girl recognized that any attempts at conversation were doomed for the moment. After a few moments the conductor stepped to the front of the car and said, "No cause for concern, folks. We've been diverted into a siding so the eastbound train can pass. Usually we'd have already crossed paths, but we're both running late and so have to wait here. It should only take a few minutes."

"But why don't they wait for us?" Kyle blurted out. He was embarrassed when everyone in the room turned to look at him.

The conductor turned a cool glance his way. "Because they're much later than we are and the track in front of us is more congested. There may be other delays as we work our way to Ogden."

Kyle looked down at the remnants of his meal, set his napkin down, and looked out the window again. He was grateful when the conversation in the room picked back up. In a few moments the ground trembled like an earthquake as a mighty locomotive rumbled past the window, steam billowing up and around the massive wheels as the superheated exhaust mixed with the freezing-cold air of the storm. Kyle watched as the oiler car passed, followed by a seemingly endless stream of passenger cars that glowed warmly through the windows.

"A penny for your thoughts?"

Kyle turned to his dinner companion. "It was bad form for me to complain. I'm sorry. I'm just so nervous about not making connections."

"I understand. We should be starting up soon. In the meantime, perhaps you can tell me how you came to be invited to play at the Tabernacle. That seems like quite an accomplishment for one so young."

Kyle blushed. "I'm not so young—almost thirty. Well, twenty-six."

"Ah . . . I guess I'm accustomed to the wrinkled old men who play at my church."

"Okay, so I am a bit young. But I've been studying for a long time now, and came about this opportunity in quite a roundabout way. You'll probably find it boring."

"Why don't you tell me the story and let me be the judge. As you can see, I don't have many other options for conversation, and it's far more pleasant talking with you than sitting by myself in a coach seat."

"All right, then. Here's the story of young Kyle Byland and the Christmas Concert."

"Kyle. That's a wonderful name."

"Oh, no, I've done it again, haven't I? Struck up a conversation with a young lady without proper introductions?"

"You spend way too much time apologizing. But to make things right my name is Martha Graham of Salt Lake City."

"Pleased to meet you, Miss," he stumbled, not knowing if she was married, "Miss Graham?"

She smiled. "It is Miss. But I'd much prefer to be called Martha since we're the same age."

This time his smile was easier. "Well, then, back to the story. Music has always been part of my life. My earliest memories are of my mother singing to me and my older sister. Even at three years old I'd sit up against the piano to hear Mom play."

"I wish I played. Fortunately we have a professional organist at our church."

Kyle gulped. He'd assumed that since Martha was from Salt Lake City she must be LDS. "Do you mind if I ask which church you attend?"

"Not at all; the First Presbyterian church on South Temple."

"Oh, yes," said Kyle excitedly. "I've had the chance to play your organ. It's a wonderful instrument with a rich and resonant timbre."

"Well, then, there you are. But you were telling me about your childhood interest in music."

"Yes. Well, at age seven I began to learn piano from my mother. I don't know why, but music just made sense to me, even at that age. In less than two years I'd worked through all the basic introductory books and practiced for hours per day. I was probably the only boy in the world whose parents told him to stop practicing and go outside to play." He was gratified when she laughed.

"At any rate, Mother took in some children to tend so she could earn enough extra money to enroll me in piano lessons with one of the best instructors in Salt Lake City. I spent the next ten years with Dr. Franks."

"I've heard him. But how did that lead to the organ?"

"Church, actually. At fourteen I was called to be the Sunday School organist for our ward—excuse me, but do you know about wards?"

This amused her. "It would be fairly impossible to grow up in Salt Lake City without knowing about wards and bishops and stakes. Many of my friends are LDS, and I've attended their weeknight activities. So you can talk freely about your church experience."

"Thank you. Well, as I was saying, I was called as the organist. At first it was extremely difficult because playing the organ is so different from the piano. The way you have to manipulate the keys is dramatically different—probably not for most people—but for one trained in classical piano it was a challenge. Professor Franks was irritated with me because he said the organ was ruining me for the piano. But my mother was adamant that I had to fulfill my calling. I tried to argue with her, but she said she guessed the Lord knew what was best for me. So I concentrated doubly hard on my regular lessons so that Dr. Franks would keep me on while I became more and more comfortable with the organ."

"I think I like your mother, even though I haven't met her. I wish my parents had insisted I play."

"I'm glad I stayed at the organ now, even though I resisted at the time. As it turns out the organ was to become not just a church assignment, but my occupation."

"Your occupation?"

"Yes. When I was a teenager we went to an organ recital at the Tabernacle. When I saw those golden 32-foot pipes I was thunderstruck. Then, when the organist played Bach, with those wonderful bass pipes shaking the whole building, I resolved that one day I would play that organ. It became my dream."

Martha marveled at the fire that had come into his eyes. Then, she watched as it suddenly went cold.

"And tonight is the night it's finally to happen. But only if there is a concert." He looked out the window again.

Now it was Martha who sighed. "But we're making great progress. I'm sure you'll make it." She smiled hopefully, but he simply pursed his lips and shrugged. The conversation stalled.

"But certainly you can't be playing the Tabernacle organ for the first time. I can't imagine anyone performing at a concert without first practicing on the instrument they're going to play."

"No, you're right. I've played it before. Many times, in fact. But only at night when no one was around. You see, when I graduated high school, I started at the university to study music. But my father was killed in an automobile accident, and I had to give up school to earn a living."

Martha could see the pain this had caused. "But something happened that qualified you to play the great organ of your dreams?"

"One night I went to Temple Square for an evening recital. Professor Franks was meeting with the choir leaders in preparation for a solo cantata he was going to play on the grand piano during one of their upcoming Sunday broadcasts. When he spied me out in the seats, he called me up and introduced me to the organist." Kyle laughed. "I'll never forget that introduction—'Gentlemen, here is a young man who showed great promise on the piano until your church introduced him to the organ. Now he has a split personality. You ought to let him play your great Tabernacle organ since you slowed down his progress so much."

Martha laughed with him. "So?"

"So they let me step up to the keyboard, and even though I was unfamiliar with the stops, my heart simply filled with joy to hear the sounds emanate from that wonderful instrument. It was love on my part, and maybe the organ felt it too because it responded with what seemed like affection to my playing." He smiled as he relived the moment.

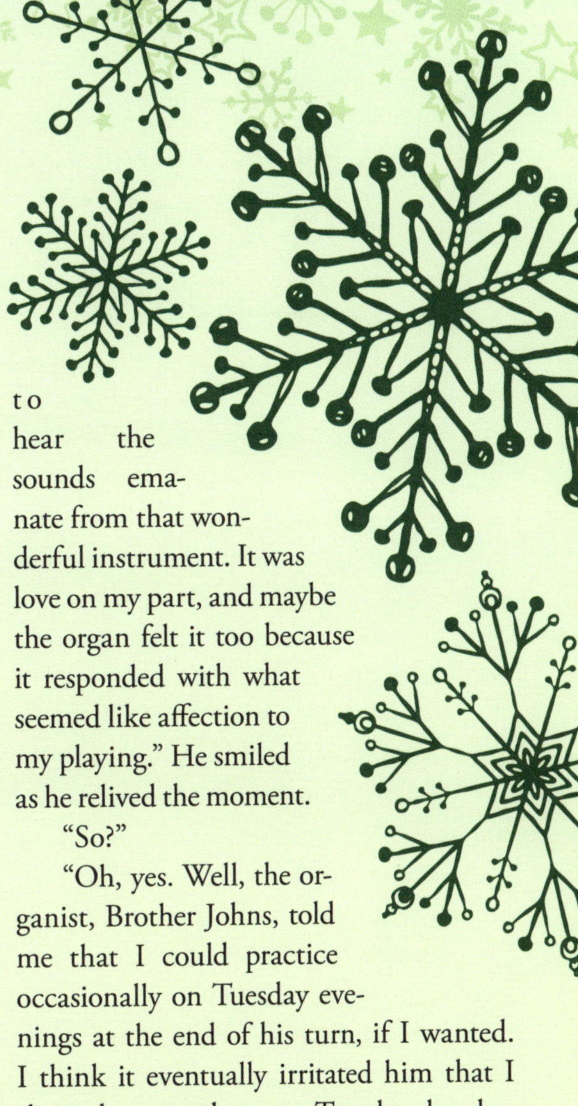

"So?"

"Oh, yes. Well, the organist, Brother Johns, told me that I could practice occasionally on Tuesday evenings at the end of his turn, if I wanted. I think it eventually irritated him that I showed up nearly every Tuesday, but before long we became friends.

"So, that led to this invitation?"

"Actually, no."

She gasped in exasperation.

"I'm getting to it, I promise. What happened is that I also met the master technician who is tasked with maintaining the organ. As I started asking questions he invited me to take a tour of the organ to see its internal workings. First, he took me downstairs to see the huge electric motors that power the blowers that keep a constant air pressure to the nearly 6,500 pipes. Then we climbed up into the catwalks to pass through an air lock into the universal wind chest that supplies air to the various ranks of pipes. It is so amazing to see row after row of pipes, including some that are square and wooden, still in use from the original organ installed by the pioneers."

By this point his eyes were shining, and Martha decided not to interrupt with a question.

"The thing that seems so miraculous to me is that you can actually lift one of the little treble pipes right out of the cabinet and blow on it with your mouth. Out comes this high pitched little tone that can be heard throughout the entire building. Is that amazing, or what?"

"It is amazing!" She laughed, even though she hadn't intended to. Then she smiled when his face went red. "Don't be embarrassed. It's just so nice to see someone become so passionate. Please, continue."

So Kyle told her all about how the organ worked and how to maintain it.

"Well, that's one of the most interesting stories I've ever heard. I just sit in the congregation and do my best to sing each Sunday while the organist plays away. Now, I have some idea of how it all happens. But, how does that relate to you?"

"I decided that what I want most in life is to be a professional organist. Since I couldn't afford college, I needed a profession that allowed me time to practice. When one of the organ maintenance workers retired, I applied for the position of apprentice. And I got it. I'm actually on my way back home from training with the factory crews at the Austin Organ Company in Hartford, Connecticut. On the way home, I got to stop in New York City and visit Carnegie Hall, which was another dream come true."

"So it's because you're a member of the technical staff that you got invited to play tonight?"

"Well, no . . ."

"Of course not. Why would I think we'll ever get to the part about your concert?"

Now he laughed easily. "We're there—honest. You see, just because you know how to work on organs doesn't mean you're qualified to play. In fact, we're supposed to stay in the background."

"And you're trying to be out front . . ."

"Exactly. The reason I got invited to perform tonight is that Dr. Franks set it up with the Choir's musical director. That's why I'm so anxious to have things go well. I really want to be in both places—in front of and behind the keyboard, so to speak. If the concert doesn't come off, I don't know if I'll get another chance . . ."

There was silence between them, but not an uncomfortable silence. When Kyle finally turned to glance at Martha, he saw that she was staring out the window. He resisted the urge to make a wisecrack about snow blindness since it almost looked like she was mentally willing the snow to stop on his behalf. He felt a wave of gratitude sweep over him.

Their reverie was interrupted by a grinding noise from the carriage underneath their feet, and once again the car jerked to the right.

"Oh, no!" she cried. "Not again."

He smiled weakly. The waiter came up silently from behind Kyle. "Folks, we need to clear the dining room for the second sitting. People in the cars ahead are getting pretty hungry."

"Of course, thank you. The food was wonderful." Then, turning to Kyle, Martha added, "The seat across from me is empty. Care to continue our conversation there?"

"Why, thank you. I will. I mean, I would . . ." She laughed to cover his embarrassment.

The train pulled into Ogden station at 2:45 p.m. after two more unscheduled sidings. "Still, we should be able to catch the 3:30," said Martha breathlessly as they hurried through the crowded terminal.

"It'll probably be sold out . . ."

"Then we'll make them sell us a ticket anyway. We'll stand in the aisles, if we have to. Now, hurry up!" But the ticket windows were closed. "Oh, for heaven's sake," said Martha. "Where is someone we can talk to?" Then, spying a conductor on the other side of the platform, Martha tripped off in short, running steps. Kyle couldn't help but marvel that she could do so with such grace, given her high heels and the snow on the platform. A few moments later, she returned. "I think it's all right. That's our train right there, and he said that a telegraph from Salt Lake City says that the storm has let up, so they've decided to chance a run." Kyle lurched as Martha grabbed his arm and pulled him towards the waiting train. It was at that moment that the engine they were standing next to let out a shrill shriek from its steam horn to announce its impending departure. Kyle and many of the people standing around jumped at the sound, but Martha hardly seemed to notice.

"Do you hear the change in the sound of the fire?" asked Martha. "They've fired all the burners."

Now that he thought about it, he did hear the change. Whereas there had been a low dull "whooshing" sort of sound a few moments earlier, now there was an angry roar, and as they passed the engineers' cabin, Kyle saw a bright crimson glow reflecting on the black-metal surfaces inside. Mounting the steps of the first available car, Martha leaned close to his ear and said, "This will be the closest to the front of the terminal when we get to Salt Lake City, so you'll have a head start on your two block dash to Temple Square."

"You've got this all figured out, haven't you? You really are an amazing person." Then, shyly, "I don't suppose your schedule would allow you to come to our concert? After all, I'd have probably died of anxiety back there if you hadn't started talking to me. I have an extra ticket. But, of course you probably have plans . . ."

"I'd love to come to your concert. But first we need this train to start moving."

"Oh, yeah, there's still the forty miles to Salt Lake to worry about. That's good because I never like to be without something to worry about."

Martha shook her head.

Only forty miles? It might as well have been four thousand, as it turns out. In spite of its weight of nearly 600,000 pounds, the massive steam locomotive struggled against the hundreds of tons of wet snow that clogged the track. But it was the gale force winds blowing huge drifts almost deeper than the train itself that finally brought them to a standstill. The earlier weather report was wrong because the storm now raged so ferociously that it felt like the train cars themselves might be tipped right off the track. The passengers were all huddled in their seats, with only an occasional worried whisper breaking into the sound of the storm. Everyone knew they were in trouble and regretted being numbered among the few who had decided to brave the trip from Ogden. Finally, as the locomotive made its last futile thrusting movement forward, the conductor made an announcement.

"Folks, we can't make any more progress. We'll back the train to a siding a thousand yards back by Lakeville. We hope to find shelter for you there. If not, we'll use what coal we have to keep a minimum amount of warmth in the cars to see us through the night. I guess what I'm saying is that while our situation is serious, you don't need to be alarmed."

The conductor's remarks were punctuated by the unsteady jerk of the engine reversing direction. Everyone held their breath, and then let it out slowly as they started moving backwards.

Up until now Kyle kept hoping that somehow things would work out for the concert. He'd offered a thousand prayers that God would intervene. After all, He parted the Red Sea for Moses. Why not clear a path through a rail corridor? "Obviously, I don't matter as much as Moses," he muttered under his breath.

"What?"

He turned and looked at Martha, whose face had lost its glow now that they were engulfed by the darkness of the storm. "Nothing."

"No, you said something about Moses."

"I just said that God parted the Red Sea for Moses but doesn't seem as interested in helping us." He tried to say it lightly, as if it was a joke, but the bitterness came through.

"You think this is as important as giving the Israelites freedom after four hundred years of slavery?" Kyle didn't respond. "Look, I know this concert means a lot to you, Kyle, but frankly there are a lot bigger problems to think about right now than that, like how many people are stranded out there in the snow. It seems to me God has plenty of more important things to take care of than your concert!"

Kyle turned on her fiercely, "Listen, Miss Graham, you've been very nice to me today, and I appreciate it. I know that my little problem is nothing compared to everything else that's going on, but that's the problem with problems. Somebody's always got a bigger problem, so we're supposed to buck up and be grateful that it's not as bad for us as it is for them. But right now this is the only problem I have to think about, and it really hurts. I've wanted this night more than anything, and now, instead of making music, I'm stuck out here." He was even angrier when a sob interfered with his ability to speak. Pursing his lips, he continued in as even a tone as possible, "This was my chance, and now it's gone. So be it. But if you don't mind I'd like to feel sorry for myself, at least for a minute or two. Now, if you'll excuse me, I won't trouble you any further." He brushed away her arm as he stood up and moved to an empty seat at the back of the car.

A few minutes later they were helped off the cars as the townspeople led them toward a small church directly next to the siding. Lakeville was small enough that it didn't even warrant its own station.

Once they were all inside, the mayor of the community, John Riley, (who was also the bishop of the Lakeville Ward) stepped forward to take control of the situation.

"Ladies and gentlemen, even though the railroad has offered, we won't take any money for food. Second, since we have approximately thirty families who live within walking distance, I propose that we combine all our Christmas Eve dinners here at the church to have a communal Christmas Eve with our guests." The people from the town quickly agreed, and the passengers from the train expressed their gratitude and a willingness to help with the set up and cooking.

"Next, we'll take as many folks into our homes as possible, but we'll need blankets and pillows for those who are left at the church.

The Relief Society president spoke up, "We've been working on quilts in Relief Society to send to Welfare Square, so we should have plenty."

"Thank you, Sister Williams."

After reviewing all of the other details required to care for a train load of unexpected visitors, the bishop turned to the group and concluded, "We have plenty of coal to keep all the stoves burning, so people will be warm. We know that you all had plans for this special night that have been interrupted, but please know that we'll do everything possible to make you feel welcome." The people from the train burst into applause at their generosity.

It was at that point that someone from the town shouted out, "Maybe we could have a Christmas Eve program with singing and scripture reading!" There was a broad murmur of consent.

"Excellent idea," replied Bishop Riley. "Our children performed the Christmas story last Sunday, and I bet they'll do it again." The Primary president quickly agreed. "As for singing, I'm afraid it will have to be a cappella since our pipe organ is out of service. But that shouldn't be a problem."

Martha turned and looked at Kyle and mouthed the words, "You can help," but he pursed his lips and shook his head. She frowned and looked away.

As the group broke up, Kyle watched her move forward to talk with the bishop. Kyle attempted to make himself invisible, pretending to be unaware, while still listening from the corner. That's when he heard her say, "Excuse me, Mr. Riley, but may I ask what's wrong with your chapel's organ?"

"We don't know, since there's no one here with any experience working on instruments like this. All I know is that there are a dozen or so keys that refuse to play as they should and others that make the most awful squawking sounds. It just became impossible to use. We've asked Salt Lake to send someone to fix it, but they tell us the cost would have to come out of our ward budget, and with this Great Depression, we just don't have the money. So we sing without accompaniment. Are you an organist or something, Sister, uh, I'm sorry I don't know your name."

"No, I'm not an organist. I was just curious. And my name is Martha Graham. I'm not a member of your church, but I appreciate your hospitality. Thank you."

"You're very welcome. This is actually pretty exciting for our little town. It will be good for us to have the chance to get together with your group. In fact, I can't think of a better way to celebrate the holiday than helping each other."

Martha smiled and thanked him again.

Turning to move toward Kyle, she saw his attempts to blend into the crowd, but she was determined to confront him—even while doubtful of the outcome.

"Kyle, I need to talk to you!"

"There's nothing to talk about."

"Yes, there is. Now, please don't make a scene. Come over here and talk with

me." Kyle scowled but followed her to the side of the hall.

"So you want to talk to me about their organ, I suppose."

"That's exactly what I want to talk to you about. These people are opening their homes and hearts to us, and meanwhile they have an organ that needs repair. Why didn't you volunteer to help?"

"Because I'm not in the mood to think about pipe organs right now. I had plans. They're ruined, so I'd like to make the best of a miserable evening if I could."

"But you can fix their problem—and after what they're doing for us, it seems the least we can do."

"The least we can do?" His sarcasm did not escape her. "Look, I'll help with the preparations and everything else that people on the train do to help with the dinner. But that's it. No more and no less than anyone else. Besides, I don't even know how to fix their organ; I've been trained to work on large instruments."

"How can you know if you can fix it when you haven't even looked at it? I know you have your tools with you because of how you protect that briefcase. Can't you see that it's wrong not to even try?" He noticed her eyes start to fill with indignant tears, but he was having none of it.

"I'm sorry, but I feel no obligation here. A person has to be in the right frame of mind to do something, and I am certainly not in that frame of mind. So if you'd please just stay out of my affairs, I'd appreciate it."

"I shouldn't have to be the one to point this out, but have you stopped to consider that maybe in the midst of this terrible storm God knew that you would be stranded here and that you might be the answer to these people's prayer for help? I'd think you'd be honored that He could put you to use that way. It's a chance for something good to come out of all this trouble. Besides, isn't this what you've been training for?"

"Oh, that's a good one. God creates a blizzard that causes me to miss a concert I've been looking forward to so that I can fix a two-bit organ in Lakeville. Sorry again, but I have problems of my own to think about. And as you said so eloquently on the train, I think He has bigger things to worry about right now. Besides, the bishop said they are getting along just fine without me stepping in."

Her eyes flashed, and more than anything Kyle wanted to get away from her and all these people. There were tears of his own that wanted to get out—bitter tears as he thought about the fact that he wasn't ever likely to get another chance like the one that was now out of reach. *Why can't she see my side of things?*

He braced for her next remark, but just as she was about to let go, he saw her face soften. After taking a moment to compose herself, she said in a very quiet voice, "Kyle, this Christmas Eve Concert at Temple Square—was it for you or was it for Jesus?"

Then, before he could respond, she turned and walked away slowly to help with the food.

It was probably five or ten minutes before Martha noticed Kyle move over to talk with Bishop Riley. The bishop put his arm on Kyle's back and guided him out of the cultural hall. When he didn't come in for dinner nearly two hours later, she slipped into the hall where she heard odd sounds from the chapel. Peeking through the door, she saw Kyle on the stand with the front of the organ console off, his hands extended inside the bowels of the cabinet, where he seemed to be manipulating an incredibly complex mechanism. Every now and then, the organ would growl out a note, followed by a series of staccato bursts until Kyle was satisfied that that particular key was working well. She listened for perhaps five minutes before walking up to the pulpit. Kyle looked up and beckoned her to come over.

"You're missing dinner."

"Oh? Guess I haven't had time to think about it. Besides, I'm not very hungry."

"Is there any hope for their poor little organ?"

"Actually, the surprising part is that it's really quite a wonderful instrument. Apparently it was donated to them nearly twenty years ago by an older member who played very well. Its size and performance is way out of line with what a ward chapel would normally have. I mean just listen to the sound of the bass pipes." He played a deep somber chord then paused, realizing that he was carrying on. "At any rate, when the old fellow died, no one knew how to maintain it, and so slowly but surely the keys stopped functioning. I've been able to fix most of them, although it will take a lot more work than I can finish tonight to get it properly tuned and fully repaired."

"But you've got it to where they can play it?"

Kyle nodded. "Yes, it's playable now. If they can hold off for another twenty minutes, I can put the console back together, and they can have a musical accompaniment to the singing."

"That's wonderful, Kyle. Really, wonderful . . ." Martha acted like she wanted to say more but didn't know what or how to say it.

Kyle put down the small mallet he was holding and turned to look at her.

"Martha, I'm sorry I yelled at you out there."

"It really was none of my business . . ." She stopped when he put his index finger up to her mouth.

"I was angry with you for forcing my hand on this issue. Frankly, I wanted my Tabernacle concert so much that I didn't care. All I could think of was all the influential people I could impress. It was to be the start of a whole new epoch in my life."

She watched as his eyes watered. "The truth is I thought only of me . . . until you said that part about Jesus. In all my grand plans I forgot that Christmas is about a baby, one who would never gain the acclaim of the world in his lifetime, even though He deserved it more than anyone who has ever lived."

He looked away for a moment. "You made me think, and while I couldn't fully erase my disappointment, at least I could try to do something in honor of Christmas. After all, the only gift you can give the Savior is to give a gift to someone else."

"I think that's wonderful. And it turns out that you had the ability all along."

"That's the interesting part. I didn't have either the knowledge or the skill. When I saw the type instrument they have, I almost panicked. We spent very little time studying this type of mechanical action, and I had no idea where to even start."

He struggled to control the emotion in his voice. "So I decided to offer a prayer requesting His help. That's kind of ironic, don't you think? I want to give Him a gift, but I need His help to do it? At any rate, I started praying for help, and before long I was pouring out my heart and apologizing for being so selfish . . ."

Martha wanted to hold him—she could see what an ordeal he'd passed through. "At any rate, when I finished my prayer I decided to take it one step at a time, to first study the action of the mechanical roller arms and squares. The damage was far beyond anything I was prepared to fix. But as I rehearsed my prayer a second time I felt my mind clear, and I was able to focus on the problems at hand. It's like I figured out more in ten minutes than I did studying all last year. Normally, it would take days to get done what I've finished tonight. I haven't had much experience getting prayers answered in such an obvious way, but I do know that He helped me tonight, and it was an amazing experience."

He smiled. "So I guess what I'm saying is that you were right. God did know that these people needed someone to help them. And I'm glad that He knew that I was available." Martha returned his smile. "At any rate, thank you for helping me get past my pride . . ."

Martha took his hands and reached up and kissed his cheek. Then she said, "I think the Lord knows that when He needs someone who can be a bit overbearing, He can always look to me." With that, they laughed, and the tension was gone. "Now, let me go get you a plate of food while you put this thing back together. The bishop hasn't said a word to anyone, so I think it's going to be a surprise."

Half an hour later the bishop announced the children's program and then added, "Then next, we'll be pleased to hear an organ Christmas Medley, played by Brother Kyle Byland of the Tabernacle organ staff." There was a gasp from the audience and heads turned to see where this Brother Byland might be. "It turns out that he was on his way home from training on how to maintain and repair organs, and he's put his skill to work on ours. Perhaps that's our own little Christmas miracle that shows that prayers are answered in the due time of the Lord."

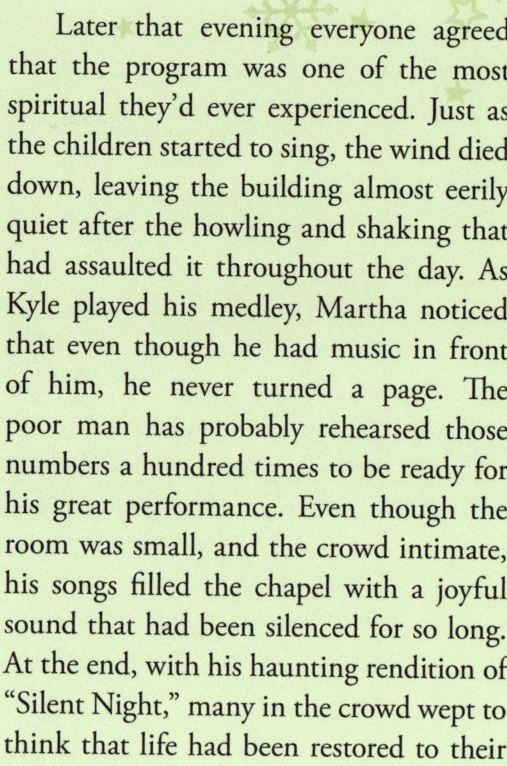

Later that evening everyone agreed that the program was one of the most spiritual they'd ever experienced. Just as the children started to sing, the wind died down, leaving the building almost eerily quiet after the howling and shaking that had assaulted it throughout the day. As Kyle played his medley, Martha noticed that even though he had music in front of him, he never turned a page. The poor man has probably rehearsed those numbers a hundred times to be ready for his great performance. Even though the room was small, and the crowd intimate, his songs filled the chapel with a joyful sound that had been silenced for so long. At the end, with his haunting rendition of "Silent Night," many in the crowd wept to think that life had been restored to their organ.

When the program finished, Martha was whisked away with the other single women to stay in local homes, while Kyle and the men bedded down in the cultural hall. She smiled in his direction and saw his acknowledging smile in return as he mouthed the words, "Merry Christmas!"

Symbolism of Christmas Holly:

The prickly green leaves of the holly are a reminder of thorns Jesus wore on the day of the Crucifixion. The bright red berries symbolized the blood of Christ spilled for the sins of mankind.

Giving, not getting, brings to full bloom the Christmas spirit. Enemies are forgiven, friends remembered, and God obeyed. The spirit of Christmas illuminates the picture window of the soul, and we look out upon the world's busy life and become more interested in people than things. To catch the real meaning of the "spirit of Christmas," we need only drop the last syllable, and it becomes the

"*Spirit of Christ.*"

~Thomas S. Monson